Jung on the East

Jung's interest in the religious and psychological ideas of the East was deep-rooted and life-long. His writings on such texts as the *I Ching* and *The Tibetan Book of the Dead*, on yoga and Zen, as well as his account of his own journey to India, show that the traditional teachings of China and India played an important role in his personal and intellectual development.

J. J. Clarke's selection for and introduction to *Jung on the East* also show that, in spite of his popular reputation, Jung was by no means an uncritical follower of the Eastern way. He acknowledged the difficulties in bridging the wide gap between Western and Eastern ways of thinking, and frequently voiced severe reservations about the use of Eastern techniques by Westerners, taking to task those who cover up their own spiritual nakedness with what he called 'the gorgeous trappings of the East'. As a critic of many aspects of modern life he saw that 'the wisdom and mysticism of the East have . . . very much to say to us', and can be useful as mirrors in which to examine our own shortcomings and uncertainties, but at the same time he warned that 'we must get at Eastern values from within and not from without, seeking them in ourselves'.

Jung on the East will appeal both to those readers seeking greater knowledge of the thought and spirituality of the East and to those who wish to deepen their understanding of Jung's work.

Also published by Routledge in this series:

Jung on Alchemy

Jung on Evil

Jung on the East

C. G. Jung

Edited and with an introduction by
J. J. Clarke

London

First published 1995
by Routledge
11 New Fetter Lane, London EC4P 4EE

Simultaneously published in the USA and Canada
by Princeton University Press

Typeset in Times by
Ponting–Green Publishing Services, Chesham, Bucks

Printed and bound in Great Britain by
Biddles Ltd, Guildford and King's Lynn

British Library Cataloguing in Publication Data
A catalogue record for this book is available from the British Library.

ISBN   0–415–11017–3

Contents

vi *Contents*

Illustrations

Introduction

In spite of their continuing popularity, Jung's writings on Eastern thought and religions evoke ambivalent reactions. On the one hand these writings inspire strong and continuing interest among a wide readership, and provide for many people an important psychological bridge to the alluring, though often elusive, spiritual traditions of the Orient. On the other hand some of Jung's own followers have been reluctant to admit their importance for an understanding of his work as a whole, and critics have sometimes been inclined to dismiss them as typifying his supposed 'mystical' bent. The publication of a selection of his writings on this subject will probably not resolve such ambivalence, but it may help to encourage further reflection, both on the relation of these writings to Jung's psychological thinking in general and on their relevance for us today.

Jung's interest in the East was certainly not a superficial matter or a passing phase, but was deep-rooted and life-long (he lived from 1875 to 1961), and a reading of the selections in this book will help to confirm both the wide range of this interest in, and the depth of his knowledge of, Eastern thought. The philosophical and religious traditions of China and India in fact played an important role in his intellectual development. Right from the early days when he was distancing himself from Freud and fashioning his own distinctive approach to psychology, up to the 1930s when his ideas were reaching their full expression and maturity, Eastern ideas and concepts wove their way in and out of his writings, and were used in various ways to clarify and substantiate his own controversial views. Concepts such as 'self', 'individuation', 'archetypes', and 'active imagination', which are central to the theory and practice of Jungian analytical psychology, were all shaped to some extent by his investigations into texts and ideas from the ancient traditions of China and India.

However, in spite of a certain popularly conceived reputation, he was by no means an uncritical follower of the Eastern way, nor an exponent of that peculiarly Western orientophilia according to which all things Eastern are sacred and beyond criticism. He acknowledged the difficulties of bridging the wide gap between Eastern and Western ways of thinking, and frequently voiced severe reservations about the use of Eastern techniques by

Westerners, taking the theosophists to task for covering up the spiritual emptiness of the West with what he called the 'the gorgeous trappings of the East'.[1] But at the same time he believed that at several levels we have much to learn from the study of Eastern thought. At the individual level he saw the teachings of Buddhism, yoga and Taoism as casting light on the structure of the human psyche, and as making important contributions to the philosophy of mind. At the broader, social level he believed that certain Oriental writings offered a useful instrument for self-examination and diagnosis with regard to the West's cultural ills, and that they suggested ways in which these ills might be treated. Jung was certainly no revolutionary seeking to subvert Western traditions or to seduce Christians from their indigenous beliefs; nor was he a romantic – in a popular sense of that many-faceted term – seeking to escape an unbearable present by reviving outworn creeds from the exotic East. But as a critic of many aspects of modern life – of its one-sided materialism, its worship of scientific rationalism, and its tendency to ego-aggrandisement – he saw Eastern philosophies as a way of exploring and redirecting the West's neglected inner psychic life. For Jung, 'The wisdom and mysticism of the East have . . . very much to say to us, even when they speak their own inimitable language. They serve to remind us that we in our culture possess something similar, which we have already forgotten, and to direct our attention to the fate of the inner man, which we set aside as trifling.' Nevertheless, in his view this 'wisdom' is not something which can be applied 'like an ointment', but must be approached from our peculiarly Western ways of thinking, mediated through our own traditions, rediscovered in terms of our own cultural modalities, and hence he insisted that 'in order to possess it, we must first earn it'.[2] Jung's approach to the East, therefore, was a complex one, both warmly enthusiastic and at the same time circumscribed by critical caution, displaying an ambivalence which reflects that of his readership, and a reflexiveness which continues to open up new ways of thought for us today.

JUNG AND THE HISTORY OF ORIENTALISM

Although Jung was in many respects a pioneer in the exploration of Eastern ideas, he was by no means the first European to engage in a dialogue with the religious and philosophical traditions of the Orient, and in order adequately to evaluate his writings in this field we need to place them in a wider historical context. From the time of Marco Polo's expedition to China in the thirteenth century to recent cults of Hari Krishna, yoga and Zen, Westerners have been fascinated by the East, and exotic images of the Orient have penetrated deeply into the Western imagination. This is not merely a matter of popular stereotypes, summed up in such phrases as 'the mystical East', 'Eastern wisdom' and 'Oriental despotism', but is a factor that has long pervaded Western art, literature and culture in general. Many people are familiar with the fashion for *chinoiserie* in the eighteenth century, with the impact of Japanese art on European painting and design in the late nineteenth century, and with the ways in which Western literature has been given an Oriental dimension, ranging from fantastic tales such as the *Arabian Nights* to the novels of Kipling, and the poetry of W. B. Yeats and Ezra Pound. Many readers of this book will recall the extraordinary efflorescence of orientomania amongst the beat and hippie generations, with their huge appetite for all things Eastern, from bells and joss-sticks to meditation and spiritual enlightenment. What is not always recognized is the extent to which the East has penetrated the *intellectual* life of the West, has entered into some of its crucial debates in the modern period, and has been commandeered to serve its various causes.

Successive waves of Eastern thought have over the past four hundred years washed over the minds of Western Christendom. First it was the philosophy of Confucius in the age of Enlightenment, when Europe became infatuated with an exalted vision of Cathay. Drawing on detailed and sympathetic reports of the Jesuit missionaries in China, Enlightenment thinkers, ranging from Bayle and Leibniz to Voltaire and Quesnay, seized upon Confucianism as a political ideal with which to subvert the existing order and as a model for a new, more rationally based, secular polity in Europe. In the Romantic period of the late eighteenth and early nineteenth centuries, attention switched from China to India. The more religiously, even mystically, inclined Romantics, reacting against the rationalism and materialism of the earlier period, found in the *Vedas* and the *Upanishads* not only an ancient, possibly pre-biblical, source of wisdom and civilization, but also a philosophy which matched their own and offered them a model of spiritual harmony and cultural wholeness that they believed was lacking in the West. Even Hegel, who was more critical than most of the enthusiasm for all things Oriental, sought for the first time to integrate Chinese and Indian thought and culture into a universal history of the human spirit. The emergence in the nineteenth century of Buddhism as an object of European interest is associated first and foremost with the German philosopher Arthur Schopenhauer, who not only incorporated large elements of Indian thought into his philosophical writings, but also helped in the propagation and popularization of Buddhist ideas in the second half of the century. These ideas had a powerful impact on such towering figures as Wagner and Nietzsche, but they also entered crucially into the debates of philosophers and theologians in that period, providing sceptics with a powerful argument against the supposed uniqueness and moral supremacy of Christianity. By the turn of the twentieth century orientalism had become well established as an academic discipline, involving the huge task of translating Eastern texts, carried out by individuals such as Friedrich Max Müller and Paul Deussen and by scholarly enterprises such as the Pali Text Society and the *Sacred Books of the East* series. This meant that a growing body of Oriental knowledge was becoming available for academic purposes, but in addition to this organizations such as the Theosophical Society and books such as

Edwin Arnold's *The Light of Asia*, not to mention the World Parliament of Religions in Chicago in 1893, were all helping to bring the ancient ideas of the East to an ever wider audience in Europe and America. Indeed, by the time Jung began his close study of Eastern religions in the inter-war period, many educated people in the West had acquired a more than superficial knowledge of Asian religious and philosophical thought, and many had turned to the East for inspiration, often as a model for the renewal of what was increasingly perceived as the declining civilization of the West.

It is within this broad framework that we need to place the writings of C. G. Jung on Eastern philosophies, for his approach is one which echoes and resonates to a whole tradition – or more strictly a sub-tradition – of Western thought, and in a sense his own particular contribution to orientalism can be seen as yet another phase in the West's repeated turnings to the East, its *orientation*. Furthermore, with the benefit of his wide educational background and cultural milieu, he was well tuned into the crescendo of popular and academic interest in Eastern thought at the turn of the century, and his close study of philosophers such as Schopenhauer and Nietzsche made him aware of the strong intellectual tradition that lay at the bottom of more recent concerns and enthusiasms for the East.

This broad cultural sweep which we have called orientalism has certainly not always been fully understood or appreciated by historians, whether general or intellectual, and as a strand of Western cultural history has not enjoyed a particularly emphatic presence within European consciousness. The role which the East has played in the formation of the modern Western mind has been, if not actively censored, at any rate conveniently marginalized. This is no doubt partly due to Europe's attainment in the past two hundred years to a position of global hegemony, which has tended to confirm, at any rate in the minds of the political establishment, the inherent superiority and historical mission of Europe in relation to the East. It may also be due to the parallel growth of scientific rationalism, which has increasingly dominated the West's intellectual agenda, and which has led to a dismissal of the 'mystical' outpourings of the East along with the outmoded ideas of pre-modern Europe. In a similar way Jung's own Oriental interests have often been misunderstood, seen as confirmation of his notorious mystical bent, or as evidence of his tired retreat from modern life into bygone creeds. Even his own followers have shown a reluctance to take this aspect of his work seriously, some sympathetic studies ignoring it or passing over it with embarrassed haste, an attitude which has been assisted by the fact that Jung's writings in this area have been spasmodic and have not added up to anything like a systematic treatment. The orientalist sub-tradition, looked at in its widest dimensions, is one that has often run against the tide, beating against accepted orthodoxy, and undermining long-laid foundations. Something of this is also true of Jung's orientalism, as we shall now see.

JUNG'S WAY TO THE EAST

It has often been suggested that Jung's involvement with the East began with his reading of Richard Wilhelm's translation of the Chinese Taoist text *The Secret of the Golden Flower* in 1928 and ended ten years later with his trip to India and Ceylon (now Sri Lanka), but in fact his interest began with his study of the history of religions and mythology in 1909, and he was still studying Buddhism in the last months of his life. Even as a small child Jung pestered his mother to read to him from a book containing stories of Brahma, Vishnu and Shiva, which he found 'an inexhaustible source of interest'.[3] In his youth Jung's imagination had been captivated by his reading of Schopenhauer, who made no secret of his admiration for and intellectual affinity with Hindu and Buddhist philosophy, and whose influence in the shaping of Jung's mature outlook was at least as great as that of Freud. There are some brief references to Oriental ideas in the so-called 'Zofingia' lectures of his student days in Basel just before the turn of the century, but by the time he came to write his first truly 'Jungian' books, *Symbols of Transformation* (1912) and *Psychological Types* (1921), he had acquired an extensive knowledge of Vedic, Buddhist and Taoist ideas and mythology, which he treated on a par, and closely interwove, with symbolic material from Western sources. The bibliographies to these books give evidence of extensive reading in primary as well as secondary texts and show familiarity with classics such as the *I Ching*, the *Ramayana* and the *Bhagavad Gita*, as well as with the writings of leading Indologists such as Max Müller, Oldenberg and Deussen. What appears to have struck him most forcibly in his reading at this stage is the dominance in Eastern thought, whether Chinese or Indian, of the ideas of duality and of the complementary nature of opposites, ideas which, transposed into psychological terms, came to play a central role in Jung's thinking as well.[4]

During the 1920s the immediate stimulus for Jung's Oriental interests came from three men: Oscar Schmitz, whose book *Psychoanalyse und Yoga* anticipated Jung's insights into the parallel between psychotherapy and Eastern spiritual practices; Hermann Keyserling, a widely travelled amateur philosopher whose book *The East and the West in their Search for a Common Truth* urged the need for some kind of synthesis between Eastern and Western thought; and, most significantly, the sinologist Richard Wilhelm. Keyserling had founded 'The School of Wisdom' at Darmstadt to study Eastern thought, and it was in 1923 on one of his visits there that Jung met Wilhelm. They immediately struck up a close friendship, which lasted until Wilhelm's death seven years later, an association which had a huge impact on Jung's intellectual development. In a memorial tribute,[5] Jung wrote that Wilhelm's life-work was 'of such immense importance to me because it clarified and confirmed so much that I had been seeking, striving for, thinking', and he felt himself 'so very much enriched by him that it seems to me as if I had received more from him than from any other man'.[6] Wilhelm had been a missionary in China, where he had devoted himself more assiduously to the study of the country's language and literature than to the conversion of its people – he once boasted to Jung that he had never actually converted a single Chinese! Jung was clearly struck by Wilhelm's empathy with the Chinese, with their literature and their philosophical outlook, which meant that he had, as Jung put it, 'the gift of being able to listen without bias to the revelations of a foreign mentality, and to accomplish that miracle of empathy which enabled him to make the intellectual treasures of China accessible to Europe'.[7] Through his translation of ancient Chinese texts he had 'created a bridge between East and West and gave to the Occident the precious heritage of a culture thousands of years old, a culture perhaps destined to disappear for ever'.[8] The first of these was published in Germany in 1929, and Jung was asked to write a psychological commentary for it, an invitation which gave him the opportunity to begin to build his own bridge of understanding by linking up the ideas of this ancient alchemical text with his emerging ideas on the self and the unconscious.[9] Some years later, long after the death of Wilhelm, he was invited to carry out a similar task for the English edition of the *I Ching*, which was published in 1950, and, as with the earlier work, he took the opportunity to tie it in closely with ideas that he was currently working on, in particular the idea of 'synchronicity'.[10]

Jung's interest in the East developed strongly in the 1930s. In addition to Wilhelm, he made the acquaintance of a number of orientalists, including the Indologists Heinrich Zimmer and J. W. Hauer. The relationship with the former was the more important, the two men becoming close friends, and Zimmer, who was Professor of Sanskrit at the University of Heidelberg, gave frequent lectures to the Zürich Psychological Club at Jung's invitation. Zimmer's importance in Jung's intellectual development lay in the field of mythological studies, and he enabled Jung to see close parallels between Indian thought and analytical psychology. 'In our work together', Jung acknowledged, 'he gave me invaluable insights into the Oriental psyche, not only through his immense technical knowledge, but above all through his brilliant grasp of the meaning and content of Indian mythology.'[11] By this time Jung had formulated his teaching concerning the self and its relation to the ego, and his friend's work enabled him to discern important affinities between his own thinking and that of Indian yoga, and to confirm that his psychological insights into this question reflected the age-old theories and practices of India. Such insights led him to exclaim: 'The philosophy of the East, although so vastly different from ours, could be an inestimable treasure for us too.'[12] Zimmer had a special interest, clearly personal as well as professional, in the contemporary Indian saint Shri Ramana Maharshi, though Jung's Foreword to Zimmer's edition of the Maharshi's writings[13] evinces a somewhat less than enthusiastic response to the saint, as we shall see shortly.

The importance for Jung of the second of these Indologists, J. W. Hauer, lay in Jung's interest in *kundalini* (or Tantric) yoga. Jung had earlier made the acquaintance of this particular form of Indian yoga through John

Woodroffe's *The Serpent Power*, and in 1932 he invited Hauer, who was Professor of Sanskrit at Tübingen University, to lecture on *kundalini* to the Zürich Psychology Club. The lecture left the audience somewhat bemused, and in order to clarify matters Jung followed it up with two lectures in which he sought to develop links between the Tantric system and his own concept of individuation.[14] By this time he was confident that a bridge of understanding between East and West could be built with the aid of concepts drawn from analytical psychology, and in his lecture he set out to show that the symbolism of the Tantric path towards enlightnment, whereby the 'serpent power' climbed up through the successive psychic centres (*chakras*), could be used to illuminate the nature of the individuation process whereby a human being endeavours to achieve psychic wholeness.

An important stage in this task of East–West bridge-building took place in 1933 with the establishment of the annual '*Eranos*' conferences, in which Zimmer and Hauer, as well as Jung, were involved. Hosted at her villa near Lake Maggiore by the theosophist Olga Fröbe-Kapteyn, these conferences originally set themselves the goal of mediating between the cultures and philosophies of East and of West, and of studying Eastern philosophies – not with a view to imitating them, but rather, in the words of Fröbe-Kapteyn, 'to rediscover the spiritual values that are most distinctively our own'. Though Jung was a prime mover in this enterprise and gave many lectures there, the conferences also drew together over the years a wide range of distinguished scholars, including the sinologist Erwin Rousselle, the philosopher of religion Rudolf Otto, the theologians Martin Buber and Paul Tillich, the anthropologist Paul Radin, and the historian of religions Mircea Eliade. 'Yoga and Eastern Meditation' was the title of the first of the conferences, and Eastern topics continued to dominate the proceedings up to their close in 1951, though as the years passed by the meetings broadened out to embrace a wide range of subjects connected with the history and psychology of religious experience and mythology. As far as Jung was concerned, these conferences gave him the opportunity to extend his understanding of Eastern philosophies while at the same time providing him with a platform on which to develop some of his central ideas concerning archetypes and the collective unconscious.

The high point, and in some ways the turning-point, of Jung's relationship with the East was his expedition to India in 1938, a three-month visit undertaken at the invitation of the British Government in India to take part in the celebrations to mark the twenty-fifth anniversary of the founding of the University of Calcutta. Aside from the formalities of the visit and a nasty bout of dysentery requiring a ten-day sojourn in hospital, Jung took the opportunity to travel widely in India and Ceylon, and made the acquaintance of a number of Indian scholars, giving lectures at various universities and visiting some of the important historical and religious sites. He was especially moved by the *stupas* (hemispherical monuments) at Sanchi, where the Buddha had delivered his 'Fire Sermon', recalling in his autobiography that he was gripped by 'an unexpected power' and overcome by a strong emotion of the kind that occurred when he encountered a thing, person or idea of whose significance he was still unconscious. The 'exquisitely obscene sculptures' of the temple at Konarak, with their larger-than-life images of love-making, impressed him in a different way, and he was struck too by the sense of deep historical rootedness that underpinned every aspect of what he called the 'dreamlike world of India'.[15]

Nevertheless, a strong feeling of ambivalence towards India pervades his account of the trip. This ambivalence was partly due to the fact that in 1938 the main focus of his interest was beginning to shift away from Eastern philosophies towards European alchemy, a shift precipitated some years earlier by his reading of the Chinese alchemical text *The Secret of the Golden Flower*. He described his journey as 'an intermezzo in the intensive study of alchemical philosophy on which I was engaged at the time',[16] and spent much of his spare time in India and on the long sea voyage studying a mediaeval European alchemical text. Prior to his return he had a powerful dream, which he interpreted as calling him back 'to the too-long-neglected concerns of the Occident', the dream reminding him that 'India was not my task, but only a part of the way'.[17] In recalling his visit many years later, he pictured himself as remaining within himself 'like a homunculus in a retort', and of pursuing his own truth in spite of the exotic and thought-provoking distractions that surrounded him. Pervading his whole Indian experience was a feeling of distance, even of alienation, towards India with its 'foreign mentality and culture', a feeling which may help to explain why Jung decided not to visit Shri Ramana Maharshi, in spite of the fact that his friend Heinrich Zimmer had strongly urged him to do so. The reasons he gave for this in his autobiography – namely, that saints of this kind could be seen all over India ('he is of a type which always was and will be. Therefore it was not necessary to seek him out'), and that 'in India he is merely the whitest spot on a white surface'[18] – do not seem to tell the whole story. It may be that Jung, in order to maintain his stance of independence, felt it necessary to avoid a man who, by repute, may well have been able to penetrate his defences, for just as he had since his boyhood refused to bend his knee to the Christian way of faith, so with regard to Eastern spirituality his attitude remained one of guarded objectivity. He could not, as he expressed it, 'accept from others what I could not attain on my own', or 'make any borrowings from the East, but must shape my life out of myself'.[19] As we shall see shortly, this attitude is one with which we need to come to terms in order to understand Jung's whole approach to Eastern thought and spirituality.

While Jung's interest as we have plotted it so far had concentrated first on Chinese Taoism, and then on Indian yoga, in the period from about 1935 a new interest emerges into prominence, namely, Buddhism. This interest bore fruit in several ways during the period leading up to the war. In 1935 he contributed a psychological commentary to the German translation of *The Tibetan Book of the Dead*,[20] and in 1939 he wrote a psychological commentary on *The Tibetan Book of the Great Liberation*,[21] the publication of which was delayed by the war. These esoteric works from the Tibetan Mahāyāna Buddhist tradition represented a new phase in the West's understanding of Asian philosophies. Hitherto, the West's knowledge of the Buddhist traditions had been confined largely to the Hinayana branch which flourished in southern Asia, but in the inter-war period this understanding was enriched by new explorations in the northern Mahāyāna schools of Tibet, China and Japan. These texts, especially the former, were to have a considerable impact on later generations, *The Tibetan Book of the Dead* becoming a special favourite among the Flower People of the 1960s. As far as Jung was concerned, they offered deep psychological insights, once the mythical and metaphysical elements had been filtered out, and provided important confirmation of his theory of the self as an ontologically primary datum and as an image of the potential and the unity of the personality as a whole. Thus, *The Tibetan Book of the Great Liberation* was seen as offering an essentially psychological insight, and as confirming his belief in the centrality of the psyche, which 'is not a nonentity devoid of all quality', as materialists would claim, but rather 'the only category of existence of which we have *immediate* knowledge'.[22]

Jung found further confirmation for these insights in Zen Buddhism. His interest in Zen dates back to the period of *Symbols of Transformation*, but was rekindled on his being introduced to the writings of D. T. Suzuki by Heinrich Zimmer. Suzuki was trained in his native Japan, but lived for a long period in America, producing throughout his long life a series of books which provided the chief source of understanding of Zen in the West. One of his most influential books, *Introduction to Zen Buddhism*, was translated into German by Zimmer, and Jung was invited to contribute a Foreword for the 1939 edition.[23] Once again Jung's interest was strictly psychological. He found the ideas of Zen 'strange', referring to their 'exotic obscurity', and admitting that at times Zen talk sounds 'like the most crashing nonsense'.[24] Nevertheless, he was convinced that Zen is not mere 'mumbo-jumbo', and that once again sense can be made of it for the Westerner by treating it in psychological terms. The central experience of *satori* (enlightenment) was one which, though difficult for the European to appreciate, could be made sense of in terms both of Christian mysticism and of psychotherapy. As with mystics, such as Meister Eckhart, the Zen techniques aim at the transformation of consciousness into a higher state, and as with psychotherapy they are concerned with the redirecting of the psychic life, its reorientation and its quest for wholeness.

In spite of Jung's shift of interest towards European alchemy in this period, a shift which led to a further immensely productive phase of his life, his involvement in Eastern ideas continued to command his attention in the final period of his life. Of all the Eastern philosophies it was Buddhism, with its concern for the healing of human suffering, that resonated most harmoniously with his own concerns with psychic healing, and which at the same time seems to have touched him most deeply, and although he never in any sense became a Buddhist, it is clear that spiritually he felt a close affinity with it in his final years. His introductory remarks for a publication in 1956 of the discourses of the Buddha[25] express a forthright acknowledgement of 'the immense help and stimulation I have received from the Buddhist teachings', and contain the admission that Buddhist teachings offer a way towards psychic healing which is superior to 'the various brands of Christianity'. He continued to study Buddhist texts right to the end of his life, and in a letter written a year before his death in 1961 he says that he had for several months embarked on a long-planned study of the Buddha's sermons, 'trying to get nearer to the remarkable psychology of the Buddha himself'.[26]

JUNG'S INVOLVEMENT WITH THE EAST

We need to look more closely at the reasons and motivations that led Jung to engage in a protracted dialogue with the East. After all, even though he may have had a personal interest in such matters, the considerable input of energy involved in studying and commenting on Oriental texts and ideas might be viewed as a wasteful distraction from his clinical work, and the publication of essays on Eastern thought might well have been seen at the time as doing his reputation as a 'scientist' no good at all.

To make sense of this we need to examine matters at several different levels. In the first place, it is important not to underestimate the extent to which the East entered into Jung's own individuation process. He did not approach these matters as a disinterested scholar, and even a superficial reading of the texts published in this volume will make clear the extent to which the subject-matter touched him personally. It is true that he was often at pains to identify himself with the Christian tradition, and there is no doubt that his attitude towards the religion of his upbringing and his culture was far from straightforward. Though Christ represented for him a symbol of the individuation process of the self, it was a symbol that left him unsatisfied, one from which he himself did not appear to derive much spiritual fulfilment. Moreover, Christian theology often appeared to him as far too rationalistic, and as lacking in the capacity to reach the deepest levels of the human psyche. The profoundly transformative experiences of his life, such as the early fantasy of God destroying Basel Cathedral, and his later encounter with the internal imaginal figures such as Philemon, had a significance for him which appeared to lie outside the bounds of Christian doctrine. In addition to this, Christ, though a symbol of the self, did not represent for him a fully fleshed-out image of wholeness or a symbol of complete psychic integration, for the Christ-image always carried with it a sense of otherworldliness which led to a discounting of embodied experience as well as of the positive role of evil in human life. While acknowledging that both paths 'are right', he admitted that compared with Christ 'Buddha is the more complete human being. He is a historical personality, and therefore easier for men to understand.

Christ is at once a historical man and God, and therefore much more difficult to comprehend.'[27] Moreover, Christianity demanded faith, and this was something that always eluded Jung. There is no doubt that he recognized in Eastern religions an inwardness and an emphasis on the validity of personal experience that seemed absent from the mainstream of the Christian tradition. His deeply personal attachment to Gnosticism, an attachment which flourished during the period of inner uncertainty and disorientation following his break with Freud, seemed to prepare him for, and lead naturally into, his dialogue with Eastern religions, and the self-discovery and self-transformation which so appealed to him in Buddhism and yoga must have represented for him a powerful echo of the Gnostic inner path. Moreover, his well-known fascination with the mandala symbol was one which was sparked not by scholarly interest, but by the need to recover and redirect his own life's path during a period of inner turmoil and disorientation. In the course of producing a large number of mandala drawings in 1918–19 he discovered, as he put it, 'the self, the wholeness of the personality', a discovery which was confirmed later when he came to realize that the ritual mandala diagrams of the East also appeared to function as instruments for psychic integration.[28] None of this implies that he in any sense committed himself to an Eastern belief system, for, as we shall see, he expressed weighty reservations about the advisability of the adoption of Eastern religious ways by Westerners. But we can speculate – no more than that – that these factors represented a significant catalyst in his own psychological growth.

What is especially striking in Jung's personal development is his ability to confront and grapple with the strange and sometimes disturbing elements within his own personality, his ability to encounter and integrate the 'shadow' within himself. His autobiographical essay gives poignant witness to his willingness, from an early age, to explore and face up to experiences which were in various ways alien and threatening. This bears on his relationship with the East in at least two ways. In the first place he found in his Oriental explorations an inclination to integrate within the totality of human experience those aspects which could be described as evil or as negative in some way. It must be remembered in this context that the recognition of the importance of opposite tendencies within the personality was a central feature of Jung's psychology and one for which he found close parallels in the philosophical systems of both India and China. This factor seems to have been prominent in his mind during his trip to India when, as he put it later, 'I was principally concerned with the question of the psychological nature of evil'; he goes on to say that he was 'very much impressed by the way this problem is integrated in Indian spiritual life'.[29] Where Christianity sought to place good and evil at opposite and irreconcilable poles, with evil as the absolute negation of good, Indian philosophies sought liberation from these and all other apparent opposites by experiencing them as complementary, and by pursuing a middle path of balance between opposing tendencies. Similarly, the opposites *yang* and *yin*, which are fundamental to the outlook of Chinese philosophy, are seen not as mutually exclusive but as complementary, and so, in Jung's words, '*Tao* is the right way . . . the middle road between the opposites, freed from them and yet uniting them in itself.'[30] Furthermore, the strange otherness of the East, which many have interpreted as a sign of relative backwardness, Jung construed as manifesting the way in which the psyche itself is polarized between opposing tendencies, and that while the West has developed and refined the extraverted aspects of the psyche, associated with rational understanding and control of the external world, the culture of the East has by contrast developed those psychological qualities associated with the understanding and control of the inner world. Psychic health meant, for Jung, a balancing of these opposing tendencies, sought by drawing the strange 'other' into some kind of accommodation.

Second, Jung's proclivity towards engaging with what is strange and different is evident in a parallel way in regard to the outer world as well, whether that of his patients or that of human cultures. Here again we see him engaging with the 'other', and involving himself in a dialogue in which he sought to relate and accommodate his own views and outlook to what at first sight appeared uncompromisingly alien. Whether dealing with schizophrenic patients, with mediaeval alchemy, with Gnosticism, or with the traditions and texts of the East, his method was consistently one of dialogue, in which he sought to construct bridges of understanding. This approach was evident early on in Jung's career when, as an intern at the Burghölzli mental hospital in Zürich, he argued, contrary to the prevailing medical opinion, that it was possible to make sense of the strange behaviour and utterances of schizophrenic patients. By carefully listening and relating to these patients he came to the conclusion that apparently crazy symptoms could be 'read' and 'interpreted' in perfectly meaningful ways. This essentially hermeneutical approach became a model for all his later dealings with patients, with whom he sought to establish a relationship of mutual rapport and dialogue rather than one of scientific objectivity and clinical authority. Therapy therefore became for him a personal relationship in which he strove to relate to the patient as one human being to another, recognizing that the analyst is as much involved in the analytic process as the patient.

We find a similar dialogical approach in his treament of cultural phenomena, the world of symbolic products and belief systems, a world which included Gnosticism, mediaeval alchemy, Christian theology, aspects of the occult, and – the philosophical texts of the East. In formulating his own distinctive theories, such as psychological types and the collective unconscious, he sought to relate his insights to a whole range of philosophical, historical and mythological precedents and parallels. This was partly a matter of enriching the empirical base from which he sought to draw his conclusions, for, as in the case of the collective unconscious, Jung was aware of the need to draw on experience from beyond purely European sources. But it was also an expression of Jung's belief that self-understanding is only possible if one can, in some sense, stand beyond oneself. The endless hermeneutical gaming which he engaged in with regard to alchemy, and to a lesser extent with Eastern religions, had as its aim the illumination of the human psyche and the further elaboration of his own psychological theories. Just as, according to Jung, a patient needs to comprehend his or her symptoms in terms of the mythological and symbolic products of humanity, a process he termed 'amplification', so also the philosophies, theologies and psychological theories of European extraction need to be placed in the wider context and compared with the theories and ideas of different times and places.

This way of looking at Jung's dealings with the East is clearly evident in Jung's first major piece of writing on Eastern thought, namely his commentary on *The Secret of the Golden Flower*. The discovery of this work through the good offices of his friend Richard Wilhelm represented a major turning-point in his life. It constituted, as he put it, 'the first event which broke through my isolation', and provided him with 'undreamed-of confirmation' of ideas concerning the human psyche on which he was working at the time.[31] The break with Freud in 1913 had not only propelled him into a personal crisis, but had also cut him adrift from the wider psychoanalytical movement, and his new and revolutionary ideas concerning the human psyche, which to a large measure had precipitated the rupture, were ones which seemed to be out of harmony with the prevailing intellectual mood of the times, and attracted little interest or support. These ideas could be summed up in terms of three basic notions. The first was that of the reality of the psyche: the belief that the psyche represented not a mere epiphenomenal extension of the material world, but a kind of microcosm in its own right which, though linked to bodily function, could not simply be reduced thereto. Allied to this, second, was the idea that the exploration, cultivation and development of this inner world was the supremely meaningful vocation of humankind. This later became associated with the concept of 'individuation', but at this stage, especially during the period of what he called his 'confrontation with the unconscious', Jung came to the conclusion that the goal of psychic development is the 'self', the latter representing for him the idea of the fullest realization of human potential, and the unity of the personality as a whole with all its disparate, opposite and often warring elements. The third was the idea that, in addition to a personal unconscious, there exists a *collective* unconscious. According to this view, the psyches of individual persons must be understood not just in terms of their own individual histories, but in terms of the history of the human race; in some sense we actually inherit patterns of psychic behaviour, just as we inherit patterns of physical behaviour. This does not mean, as is sometimes supposed, that we inherit actual memories, but rather that the contents of the collective unconscious, which he saw as archetypes, are patterns of *potential* behaviour, not actual images or thoughts. Thus as members of the human race we inherit the capacity or disposition to develop distinctive psychic attitudes which, though in one sense unique to us as individuals, are also recognizable traits of humanity as such.

These ideas appeared to fly in the face of accepted orthodoxy, and moreover, as Jung was acutely aware, they rested on a rather narrow empirical base. He admitted that his results, based on fifteen years of work, 'seemed inconclusive, because no possibility of comparison offered itself', for he 'knew of no realm of human experience with which I might have backed up my findings with some degree of assurance', except for the scattered and fragmentary reports from early Christian Gnostics.[32] His meeting with Richard Wilhelm in 1923 represented the breakthrough that he had been seeking for some years, for it offered, so he believed, the crucial evidence in support of his theory of the archetypes of the collective unconscious, helping to confirm him in his view that 'the human psyche possesses a common substratum transcending all differences in culture and consciousness'.[33] There were further bonuses. In the first place his reading of *The Secret of the Golden Flower* acquainted him with a culture which, to a far greater extent than that of the West, recognized the depth and complexity of the human psyche and believed in the vital importance of its investigation and cultivation. The Chinese, judging by this text, had long understood that it is 'far more reasonable to accord the psyche the same validity as the empirical world, and to admit that the former has just as much "reality" as the latter'.[34] Their appreciation of its subtle depths and nuances, of its inner dynamics and tensions, and of its tendency towards a state of balance and harmony all offered confirmation to Jung of the conception of the psyche that he was elaborating at that time. And, second, their capacity for introspection and their grasp of the basic psychic need for inner transformation and self-realization seemed to be remarkably analogous to his own therapeutic endeavours and to confirm him in the basic correctness of his clinical methods. Indeed he was led to conclude that in his professional work he 'had been unconsciously following that secret way which for centuries had been the preoccupation of the best minds of the East'.[35]

Jung's initial experience on meeting Wilhelm and working with *The Secret of the Golden Flower* became a model for much of his subsequent dealings with Eastern texts. Thus in his psychological commentary on *The Tibetan Book of the Dead* we find him reading it not as a (to the Westerner) strange metaphysical or even mythological narrative, but rather as a work of deep psychological insight which can help initiate us into the way of individuation and wholeness. What appears at one level as a book of instructions for the dead and dying can be read as an initiation into the encounter with the unconscious mind. He is similarly dismissive of all metaphysical claims in his commentary on *The Tibetan Book of the Great Liberation*, and sees its value as lying in its capacity to teach us about the reality of the psyche and to correct the one-sidedness of the Western materialist/reductionist outlook. In this text, with its strong introspective and introverted tendencies, Jung finds confirmation of his belief that 'matter is an hypothesis' not a primary reality, and that 'Psychic existence is the only category of existence of which we have *immediate* knowledge, since nothing can be known unless it first appears as a psychic image'.[36]

In a similar way, Jung's writings on yoga and Zen seek to throw across the East–West divide a bridge of understanding by relating these Oriental traditions to Western philosophical and psychological concerns. Thus in the case of yoga his aim is to transpose the 'rich metaphysic and symbolism of the East' into terms which relate to the psychological and spiritual needs of the West, and to show how the various dualisms that rack Western culture – science versus religion, body versus mind, reason versus emotion – can be mediated by means of the ideas and practices of yoga. In the case of Zen, the idea of *satori* (enlightenment) and the technique of the *koan* (verbal paradoxes to aid enlightenment) seem at first glance to be so much 'crashing nonsense', strange notions which seem 'more or less unassimilable for ordinary Europeans'.[37] Here again Jung starts from the premiss that Eastern ideas arise from a totally different conceptual framework from that of the West; yet a fruitful dialogue is not only possible but highly desirable, for even though we cannot simply assimilate Japanese Zen, the idea of *satori* as a process of self-knowledge, a psychological breakthrough, a sudden awakening, can cast interesting light on parallel processes occurring within Western psychotherapy.

In the case of the *I Ching*, Jung's dialogical encounter with the East takes on a quite literal significance. He had become acquainted in the early 1920s with this classic Chinese text in the translation by James Legge and had embarked on a series of experiments with it, obtaining, as he put it, 'All sorts of undeniably remarkable results . . . meaningful connections with my own thought processes which I could not explain to myself'.[38] Some years later he was invited to contribute a psychological commentary to the English edition of Wilhelm's translation of the *I Ching*, and he took the opportunity to conduct a systematic dialogue with it, engaging in a remarkable question-and-answer exchange with the text, an experiment which, as readers can see for themselves, produced some interesting results. Here again he confronts a strange ancient text, despised even by modern Chinese, which to many appears to be little more than 'a collection of magic spells', and manages to make sense of it in a way that directly parallels his earlier treatment of schizophrenic patients. Furthermore, the work also had significance for him at a theoretical level, for it presented him with a way of seeing the world in terms of the correlations of meanings rather than of mechanical causation, an idea which was to provide the basis for his theory of synchronicity, or meaningful coincidence.[39]

What is evident so far is that much of Jung's concern in these dialogues was with the search for a means of making sense of and enhancing the goal of psychological integration. But in his view this had wider implications for modern Western culture as a whole, and here we begin to explore yet another level of Jung's engagement with the East, one which moves on to a global plane. Jung recognized from an early stage of his investigations into the individual human psyche that his patients' problems could not be dissociated from wider social, cultural and political issues, and indeed that a good analyst is one who is able to view matters in a broad historical perspective. He often expressed the need to bring the experiences of medical specialists out of their narrow setting into a wider context, and sought to underline the relevance of his psychological theories to philosophy and the history of ideas. His preoccupation with the broader moral and social questions surrounding psychotherapy was evident as early as 1912, when he wrote that 'in the patient a conflict . . . is connected with the great problems of society', and that neurosis 'is intimately bound up with the problem of our time'.[40] This concern developed over the following decades, with their history of apocalyptic events – a period coinciding with his growing involvement with Eastern thought, and expressed in his popular collection of essays *Modern Man in Search of a Soul*, first published in 1933. What, then, was the nature of this broad concern, and how did it link with his Oriental interests?

In brief, Jung became convinced in this period that European civilization and Christianity were undergoing an unprecedented crisis. In 1931 he wrote: 'We are living undeniably in a period of the greatest restlessness, nervous tension, confusion and disorientation of outlook' and that 'everywhere the mental state of European man shows an alarming lack of balance'.[41] In his consulting room he had come to see that 'Christian tenets have lost their authority and their psychological justification.'[42] Traditional metaphysical certainties and inherited truths had ceased to convince. The cultivation of rational consciousness in the West was tending to detach us from our instinctive roots in the collective unconscious. Science had torn to shreds the supportive fabric of belief that had so laboriously been woven together in an earlier age. And on the political level the individual was increasingly being caught up in a 'collective possession' and subjected to a 'psychic epidemic'. This crisis was not, though, of recent origin, for according to Jung it can be traced back to the period of the Reformation, the Scientific Revolution, and the Enlightenment, a period when European culture turned its back on its ancient traditions with their rich store of archetypal myths, images and rituals. The modern period has often been characterized as one of progress and liberation, but for Jung it also represented a period when European culture was set adrift from its traditional cultural and psychological roots, and when the cultivation of scientific rationalism and technology had led to a one-sided development of human faculties that focused our attention on the external world at the expense of the inner life of the spirit. The result was the 'breathless drive for power and aggrandisement'. 'No-one', he lamented, 'has any time for self-knowledge or believes that it could serve any sensible purpose . . . . We believe exclusively in doing and do not ask about the doer.'[43]

Jung's interest in Eastern philosophies must be understood in the light of these concerns. While wary of what he deprecatingly called 'the allurements of the odorous East', he explicitly sought an understanding with the East that would help in the formulation of a spiritual cure for the West. In alchemical terms, the East represented not the gold, but rather the philosopher's stone, the catalyst through which spiritual transformation might take place; the East was, he believed, 'at the bottom of the spiritual change we are passing through today', and out of its depths 'new spiritual forms will arise'.[44] At the heart of Jung's thinking on this question lay his conviction concerning the unbalanced nature of the Western psyche. The one-sided emphasis in the West on the extraverted attitude needs to be balanced in favour of the introverted attitude, and the functions of feeling and intuition given parity with thinking and sensation. The East represented for Jung a different point of view which would compensate for what he called the 'barbarous one-sidedness' of the Western outlook. In his view, Eastern philosophies and practices offered the West a model of self-awareness which had the potential for uncovering and releasing the self-liberating powers of the mind and thereby opening the way towards a more adequate level of psychic integration and wholeness. However, this did not mean that for Jung the East had achieved the desired psychic balance that increasingly eluded the West. He frequently pointed out that in practice the East is as one-sided as the West, for it has tended to overstress the introvertive aspects of the psyche just as the modern West has overstressed its extravertive aspects. He observed that the two standpoints, however contradictory, each have their psychological justification, that both 'are one-sided in that they fail to see and take account of those factors which do not fit in with their typical attitude', the one underrating the world of consciousness, the other the world of mind.[45] Nevertheless, for Jung the West's situation is inherently more dangerous, because more extreme and politically more explosive, in addition to which, as a European himself, he saw it as his special vocation to deal with the problems that faced his own culture.

JUNG'S RESERVATIONS AND QUALIFICATIONS

It will be evident from the foregoing that Jung was not proposing that the West should, as some of his contemporaries were beginning to advocate, overthrow entirely our Western Christian heritage and replace it with *Vedanta* philosophy or with Buddhism. In the face of the spiritual crisis in the West, many have turned towards the East in search of a substitute for the god that has failed them, but the danger with this sort of strategy, Jung believed, was that it failed to strike at the root cause of the disease, which lay within ourselves. 'Study yoga', he advised, for 'you will learn an infinite amount from it – but do not try to apply it.'[46] Such reservations come as something of a shock to the unwary reader, who may have been led to believe that Jung was one of the twentieth century's chief advocates of the adoption of the ways of Oriental widsom. Jung has often been seen as a kind of Pied Piper leading an ever-growing trail of young people in this century on a pilgrimage to the East. This represents a complete misunderstanding of Jung's position, and fails to take account of the trenchant reservations and qualifications with which he surrounded his Oriental explorations. To be sure he was a great admirer of Eastern philosophies, referring to 'this spiritual achievement of the East as one of the greatest things the human mind has ever created',[47] often appearing to rank it above Western culture, and using it as a tool for criticizing the European cultural tradition. He was convinced that in some sense the West needed the East, and had much to learn from it in the context of its current spiritual crisis. Nevertheless, he took care to distance himself from it, and kept his enthusiasm for it within well-defined limits.

The first of these limits concerns the very metaphysical foundations of Eastern philosophy. In approaching *all* varieties of religious and metaphysical belief, Western as well as Eastern, from alchemy and astrology to Christian theology, Jung explicitly adopted a *phenomenological* approach, which meant placing all transcendental assumptions that go beyond experience into parentheses, and dealing solely with the experience as such. 'Our psychology', he insisted, 'is, therefore, a science of mere phenomena without any metaphysical implications';[48] 'I strip things of their metaphysical wrappings in order to make them objects of psychology.'[49] Thus, to take an example from Christian theology, in dealing with the doctrine of the Resurrection he addressed himself not to its supposed transcendent or theological significance, but rather to its symbolic or psychological meaning. Likewise, in his extensive dealings with alchemy he was not concerned with the metaphysical doctrines that were claimed to underpin it, but rather with its signficance for the experience of psychological transformation. In this respect his methodology was similar to that of an anthropologist who studies, say, the religious beliefs of a culture, while endeavouring to take no position on the question of the truth or validity of such beliefs.

This is the line he took with regard to the teachings of Eastern religions. Here, too, he sought to lay aside all metaphysical claims, taking up an agnostic position towards them, and concentrating his attention instead on their psychological significance. He maintained that his psychology was a purely *empirical* inquiry, based solely on the deliverances of human experience, and therefore it 'treats all metaphysical claims and assertions as mental phenomena, and regards them as statements about the mind and its structure'.[50] Thus in his commentary on *The Tibetan Book of the Dead* he reads the account of the experiences of the dead soul in its passage from death to rebirth in psychological terms, and in his discussion of the *I Ching* he describes his approach as 'psychological phenomenology', insisting that his use of the text is purely 'pragmatic', and that therefore 'nothing "occult" is to be inferred'.[51] This distancing of his inquiry from the truth-claims of Eastern philosophies, as well as his hermeneutical intentions towards them, is well summed up by Jung in a letter of 1935 where he writes:

I am first and foremost an empiricist who was led to the question of Western and Eastern mysticism only for empirical reasons. For instance I do not by any means take my stand by the Tao or any yoga technique, but have found that Taoist philosophy as well as yoga have very many parallels with the psychic processes we observe in Western man.[52]

At times, however, Jung takes a more radical, reductionist, stance, appearing to claim that metaphysical statements must be treated as *nothing but* psychological statements. Thus in his commentary on *The Secret of the Golden Flower* he writes that his 'admiration for the great philosophers of the East is as genuine as my attitude towards their metaphysics is irreverent. I suspect them of being symbolical psychologists, to whom no greater wrong could be done than to take them literally.'[53] Even more unequivocal is his claim: 'The world of gods and spirits is truly "nothing but" the collective unconscious inside me.'[54] These remarks seem to suggest not just that metaphysical claims are to be placed within agnostic parentheses, but that such claims are not really metaphysical claims at all, a view borne out by his advice: 'Every statement about the transcendental is to be avoided because it is only a laughable presumption on the part of a human mind unconscious of its limitations.'[55] The word 'limitations' here is important, and leads to further qualifications, for it points to the fact that Jung's whole philosophical outlook is deeply infused with the Kantian critique of human reason, according to which claims to knowledge cannot extend beyond certain circumscribed boundaries. Metaphysical claims, whether Eastern or Western, overstep these boundaries, and in Jung's view some Eastern philosophies are especially inclined to do so. He thought that Indian metaphysical speculations lack a firm empirical grounding and are based implicitly on pre-Kantian assumptions about the virtually limitless scope of human knowledge. At certain crucial points 'Eastern intuition has overreached itself',[56] and yoga philosophy in particular suffers 'a curious detachment from the world of concrete particulars we call reality'.[57]

This overreaching and detachment from reality were evident, to Jung's way of thinking, in the yoga teachings concerning the *self*. He was convinced that his own conception of the psyche bore a close analogy to the central theme of yoga philosophy concerning the self, and that the Indian concept of *atman* formed an exact parallel to the psychological idea of the self. For Jung the self represented the realization of the fullest potential of the human psyche, and, by contrast with the Freudian tradition, he saw the ego not as potentially an absolute monarch ruling the forces within the psyche, but as an integral part of a dynamic system. He therefore felt great sympathy with the yoga teaching concerning the need to transcend the narrowness of the individual ego and to attain a higher selfhood where the individual experiences identity with pure cosmic consciousness. But at this point a deep division becomes evident in the dialogue between the Western thinker and his Eastern counterparts. The ultimate goal of yoga is not simply the integration of the ego within the totality of the self, but rather a state of complete absorption (*samādhi*) where to all intents and purposes the individual person ceases to exist as such. The goal of yoga, he believed, is identity with '"universal consciousness" [which] is logically identical with unconsciousness . . . a state in which subject and object are almost completely identical'.[58]

Jung had two main difficulties with this. The first was a theoretical one, for in the final analysis he could not make logical sense of it. Whereas yoga philosophy has no problem in conceiving the idea of a self in which the individual ego has been absorbed into a higher totality, Jung on the contrary could not 'imagine a conscious mental state that does not relate to a subject, that is, to an ego', for '[if] there is no ego there is nobody to be conscious of anything'.[59] In order that a higher selfhood should be attained there must remain an individual consciousness, an ego, that does the attaining; there must 'always be somebody or something left over to experience the real-ization, to say "I know at-one-ment, I know there is no distinction"'.[60] Thus for Jung the Indian doctrine of non-duality, of the ultimate obliteration of the distinction between subject and object, is quite simply a contradiction in terms. He remained finally and obstinately pluralistic in the face of Eastern monism, claiming that beneath the Indians' non-dualistic standpoint 'there nevertheless lies hidden the whole unabolished pluralistic universe and its unconquered reality'.[61]

One consequence of this theoretical difference was that Jung rejected the possibility of any final and fully realized state of self-illumination. According to yoga philosophy it is possible, albeit very difficult, for the self to attain a state of illumination in which the psyche becomes completely transparent to itself and the ego is completely absorbed into the higher self. But according to Jung the totality of the self – conscious and unconscious – can never become fully luminous to the ego. According to his view the life of the psyche, though capable of increasing integration and harmony, is inescapably one of inner tension and dialectical opposition. As he puts it: 'The life of the unconscious goes on and continually produces problematical situations . . . . There is no change which is unconditionally valid over a long period of time. Life has always to be tackled anew.'[62] This view is plainly at odds with Buddhism as well as with yoga, for both hold out the hope of an ultimate state of illumination in which suffering is irreversibly transcended. By contrast, Jung held the view that 'Complete redemption from the sufferings of this world is and must remain an illusion';[63] indeed 'Complete liberation means death.'[64]

This leads to the second type of difficulty that Jung had with Eastern philosophies, which is of a more practical kind. We have already quoted Jung as proclaiming that, in spite of its great store of wisdom, Eastern philosophies such as yoga should not be imitated by Westerners, and going so far as to suggest that such an attempt would be positively dangerous. Thus, concerning the practice of Zen, he proclaimed that its 'direct transplantation . . . to our Western conditions is neither commendable nor even possible',[65] and warned against 'the oft-attempted imitation of Indian practices and sentiments'.[66] Why did he hold such a view, and how can it be reconciled with his evident enthusiasm for the psychological insights of the East? Certainly not because he was convinced of the superiority of the West: 'If I remain so critically averse to yoga, it does not mean that I do not regard this spiritual achievement of the East as one of the greatest things the human mind has ever created';[67] and he often repeated sentiments such as: 'The East teaches us another, broader, more profound and higher understanding.'[68]

To make sense of this seeming contradiction in Jung's thinking, we need to understand that Jung had a strong sense of the cultural and historical embeddedness of religious and philosophical beliefs. He saw cultures, such as the Indian, the Chinese, and the European, with their complex patterns of thought, ritual and emotional response, as firmly rooted in their own specific histories and traditions. For him they were like living organisms, and human consciousness itself is like an organism which is adapted to and grows within a unique environment; hence it is wrong to imagine that Westerners can detach themselves from their own historical roots and graft themselves on to another. Such an attempt leads at best to superficial imitation, without ever really being able to integrate and fully understand another culture, and at worst it may lead to severe psychological disorientation and even psychosis. It was for this reason that he was so consistently critical of what he described as the attempt 'to put on, like a new suit of clothes, ready-made symbols grown on foreign soil', for 'If we now try to cover our nakedness with the gorgeous trappings of the East, as the theosophists do, we would be playing our own history false.'[69] Often such an attempt on the part of Westerners was symptomatic of a kind of consumerist attitude, which betrayed a propensity to escape from their present ills by adopting palliatives acquired from exotic foreign parts. Our 'imitative urge' misleads us into 'snatching at such "magical" ideas and applying them externally, like an ointment'.[70] The consequences of this can, indeed, in some cases be quite disastrous, according to Jung. The trance-like states sought in yoga and the powerful methods of the Tantric system were especially to be feared, for there was a real danger that the Westerner, lacking the cultural supports provided within the traditional Indian way of life, could be precipitated into a psychotic state.

What we should be doing, on the contrary, is facing our own problems in our own terms, Jung maintained. Yoga and its philosophy can inspire and motivate us, but to be true to ourselves and our cultural heritage we must seek a path of psychological growth and spiritual development which comes from our own inner resources. We must therefore 'build on our own ground with our own methods', seeking to 'get at the Eastern values from within and not from without, seeking them in ourselves'.[71] In the course of the centuries, he believed, the West would produce its own form of yoga, which would arise from the West's own indigenous cultural resources, psychotherapy representing a significant move in this direction.

QUESTIONS ADDRESSED TO JUNG

At this point a number of questions and issues inevitably arise. In the light of the above considerations we might begin to wonder why, from Jung's point

of view, it is desirable, or even possible, to engage with the East at all, for
if its ways of spiritual growth are so entirely alien to our own, what benefit
is there in embarking upon a dialogue with it? In the first place it may
be wondered whether Jung's whole approach to the East was in a sense too
cautious, altogether too Eurocentric. In the light of subsequent history, his
misgivings, voiced in the 1930s, may appear to be unnecessarily restrictive.
After all, the pursuit of the ideals and practices of yoga and Zen has grown
at an exponential rate since the time when Jung issued his warnings. It is
true that there are dangers, as he rightly pointed out, in the 'unthinking'
adoption of Eastern practices; many psychiatrists in the 1960s had to deal
with young people whose total immersion in Eastern practices led to mental
breakdown. But all the evidence suggests that by and large the yoga
techniques of Hinduism, Buddhism and Taoism can be successfully integrated into Western culture, and that their effects can be beneficial in a
variety of contexts. To be fair to Jung, he could hardly be expected to have
anticipated the cultural explosion that followed the Second World War, or
the extent to which the different cultures of the world would become
increasingly interconnected, but his project for 'creating our own yoga' has
to all intents and purposes already begun in a thousand different ways in
such fields as general health, psychotherapy, personal growth and professional training.

Jung may also have exaggerated the extent to which individuals are
'rooted' in their own cultures and hence are barred from participating
meaningfully in another. In his attempt to emphasize the fundamental
differences between East and West he falls into ways of thinking about
cultures and cultural differences which now appear to us naïve. Too often he
seems to be reinforcing popular stereotypes when employing such phrases as
'the mysterious Orient', 'the baffling mind of the East', 'the unfathomableness of India', and 'the dreamlike world of India', and his repeated references
to 'the strangeness' and the 'incomprehensibility' of the Eastern psyche are
in danger of locking us into all kinds of prejudices from which since his day
we have sought to liberate ourselves. The danger here is not merely that we
oversimplify the differences, as in his characterization of the West as
'extraverted' and the East as 'introverted', but that we encourage the view
that there are some fundamental, essential differences between the mentalities
of Orientals and Occidentals – an attitude that can easily slide into racism of
one sort or another. Jung himself came dangerously close to this in the 1930s,
when he sought to develop a psychology of national differences, arguing that
Jews and Aryans are constituted differently psychologically. In his own
defence Jung argued that the attempt to differentiate between Germanic and
Jewish psychology expressed no value judgement, and implied 'no depreciation of Semitic psychology, any more than it is a depreciation of the Chinese
to speak of the peculiar psychology of the Oriental'.[72] Nevertheless, it might
seem to us now that his talk of 'the peculiar psychology of the Oriental' is
as objectionable as his talk of the peculiar psychology of the Jews.

A converse criticism arises from the fact that, having decided that the East lies in some conceptual terrain that is totally 'other', he then proceeds to try and make sense of it in terms of his own psychological theory. When we examine Jung's own attempt at dialogue we cannot but question whether he has simply assimilated ancient Eastern spiritual traditions to his own Western psychological theories. His stated aim of constructing 'a bridge of understanding' between East and West is an admirable one, and his constantly reiterated praise for Eastern philosophies represents a refreshing antidote to Western arrogance, but his attempts to transpose Eastern wisdom into the language of analytical psychology sometimes renders his 'dialogue' a somewhat one-sided affair. This is an issue which takes us beyond Jung, for critics have often in recent years raised the question whether there can ever be a genuine dialogue between East and West so long as one of the sides remains in a position of virtual control, where the European mode of thinking retains the status of planetary domination. Jung's own approach points up this issue sharply. His attempt to place Eastern metaphysical claims in parentheses, and to deal with them in purely phenomenological terms, sounds innocent enough, but, as we have seen, this approach slides imperceptibly into a reductionist stance which refuses to take seriously Eastern philosophy on its own terms.

This line of criticism applies to both the theoretical and the practical level. At the theoretical level we are left wondering about the extent to which Jung had an adequate grasp of Eastern metaphysics. We have already taken note of Jung's doubts concerning the notion of *samādhi*, where, it is believed, the individual is absorbed into a higher state. Might it not be the case, as critics such as Alan Watts have suggested, that in this instance Jung is simply trapped within his own Western conceptual framework, with its categorical insistence on the duality of subject and object, a duality supported by the very subject–predicate structure of our Western languages? Jung tended to think of the absorption of the ego as a regression to a more primitive state, a state disastrously manifested in the mass hysteria of Nazi Germany, but yoga philosophy points in a different direction and asks us to conceive of the possibility of a higher state of consciousness in which awareness is not obliterated, but is transformed into a condition where the concerns and limitations of the indiviudal ego cease to be of importance. This latter could be described as a spiritual state, one which transcends ordinary states of consciousness, and Jung's attempt to compare it with the process of individuation, which is a purely psychological one, may well result in a distortion of both conceptions.

This is closely linked to more practical questions concerning meditation. Jung's reservations about the employment of yoga practices are, as I have suggested, not entirely groundless, even in an age when meditation has become quite widely practised in the West. Nevertheless, there remains the nagging suspicion that Jung misunderstood the nature of meditation, or at any rate conceived of it rather too narrowly. The criticism often levelled here is that he understood this central Eastern spiritual practice in terms of concentration and absorption, leading to a trance-like state in which the practitioner withdraws from the world and surrenders to the unconscious, resulting in the dissolution of the ego and leading back to an experience of oneness and timelessness. This sort of criticism is not entirely accurate, since, in his discussion of Zen meditation, Jung specifically attributed to *zazen* (meditation) the aim of refining consciousness rather than transcending it: 'It is not that something different is seen, but that one sees differently', he argues; and he spoke of *satori* as an 'illumination', a 'revelation', and an insight into the self.[73] Nevertheless, it is true that his accounts of meditation generally emphasize the loss of rational, conscious awareness and a withdrawal from the external world, from the body, the senses, and all practical concerns, speaking of it as 'the void of deep sleep', an 'autohypnotic condition, which removes [one] from the world and its illusions'.[74] Such a view, though accurate with regard to some yoga methods and schools, does not in fact do justice to the whole range of such practices to be found in Asia, and at the same time tends to perpetuate certain rather unfortunate myths and stereotypes in Western thinking about Eastern religions.

In this regard it must be recognized that Jung's interpretations of Eastern philosophies, though often bold and original, were in many respects conditioned by the age in which he lived and by the state of scholarship that prevailed in his day. Some of the problems of interpretation we have just been discussing stem from the fact that during the period in which Jung was developing his ideas early in this century the Western view of Indian philosophy was dominated by the nineteenth-century neo-Kantian, neo-Romantic view that saw Indian philosophy as based on the belief that the world is an illusion. The ultimate aim is to penetrate the veil of *māyā* and to achieve identity with the timeless world beyond, an interpretation which has undergone considerable transformation in the second half of this century. Moreover, the translations of Eastern texts that he was working with can now be seen to be in many respects inadequate and even corrupt. For example, Richard Wilhelm's translation of *The Secret of the Golden Flower*, however valuable it may have been in introducing the West to Taoist thinking, has come to be seen by scholars as in many respects an inadequate rendering of a text which itself was a truncated and expurgated version of the original. Similarly, the translations of Tibetan texts by Evans-Wentz on which Jung wrote psychological commentaries are now seen to be fundamentally flawed owing to the technical deficiencies of the translator – he was a Celtic scholar who knew little Tibetan – and the fact that his whole approach to the text was coloured by his theosophical beliefs. Even in the case of secondary sources, such as Suzuki's *Introduction to Zen Buddhism*, there are problems of a similar nature. It would be impossible to overestimate the historical importance of Suzuki's role in introducing Zen to the West, but his views on this matter have in recent decades become the subject of some controversy, in particular his emphasis on the *koan* technique at the expense of *zazen* meditation, a bias which inevitably filters through into Jung's own reading, which emphasizes the sudden and irrational nature of the enlightenment experience. Jung was not aware of any of the deficiencies in the translations he was using and cannot be held responsible for the fact that Oriental scholarship has moved on since his day. But these considerations must inevitably affect the way we read Jung's writings on this subject today.

JUNG FOR TODAY

There are, then, important question-marks over Jung's method, over his actual interpretations, and over the texts that he was using. Nevertheless, from a historical standpoint, Jung's engagement with the East must certainly be regarded as a significant undertaking, moving as it does into uncharted seas, and risking his reputation in so doing. He certainly learned from, and stood on the shoulders of, those giants (such as Leibniz and Schopenhauer) who from the Enlightenment onwards had sought to integrate European thought within a wider global context, but his attempts to relate psychotherapy, then in its fragile infancy, with Buddhism and yoga had a significance in the intellectual life of the West which was quite new and original and which will reverberate for a long time to come. It is difficult to evaluate precisely the influence of Jung's hermeneutical engagement with the East in the wider academic context. A list of the thinkers who have engaged, not always uncritically, with Jung's ideas in this field is long and distinguished and includes the historian Arnold Toynbee, the anthropologists Mary Douglas and Rodney Needham, the theologian Paul Tillich, and the historians of religions R. C. Zaehner and Edward Conze. Toynbee, for example, made much of his debt to Jung's ideas about Eastern philosophies in his attempt to build his own bridge of understanding between East and West; and the distinguished orientalist Zaehner drew heavily on Jung's ideas because, as he put it, 'they seem to illumine much in Oriental religion that had previously been obscure'. Jung's influence is evident, too, in the burgeoning field of comparative religion, where his pioneering example has frequently been acknowledged in the ever more urgent attempts to encourage dialogue between the great religions of the world. And in spite of all the reservations and warnings with which Jung sought to surround his remarks on these matters, his writings on Eastern religions have undoubtedly been a major attraction for many young Westerners since the beat and hippie generations who, disillusioned with their own indigenous traditions, have sought inspiration from the East.

But what of Jung's significance today? Scholarship has moved on, the dialogue of religions has its own impetus, and the heady enthusiasms of the 1950s and 1960s are now matters of history. Nevertheless, his writings on the East are still highly relevant for the present times and can still be read with great profit from a number of different perspectives. Even if we do not agree with all his interpretations and conclusions, the sheer intellectual zest with which he confronted what were then strange and even alien texts from remote cultures, and his prescient insight into many of the issues which continue to tax the minds of those engaged in comparative studies, constitute a model for today's intellectual explorers. As I have tried to show in this introduction, Jung's approach to the ideas and texts of the East was far more critical and reflexive than is often supposed. He was acutely aware of the conceptual problems involved in transposing crucial Oriental terms into Western languages, and his recognition of the necessity to maintain the 'otherness' of the writings and cultures he was dealing with has echoes in important current intellectual debates. The criticisms of people like Watts that we noted above may miss the point that Jung was engaging in a philosophical debate with the East, not merely swallowing uncritically its supposed eternal verities. It is significant that the title of the first section of his commentary on *The Secret of the Golden Flower*, perhaps his most important contribution in this field, is 'Difficulties Encountered by a European in Trying to Understand the East', a title which clearly flags up, right at the start of his intense period of hermeneutical engagement with the East, that his approach is one of thoughtful encounter rather than blind commitment. This approach is one which, as much as anything else, allows Jung to continue to speak to us today.

But there are more substantial reasons for perpetuating our own dialogue with Jung. The period in which he wrote the majority of his pieces on Eastern thought was one in which the modernist outlooks of positivism and Marxism were in their heyday. Both were implacably hostile not only to religion in general but to anything that smacked of mysticism, and both encouraged an aggressive confrontation with modes of thought which did not fall within the tightly prescribed limits of scientific rationalism. But the intellectual climate has changed dramatically. A more pluralistic, relativistic epistemology has emerged in the last decades of the twentieth century, in which recognition is given to the possibility of divergent and competing modes of discourse; and though the age of grand system-building is now seen to be past, there is a growing willingness to re-engage, in a spirit of sympathetic dialogue, with what until recently appeared to be outworn and discarded modes of thought and experience. A case in point is the recognition in some quarters that developments in the new physics bear striking analogies with the so-called 'mystical' ideas of the ancient Taoists, an insight which was anticipated by Jung in his speculations on synchronicity and the *I Ching*. Another is the attempt to formulate a new holistic paradigm which is more compatible with the ecological and environmentalist values of the age, an endeavour which has often turned to the East for inspiration and where, too, Jung had already begun to make explorations.

Moreover, although it would be a mistake to identify Jung with the so-called postmodern outlook – his concern with the self as life's goal and with universal archetypal structures prevents that – his hermeneutical approach to

Eastern thought is one which bears a marked affinity in certain respects with recent intellectual attitudes. This affinity is evident in a variety of ways: in his irreverent, even deconstructive, attitude towards Eastern metaphysics, in his refusal to give any privileged status to Western consciousness, in his rejection of the idea of the detached observer and, perhaps most noticeably, in his recognition that any attempt to interpret texts and ideas from the East inevitably runs into a tangle of linguistic and symbolic ambiguity. He is perhaps closest to this way of thinking when, in the final paragraph of his autobiography, he quotes Lao-tzu: 'All are clear, I alone am clouded.'

Above all, though, Jung's voice will still be heard sympathetically by those who continue to turn Eastward in their quest for self-understanding, personal growth, and spiritual enlightenment. The exaggerated adulation conferred on Eastern wisdom, which has characterized various movements in the West from the theosophists to the hippies, has in many respects given way to a more measured, more reflective approach, no less widespread in its appeal, no less serious in its desire to address the public and private discontents of the age, but one in which many have increasingly been prepared to engage and experiment in an open-ended way with ideas and practices from a variety of non-Western cultures without impetuously casting off their own cultural inheritance. It is interesting to speculate whether Jung, had he witnessed these developments, might have moderated some of his reservations and seen in them a continuation of his project to build a bridge of understanding between East and West.

NOTES

Unless otherwise stated, page numbers in these notes refer to pages in the present work.

1 P. 65.
2 'The Holy Men of India', *The Collected Works of C. G. Jung*, Vol. 11, paras 963 and 961. *The Collected Works of C. G. Jung* (1953–83), referred to hereafter as 'CW', are edited by H. Read, M. Fordham and G. Adler, translated by R. F. C. Hull, and are published by Routledge, London, and Princeton University Press, Princeton, New Jersey.
3 *Memories, Dreams, Reflections*, recorded and edited by A. Jaffé, translated by R. and C. Winston, (London: Fontana, 1983), p. 32.
4 See pp. 77–81.
5 See pp. 41–8.
6 Pp. 47–8.
7 *Memories, Dreams, Reflections*, p. 407.
8 P. 41.
9 See pp. 82–119.
10 See pp. 121–36.
11 P. 49.
12 P. 55.
13 See pp. 49–56.
14 See pp. 151–8.

15 See pp. 33–40.
16 P. 33.
17 P. 38.
18 Pp. 49–50.
19 P. 33.
20 See pp. 183–96.
21 See pp. 197–211.
22 P. 201.
23 See pp. 212–27.
24 P. 214.
25 See pp. 234–6.
26 *C. G. Jung: Letters*, edited and selected by G. Adler and A. Jaffé, translated by R. F. C. Hull, 2 vols (London: Routledge; and Princeton, New Jersey: Princeton University Press, 1973–5), Vol. 2, p. 548.
27 P. 36.
28 See pp. 228–33.
29 P. 34.
30 P. 140.
31 P. 229.
32 CW13, p. 3.
33 P. 85.
34 P. 114.
35 P. 85.
36 P. 201.
37 P. 212.
38 P. 120.
39 See pp. 120–36.
40 CW7, paras 438 and 430.
41 *Modern Man in Search of a Soul* (London: Routledge, 1984), p. 266.
42 ibid., p. 268.
43 CW14, para. 709.
44 *Modern Man in Search of a Soul*, p. 250.
45 P. 210.
46 P. 163.
47 P. 165.
48 P. 197.
49 P. 113.
50 P. 197.
51 P. 130.
52 *Letters*, Vol. 1, p. 195.
53 P. 113.
54 P. 195.
55 Pp. 116–17.
56 CW11, para. 818.
57 *Letters*, Vol. 2, p. 438.
58 CW9i, para. 520.
59 P. 240.
60 CW11, para. 818.
61 ibid.
62 CW8, para. 142.
63 CW16, para. 400.
64 *Letters*, Vol. 2, p. 247.
65 P. 223.
66 P. 174.

67 P. 165.
68 P. 82.
69 P. 65.
70 CW12, para. 126.
71 P. 203.
72 CW10, para. 1014.
73 P. 217.
74 *Letters*, Vol. 1, p. 311.

EDITORIAL NOTE

Throughout this book the footnotes appended to Jung's writings are his own, except for those in square brackets which have been added by the editors and translators of the editions from which these writings are drawn.

Part I

The way to the East

1 Jung's passage to India

From: Memories, Dreams, Reflections

My journey to India, in 1938, was not taken on my own initiative. It arose out of an invitation from the British Government of India to take part in the celebrations connected with the twenty-fifth anniversary of the University of Calcutta.

By that time I had read a great deal about Indian philosophy and religious history, and was deeply convinced of the value of Oriental wisdom. But I had to travel in order to form my own conclusions, and remained within myself like a homunculus in a retort. India affected me like a dream, for I was and remained in search of myself, of the truth peculiar to myself.

The journey formed an intermezzo in the intensive study of alchemical philosophy on which I was engaged at the time. This had so strong a grip upon me that I took along the first volume of *Theatrum chemicum* of 1602, which contains the principal writings of Gerardus Dorneus. In the course of the voyage I studied the book from beginning to end. Thus it was that this material belonging to the fundamental strata of European thought was constantly counterpointed by my impressions of a foreign mentality and culture. Both had emerged from original psychic experiences of the un-conscious, and therefore had produced the same, similar or at least com-parable insights.

India gave me my first direct experience of an alien, highly differentiated culture. Altogether different elements had ruled my Central African journey; culture had not predominated. As for North Africa, I had the opportunity there to talk with a person capable of putting his culture into words. In India, however, I had the chance to speak with representatives of the Indian mentality, and to compare it with the European. I had searching talks with S. Subramanya Iyer, the guru of the Maharajah of Mysore, whose guest I was for some time; also with many others, whose names unfortunately have escaped me. On the other hand, I studiously avoided all so-called 'holy men'. I did so because I had to make do with my own truth, not accept from others what I could not attain on my own. I would have felt it as a theft had I attempted to learn from the holy men and to accept their truth for myself. Nor in Europe can I make any borrowings from the East, but must shape my life out of myself – out of what my inner being tells me, or what nature brings to me.

In India I was principally concerned with the question of the psychological nature of evil. I had been very much impressed by the way this problem is integrated in Indian spiritual life, and I saw it in a new light. In a conversation with a cultivated Chinese I was also impressed, again and again, by the fact that these people are able to integrate so-called 'evil' without 'losing face'. In the West we cannot do this. For the Oriental the problem of morality does not appear to take first place, as it does for us. To the Oriental, good and evil are meaningfully contained in nature, and are merely varying degrees of the same thing.

I saw that Indian spirituality contains as much of evil as of good. The Christian strives for good and succumbs to evil; the Indian feels himself to be outside good and evil, and seeks to realize this state by meditation or yoga. My objection is that, given such an attitude, neither good nor evil takes on any real outline, and this produces a certain stasis. One does not really believe in evil, and one does not really believe in good. Good or evil is then regarded at most as *my* good or *my* evil, as whatever seems to me good or evil – which leaves us with the paradoxical statement that Indian spirituality lacks both evil and good, or is so burdened by contradictions that it needs *nirdvandva*, the liberation from opposites and from the ten thousand things.

The Indian's goal is not moral perfection, but the condition of *nirdvandva*. He wishes to free himself from nature; in keeping with this aim, he seeks in meditation the condition of imagelessness and emptiness. I, on the other hand, wish to persist in the state of lively contemplation of nature and of the psychic images. I want to be freed neither from human beings, nor from myself, nor from nature; for all these appear to me the greatest of miracles. Nature, the psyche, and life appear to me like divinity unfolded – and what more could I wish for? To me the supreme meaning of Being can consist only in the fact that it *is*, not that it is not or is no longer.

To me there is no liberation *à tout prix*. I cannot be liberated from anything that I do not possess, have not done or experienced. Real liberation becomes possible for me only when I have done all that I was able to do, when I have completely devoted myself to a thing and participated in it to the utmost. If I withdraw from participation, I am virtually amputating the corresponding part of my psyche. Naturally, there may be good reasons for my not immersing myself in a given experience. But then I am forced to confess my inability, and must know that I may have neglected to do something of vital importance. In this way I make amends for the lack of a positive act by the clear knowledge of my incompetence.

A man who has not passed through the inferno of his passions has never overcome them. They then dwell in the house next door, and at any moment a flame may dart out and set fire to his own house. Whenever we give up, leave behind, and forget too much, there is always the danger that the things we have neglected will return with added force.

In Konarak (Orissa) I met a pandit who obligingly offered to come with me on my visit to the temple and the great temple car. The pagoda is covered from base to pinnacle with exquisitely obscene sculptures. We talked for a long time about this extraordinary fact, which he explained to me as a means to achieve spiritualization. I objected – pointing to a group of young peasants who were standing open-mouthed before the monument, admiring these splendours – that such young men were scarcely undergoing spiritualization at the moment, but were much more likely having their heads filled with sexual fantasies. Whereupon he replied, 'But this is just the point. How can they ever become spiritualized if they do not first fulfil their karma? These admittedly obscene images are here for the very purpose of recalling to the people their *dharma* (law); otherwise these unconscious fellows might forget it.'

I thought it an odd notion that young men might forget their sexuality, like animals out of rutting time. My sage, however, resolutely maintained that they were as unconscious as animals and actually in need of urgent admonishments. To this end, he said, before they set foot inside the temple they were reminded of their *dharma* by the exterior decorations; for unless they were made conscious of their *dharma* and fulfilled it, they could not partake of spiritualization.

As we entered through the gate of the temple, my companion pointed to the two 'temptresses', statues of two dancing girls with seductively curved hips who smilingly greeted all who entered. 'Do you see these two dancing girls?' he said. 'Their meaning is the same. Naturally, this does not apply to people like you and me, for we have attained to a level of consciousness which is above this sort of thing. But for these peasant boys it is an indispensable instruction and admonishment.'

When we left the temple and were walking down a lingam lane, he suddenly said, 'Do you see these stones? Do you know what they mean? I will tell you a great secret.' I was astonished, for I thought that the phallic nature of these monuments was known to every child. But he whispered into my ear with the greatest seriousness, 'These stones are man's private parts.' I had expected him to tell me that they signified the great god Shiva. I looked at him dumbfounded, but he only nodded self-importantly, as if to say, 'Yes, that is how it is. No doubt you in your European ignorance would never have thought so!' When I told this story to Heinrich Zimmer, he exclaimed in delight, 'At last I have heard something real about India for a change!'

When I visited the *stupas* of Sanchi, where Buddha delivered his fire sermon, I was overcome by a strong emotion of the kind that frequently develops in me when I encounter a thing, person or idea of whose significance I am still unconscious. The *stupas* are situated on a rocky hill whose peak can be reached by a pleasant path of great stone slabs laid down through a green meadow. The *stupas* are tombs or containers of relics, hemispherical in shape, like two gigantic rice bowls placed one on top of the other (concavity upon concavity), according to the prescripts of the Buddha himself in the *Mahā-Parinibbāna-Sutta*. The British have done their restoration work in a most respectful spirit. The largest of these buildings is surrounded by a wall which has four elaborate gates. You come in by one of these and the path turns to the left, then leads into a clockwise circumambulation around the *stupa*. At the four cardinal points stand statues of the Buddha. When you have completed one circumambulation, you enter a second, higher circuit which runs in the same direction. The distant prospect over the plain, the *stupas* themselves, the temple ruins, and the solitary stillness of this holy site held me in a spell. I took leave of my companion and submerged myself in the overpowering mood of the place.

After a while I heard rhythmic gong tones approaching from the distance. A group of Japanese pilgrims came marching up one behind the other, each striking a small gong. They were beating out the rhythm of the age-old prayer *Om mani padme hum*, the stroke of the gong falling upon the *hum*. Outside the *stupas* they bowed low, then passed through the gate. There they bowed again before the statue of the Buddha, intoning a chorale-like song. They completed the double circumambulation, singing a hymn before each statue of the Buddha. As I watched them, my mind and spirit were with them, and something within me silently thanked them for having so wonderfully come to the aid of my inarticulate feelings.

The intensity of my emotion showed that the hill of Sanchi meant something central to me. A new side of Buddhism was revealed to me there. I grasped the life of the Buddha as the reality of the self which had broken through and laid claim to a personal life. For Buddha, the self stands above all gods, an *unus mundus* which represents the essence of human existence and of the world as a whole. The self embodies both the aspect of intrinsic being and the aspect of its being known, without which no world exists. Buddha saw and grasped the cosmogonic dignity of human consciousness; for that reason he saw clearly that if a man succeeded in extinguishing this light, the world would sink into nothingness. Schopenhauer's great achievement lay in his also recognizing this, or in rediscovering it independently.

Christ – like Buddha – is an embodiment of the self, but in an altogether different sense. Both stood for an overcoming of the world: Buddha out of rational insight; Christ as a foredoomed sacrifice. In Christianity more is suffered; in Buddhism more is seen and done. Both paths are right, but in the Indian sense Buddha is the more complete human being. He is a historical personality, and therefore easier for men to understand. Christ is at once a historical man and God, and therefore much more difficult to comprehend. At bottom he was not comprehensible even to himself; he knew only that he had to sacrifice himself, that this course was imposed upon him from within. His sacrifice happened to him like an act of destiny. Buddha lived out his life and died at an advanced age, whereas Christ's activity as Christ probably lasted no more than a year.

Later, Buddhism underwent the same transformation as Christianity: Buddha became, as it were, the image of the development of the self; he became a model for men to imitate, whereas actually he had preached that by overcoming the *nidāna*-chain every human being could become an illuminate, a buddha. Similarly in Christianity, Christ is an exemplar who dwells in every Christian as his integral personality. But historical trends led to the *imitatio Christi*, whereby the individual does not pursue his own destined road to wholeness, but attempts to imitate the way taken by Christ. Similarly in the East, historical trends led to a devout imitation of the Buddha. That Buddha should have become a model to be imitated was in itself a weakening of his idea, just as the *imitatio Christi* was a forerunner of the fateful stasis in the evolution of the Christian idea. As Buddha, by virtue of his insight, was far in advance of the Brahma gods, so Christ cried out to the Jews, 'You are gods' (John 10:34); but men were incapable of understanding what he meant. Instead we find that the so-called Christian West, far from creating a new world, is moving with giant strides towards the possibility of destroying the world we have.[1]

India honoured me with three doctorates, from Allahabad, Benares and Calcutta – representatives of Islam, of Hinduism, and of British-Indian medicine and science. It was a little too much of a good thing, and I needed a retreat. A ten-day spell in the hospital offered it to me, for in Calcutta I finally came down with dysentery. This was a blessed island in the wild sea of new impressions, and I found a place to stand on from which I could contemplate the ten thousand things and their bewildering turmoil.

When I returned to the hotel, in tolerably good health, I had a dream so characteristic that I wish to set it down here. I found myself, with a large number of my Zürich friends and acquaintances, on an unknown island, presumably situated not far off the coast of southern England. It was small and almost uninhabited. The island was narrow, a strip of land about twenty miles long, running in a north–south direction. On the rocky coast at the southern end of the island was a mediaeval castle. We stood in a courtyard, a group of sightseeing tourists. Before us rose an imposing *belfroi*, through whose gate a wide stone staircase was visible. We could just manage to see that it terminated above in a columned hall. This hall was dimly illuminated by candlelight. I understood that this was the castle of the Grail, and that this evening there would be a 'celebration of the Grail' here. This information seemed to be of a secret character, for a German professor among us, who strikingly resembled old Mommsen, knew nothing about it. I talked most animatedly with him, and was impressed by his learning and sparkling intelligence. Only one thing disturbed me: he spoke constantly about a dead past and lectured very learnedly on the relationship of the British to the French sources of the Grail story. Apparently he was not conscious of the meaning of the legend, nor of its living presentness, whereas I was intensely aware of both. Also, he did not seem to perceive our immediate, actual surroundings, for he behaved as though he were in a classroom, lecturing to his students. In vain I tried to call his attention to the peculiarity of the situation. He did not see the stairs or the festive glow in the hall.

I looked around somewhat helplessly, and discovered that I was standing by the wall of a tall castle; the lower portion of the wall was covered by a kind of trellis, not made of the usual wood, but of black iron artfully formed into a grapevine complete with leaves, twining tendrils and grapes. At intervals of six feet on the horizontal branches were tiny houses, likewise of iron, like birdhouses. Suddenly I saw a movement in the foliage; at first it seemed to be that of a mouse, but then I saw distinctly a tiny, iron, hooded gnome, a *cucullatus*, scurrying from one little house to the next. 'Well', I exclaimed in astonishment to the professor, 'now look at that, will you . . .'

At that moment a hiatus occurred, and the dream changed. We – the same company as before, but without the professor – were outside the castle, in a treeless, rocky landscape. I knew that something had to happen, for the Grail was not yet in the castle and still had to be celebrated that same evening. It was said to be in the northern part of the island, hidden in a small, uninhabited house, the only house there. I knew that it was our task to bring the Grail to the castle. There were about six of us who set out and tramped northwards.

After several hours of strenuous hiking, we reached the narrowest part of the island, and I discovered that the island was actually divided into two halves by an arm of the sea. At the smallest part of this strait the width of the water was about a hundred yards. The sun had set, and night descended. Wearily, we camped on the ground. The region was unpopulated and desolate; far and wide there was not a tree or shrub, nothing but grass and rocks. There was no bridge, no boat. It was very cold; my companions fell asleep, one after the other. I considered what could be done, and came to the conclusion that I alone must swim across the channel and fetch the Grail. I took off my clothes. At that point I awoke.

Here was this essentially European dream emerging when I had barely worked my way out of the overwhelming mass of Indian impressions. Some ten years before, I had discovered that in many places in England the myth of the Grail was still a living thing, in spite of all the scholarship that has accumulated around this tradition. This fact had impressed me all the more when I realized the concordance between this poetic myth and what alchemy had to say about the *unum vas*, the *una medicina* and the *unus lapis*. Myths which day has forgotten continue to be told by night, and powerful figures which consciousness has reduced to banality and ridiculous triviality are recognized again by poets and prophetically revived; therefore they can also be recognized 'in changed form' by the thoughtful person. The great ones of the past have not died, as we think; they have merely changed their names. 'Small and slight, but great in might', the veiled Kabir enters a new house.

Imperiously, the dream wiped away all the intense impressions of India and swept me back to the too-long-neglected concerns of the Occident, which had formerly been expressed in the quest for the Holy Grail as well as in the search for the philosophers' stone. I was taken out of the world of India, and reminded that India was not my task, but only a part of the way – admittedly a significant one – which should carry me closer to my goal. It was as though the dream were asking me, 'What are you doing in India? Rather seek for yourself and your fellows the healing vessel, the *servator mundi*, which you urgently need. For your state is perilous; you are all in imminent danger of destroying all that centuries have built up.'

Ceylon, the last stage of my journey, struck me as no longer India; there is already something of the South Seas about it, and a touch of paradise, in which one cannot linger too long. Colombo is a busy international port where every day between five and six o'clock a massive downpour descends from a clear sky. We soon left it behind and headed for the hilly country of the interior. There Kandy, the old royal city, is swathed in a fine mist whose tepid humidity sustains a luxuriant vegetation. The Dalada-Maligawa Temple, which contains the relic of the Holy Tooth (of Buddha), is small, but radiates a special charm. I spent a considerable time in its library, talking with the monks, and looking at the texts of the Buddhist canon engraved on silver leaves.

There I witnessed a memorable evening ceremony. Young men and girls poured out enormous mounds of jasmine flowers in front of the altars, at the same time singing a prayer under their breath: a *mantram*. I thought they were praying to Buddha, but the monk who was guiding me explained, 'No, Buddha is no more; He is in nirvana; we cannot pray to him. They are singing: "This life is transitory as the beauty of these flowers. May my God[2] share with me the merit of this offering."'

As a prelude to the ceremony a one-hour drum concert was performed in the *mandapam*, or what in Indian temples is called the hall of waiting. There were five drummers; one stood in each corner of the square hall, and the fifth, a young man, stood in the middle. He was the soloist, and a very fine drummer. Naked to the waist, his dark-brown trunk glistening, with a red girdle, white *shoka* (a long skirt reaching to the feet), and white turban, arms covered with shining bracelets, he stepped up to the golden Buddha, bearing a double drum, 'to sacrifice the music'. There, with beautiful movements of body and arms, he drummed alone a strange melody, artistically perfect. I watched him from behind; he stood in front of the entrance to the *mandapam*, which was covered with little oil lamps. The drum speaks the ancient language of the belly and solar plexus; the belly does not 'pray' but engenders the 'meritorious' *mantram* or meditative utterance. It is therefore not ador-ation of a non-existent Buddha, but one of the many acts of self-redemption performed by the awakened human being.

Towards the beginning of spring I set out on my homeward voyage, with such a plethora of impressions that I did not have any desire to leave the ship to see Bombay. Instead, I buried myself in my Latin alchemical texts. But India did not pass me by without a trace; it left tracks which lead from one infinity into another infinity.

NOTES

1 On the problem of the *imitatio*, cf. *Psychology and Alchemy*, Part I.
2 God = *deva* = guardian angel.

2 Jung's way to China

From: 'Richard Wilhelm: In Memoriam'[1]

74   It is no easy task for me to speak of Richard Wilhelm and his work, because, starting very far away from one another, our paths crossed in comet-like fashion. His life-work has a range that lies outside my compass. I have never seen the China that first moulded his thought and later continued to engross him, nor am I familiar with its language, the living expression of the Chinese East. I stand indeed as a stranger outside that vast realm of knowledge and experience in which Wilhelm worked as a master of his profession. He as a sinologist and I as a doctor would probably never have come into contact had we remained specialists. But we met in a field of humanity which begins beyond the academic boundary posts. There lay our point of contact; there the spark leapt across and kindled a light that was to become for me one of the most significant events of my life. Because of this I may perhaps speak of Wilhelm and his work, thinking with grateful respect of this mind which created a bridge between East and West and gave to the Occident the precious heritage of a culture thousands of years old, a culture perhaps destined to disappear forever.

75   Wilhelm possessed the kind of mastery which is won only by a man who goes beyond his speciality, and so his striving for knowledge became a concern touching all mankind. Or, rather, it had been that from the beginning and remained so always. What else could have liberated him so completely from the narrow horizon of the European – and, indeed, of the missionary – that no sooner had he delved into the secrets of the Chinese mind than he perceived the treasure hidden there for us, and sacrificed his European prejudices for the sake of this rare pearl? Only an all-embracing humanity, a greatness of heart that glimpses the whole, could have enabled him to open himself without reserve to a profoundly alien spirit, and to further its influence by putting his manifold gifts and capacities at its service. The understanding with which he devoted himself to this task, with no trace of Christian resentment or European arrogance, bears witness to a truly great mind; for all mediocre minds in contact with a foreign culture either perish in the blind attempt to deracinate themselves or else they indulge in an uncomprehending and presumptuous passion for criticism. Toying only with the surface and externals of the foreign culture,

they never eat its bread or drink its wine, and so never enter into a real communion of minds, that most intimate transfusion and interpenetration which generates a new birth.

76   As a rule, the specialist's is a purely masculine mind, an intellect to which fecundity is an alien and unnatural process; it is therefore an especially ill-adapted tool for giving rebirth to a foreign spirit. But a larger mind bears the stamp of the feminine; it is endowed with a receptive and fruitful womb which can reshape what is strange and give it a familiar form. Wilhelm possessed the rare gift of a maternal intellect. To it he owed his unequalled ability to feel his way into the spirit of the East and to make his incomparable translations.

77   To me the greatest of his achievements is his translation of, and commentary on, the *I Ching*.[2] Before I came to know Wilhelm's translation, I had worked for years with Legge's inadequate rendering,[3] and I was therefore fully able to appreciate the extraordinary difference between the two. Wilhelm has succeeded in bringing to life again, in new form, this ancient work in which not only many sinologists but most of the modern Chinese see nothing more than a collection of absurd magical spells. This book embodies, as perhaps no other, the living spirit of Chinese civilization, for the best minds of China have collaborated on it and contributed to it for thousands of years. Despite its fabulous age it has never grown old, but still lives and works, at least for those who seek to understand its meaning. That we too belong to this favoured group we owe to the creative achievement of Wilhelm. He has brought the book closer to us by his careful translation and personal experience both as a pupil of a Chinese master of the old school and as an initiate in the psychology of Chinese yoga, who made constant use of the *I Ching* in practice.

78   But together with these rich gifts, Wilhelm has bequeathed to us a task whose magnitude we can only surmise at present, but cannot fully apprehend. Anyone who, like myself, has had the rare good fortune to experience in association with Wilhelm the divinatory power of the *I Ching* cannot remain ignorant of the fact that we have here an Archimedean point from which our Western attitude of mind could be lifted off its foundations. It is no small service to have given us, as Wilhelm did, such a comprehensive and richly coloured picture of a foreign culture. What is even more important is that he has inoculated us with the living germ of the Chinese spirit, capable of working a fundamental change in our view of the world. We are no longer reduced to being admiring or critical observers, but find ourselves partaking of the spirit of the East to the extent that we succeed in experiencing the living power of the *I Ching*.

79   The principle on which the use of the *I Ching* is based appears at first sight to be in complete contradiction to our scientific and causal thinking. For us it is unscientific in the extreme, almost taboo, and therefore outside the scope of our scientific judgement, indeed incomprehensible to it.

80   Some years ago, the then president of the British Anthropological

Society asked me how it was that so highly intelligent a people as the Chinese had produced no science. I replied that this must be an optical illusion, since the Chinese did have a science whose standard textbook was the *I Ching*, but that the principle of this science, like so much else in China, was altogether different from the principle of our science.

81   The science of the *I Ching* is based not on the causality principle but on one which – hitherto unnamed because not familiar to us – I have tentatively called the *synchronistic* principle. My researches into the psychology of unconscious processes long ago compelled me to look around for another principle of explanation, since the causality principle seemed to me insufficient to explain certain remarkable manifestations of the unconscious. I found that there are psychic parallelisms which simply cannot be related to each other causally, but must be connected by another kind of principle altogether. This connection seemed to lie essentially in the relative simultaneity of the events, hence the term 'synchronistic'. It seems as though time, far from being an abstraction, is a concrete continuum which possesses qualities or basic conditions capable of manifesting themselves simultaneously in different places by means of an acausal parallelism, such as we find, for instance, in the simultaneous occurrence of identical thoughts, symbols or psychic states. Another example, pointed out by Wilhelm, would be the coincidence of Chinese and European periods of style, which cannot have been causally related to one another. Astrology would be an example of synchronicity on a grand scale if only there were enough thoroughly tested findings to support it. But at least we have at our disposal a number of well-tested and statistically verifiable facts which make the problem of astrology seem worthy of scientific investigation. Its value is obvious enough to the psychologist, since astrology represents the sum of all the psychological knowledge of antiquity.

82   The fact that it is possible to reconstruct a person's character fairly accurately from his birth data shows the relative validity of astrology. It must be remembered, however, that the birth data are in no way dependent on the actual astronomical constellations, but are based on an arbitrary, purely conceptual time system. Owing to the precession of the equinoxes, the spring-point has long since moved out of the constellation of Aries into Pisces, so that the astrological zodiac on which horoscopes are calculated no longer corresponds to the heavenly one. If there are any astrological diagnoses of character that are in fact correct, this is due not to the influence of the stars but to our own hypothetical time qualities. In other words, whatever is born or done at this particular moment of time has the quality of this moment of time.

83   Here we have the basic formula for the use of *I Ching*. As you know, the hexagram that characterizes the moment of time, and gives us insight into it, is obtained by manipulating a bundle of yarrow stalks or by throwing three coins. The division of the yarrow stalks or the fall of the

coins depends on pure chance. The runic stalks or coins fall into the pattern of the moment. The only question is: 'Did King Wen and the Duke of Chou, who lived a thousand years before the birth of Christ, interpret these chance patterns correctly?'[4] Experience alone can decide.

84   At his first lecture at the Psychological Club in Zürich, Wilhelm, at my request, demonstrated the use of the *I Ching* and at the same time made a prognosis which, in less than two years, was fulfilled to the letter and with the utmost clarity. Predictions of this kind could be further confirmed by numerous parallel experiences. However, I am not concerned with establishing objectively the validity of the *I Ching*'s statements, but take it simply as a premiss, just as Wilhelm did. I am concerned only with the astonishing fact that the hidden qualities of the moment become legible in the hexagram. The interconnection of events made evident by the *I Ching* is essentially analogous to what we find in astrology. There the moment of birth corresponds to the fall of the coins, the constellation to the hexagram, and the astrological interpretation of the birth data corresponds to the text assigned to the hexagram.

85   The type of thinking based on the synchronistic principle, which reached its climax in the *I Ching*, is the purest expression of Chinese thinking in general. In the West it has been absent from the history of philosophy since the time of Heraclitus, and reappears only as a faint echo in Leibniz.[5] However, in the interim it was not altogether extinguished, but lingered on in the twilight of astrological speculation, and it still remains on that level today.

86   At this point the *I Ching* responds to something in us that is in need of further development. Occultism has enjoyed a renaissance in our times that is without parallel – the light of the Western mind is nearly darkened by it. I am not thinking now of our seats of learning and their representatives. As a doctor who deals with ordinary people, I know that the universities have ceased to act as disseminators of light. People are weary of scientific specialization and rationalism and intellectualism. They want to hear truths that broaden rather than restrict, that do not obscure but enlighten, that do not run off them like water but penetrate them to the marrow. This search is only too likely to lead a large if anonymous public astray.

87   When I think of the significance of Wilhelm's achievement, I am always reminded of Anquetil Duperron, the Frenchman who brought the first translation of the Upanishads to Europe. This was at the very time when, after almost eighteen hundred years, the inconceivable happened and the Goddess of Reason drove the Christian God from his throne in Notre-Dame. Today, when far more inconceivable things are happening in Russia than ever did in Paris, and Christianity has become so debilitated that even the Buddhists think it is high time they sent missionaries to Europe, it is Wilhelm who brings new light from the East. This was the cultural task to which he felt himself called, recognizing how much the East had to offer in our spiritual need.

88   A beggar is not helped by having alms, great or small, pressed into his hand, even though this may be what he wants. He is far better helped if we show him how he can permanently rid himself of his beggary by work. Unfortunately, the spiritual beggars of our time are too inclined to accept the alms of the East in bulk and to imitate its ways unthinkingly. This is a danger about which too many warnings cannot be uttered, and one which Wilhelm felt very clearly. The spirit of Europe is not helped merely by new sensations or a titillation of the nerves. What it has taken China thousands of years to build cannot be acquired by theft. If we want to possess it, we must earn the right to it by working on ourselves. Of what use to us is the wisdom of the Upanishads or the insight of Chinese yoga if we desert our own foundations as though they were errors outlived, and, like homeless pirates, settle with thievish intent on foreign shores? The insights of the East, and in particular the wisdom of the *I Ching*, have no meaning for us if we close our minds to our own problems, jog along with our conventional prejudices, and veil from ourselves our real human nature with all its dangerous undercurrents and darknesses. The light of this wisdom shines only in the dark, not in the brightly lit theatre of our European consciousness and will. The wisdom of the *I Ching* issued from a background of whose horrors we have a faint inkling when we read of Chinese massacres, of the sinister power of Chinese secret societies, or of the nameless poverty, hopeless filth and vices of the Chinese masses.

89   We need to have a firmly based, three-dimensional life of our own before we can experience the wisdom of the East as a living thing. Therefore, our prime need is to learn a few European truths about ourselves. Our way begins with European reality and not with yoga exercises which would only delude us about our own reality. We must continue Wilhelm's work of translation in a wider sense if we wish to show ourselves worthy pupils of the master. The central concept of Chinese philosophy is Tao, which Wilhelm translated as 'meaning'. Just as Wilhelm gave the spiritual treasure of the East a European meaning, so we should translate this meaning into life. To do this – that is, to realize Tao – would be the true task of the pupil.

90   If we turn our eyes to the East, we see an overwhelming destiny fulfilling itself. The guns of Europe have burst open the gates of Asia; European science and technology, European materialism and cupidity, are flooding China. We have conquered the East politically. And what happened when Rome did the same thing to the Near East? The spirit of the East entered Rome. Mithras, the Persian god of light, became the god of the Roman legions, and out of the most unlikely corner of Asia Minor a new spiritual Rome arose. Would it be unthinkable that the same thing might happen today and find us just as blind as the cultured Romans who marvelled at the superstitions of the Christians? It is worth noticing that England and Holland, the two main colonizing powers in Asia, are also the two most infected with Hindu theosophy. I know that our unconscious

is full of Eastern symbolism. The spirit of the East is really at our gates. Therefore it seems to me that the search for Tao, for a meaning in life, has already become a collective phenomenon among us, and to a far greater extent than is generally realized. The fact that Wilhelm and the indologist Hauer were asked to lecture on yoga at this year's congress of German psychotherapists is a most significant sign of the times. Imagine what it means when a practising physician, who has to deal with people at their most sensitive and receptive, establishes contact with an Eastern system of healing! In this way the spirit of the East penetrates through all our pores and reaches the most vulnerable places of Europe. It could be a dangerous infection, but it might also be a remedy. The Babylonian confusion of tongues in the West has created such a disorientation that everyone longs for simpler truths, or at least for guiding ideas which speak not to the head alone but also to the heart, which bring clarity to the contemplative spirit and peace to the restless pressure of our feelings. Like ancient Rome, we today are once more importing every form of exotic superstition in the hope of finding the right remedy for our sickness.

91   Human instinct knows that all great truth is simple. The man whose instincts are atrophied therefore supposes that it is found in cheap simplifications and platitudes; or, as a result of his disappointment, he falls into the opposite error of thinking that it must be as obscure and complicated as possible. Today we have a Gnostic movement in the anonymous masses which is the exact psychological counterpart of the Gnostic movement nineteen hundred years ago. Then, as today, solitary wanderers like Apollonius of Tyana spun the spiritual threads from Europe to Asia, perhaps to remotest India. Viewing him in this historical perspective, I see Wilhelm as one of those great Gnostic intermediaries who brought the Hellenic spirit into contact with the cultural heritage of the East and thereby caused a new world to rise out of the ruins of the Roman Empire.

92   In the midst of the jarring disharmony of European opinion and the shouts of false prophets, it is indeed a blessing to hear the simple language of Wilhelm, the messenger from China. One notices at once that it is schooled in the plant-like spontaneity of the Chinese mind, which is able to express profound things in simple language. It disloses something of the simplicity of great truth, the ingenuousness of deep meaning, and it carries to us the delicate perfume of the Golden Flower. Penetrating gently, it has set in the soil of Europe a tender seedling, giving us a new intuition of life and its meaning, far removed from the tension and arrogance of the European will.

93   Faced with the alien culture of the East, Wilhelm showed a degree of modesty highly unusual in a European. He approached it freely, without prejudice, without the assumption of knowing better; he opened his heart and mind to it. He let himself be gripped and shaped by it, so that when he came back to Europe he brought us, not only in his spirit but in his

whole being, a true image of the East. This deep transformation was certainly not won without great sacrifice, for our historical premises are so entirely different. The keenness of Western consciousness and its harsh problems had to soften before the more universal, more equable nature of the East; Western rationalism and one-sided differentiation had to yield to Eastern breadth and simplicity. For Wilhelm this change meant not only a shifting of the intellectual standpoint but a radical rearrangement of the components of his personality. The picture of the East he has given us, free of ulterior motive and all trace of tendentiousness, could never have been painted in such perfection had he not been able to let the European in him slip into the background. If he had allowed East and West to clash together with unyielding harshness, he could not have fulfilled his mission of conveying to us a true picture of China. The sacrifice of the European was unavoidable, and necessary for the fulfilment of the task fate laid upon him.

94   Wilhelm accomplished his mission in every sense of the word. Not only did he make accessible to us the cultural treasure of ancient China, but, as I have said, he brought us its spiritual root, the root that has remained alive all these thousands of years, and planted it in the soil of Europe. With the completion of this task, his mission reached its climax and, unfortunately, its end. According to the law of *enantiodromia*, so well understood by the Chinese, the end of one phase is the beginning of its opposite. Thus *yang* at its highest point changes into *yin*, and positive into negative. I came closer to Wilhelm only in the last years of his life, and I could observe how, with the completion of his life-work, Europe and European man hemmed him in more and more closely, beset him in fact. And at the same time there grew in him the feeling that he stood on the brink of a great change, an upheaval whose nature he could not clearly grasp. He only knew that he faced a decisive crisis. His physical illness went parallel with this development. His dreams were filled with memories of China, but the images were always sad and gloomy, a clear proof that the Chinese contents of his mind had become negative.

95   Nothing can be sacrificed for ever. Everything returns later in changed form, and when once a great sacrifice has been made, the sacrificed thing when it returns must meet with a healthy and resistant body that can take the shock. Therefore, a spiritual crisis of these dimensions often means death if it takes place in a body weakened by disease. For now the sacrificial knife is in the hand of him who was sacrificed, and a death is demanded of the erstwhile sacrificer.

96   As you see, I have not withheld my personal views, for if I had not told you what Wilhelm meant to me, how would it have been possible for me to speak of him? Wilhelm's life-work is of such immense importance to me because it clarified and confirmed so much that I had been seeking, striving for, thinking and doing in my efforts to alleviate the psychic sufferings of Europeans. It was a tremendous experience for me to hear

through him, in clear language, things that I had dimly divined in the confusion of our European unconscious. Indeed, I feel myself so very much enriched by him that it seems to me as if I had received more from him than from any other man. That is also the reason why I do not feel it a presumption if I am the one to offer on the altar of his memory the gratitude and respect of all of us.

NOTES

1 [Originally delivered as the principal address at a memorial service held in Munich in May 1930, for Wilhelm, who had died the previous 1 March. Published as 'Nachruf für Richard Wilhelm', *Neue Zürcher Zeitung*, CLI:1 (6 March 1930), and in the *Chinesisch–Deutscher Almanach* (Frankfurt a. M., 1931). Republished in the 2nd edition of Jung and Wilhelm, *Das Geheimnis der goldenen Blüte: Ein chinesisches Lebensbuch* (Zürich, 1938). Previously translated by Cary F. Baynes as an appendix to Jung and Wilhelm, *The Secret of the Golden Flower* (London and New York, 1931; revised and augmented edition, 1962). Grateful acknowledgement is made here to Mrs Baynes for permission to draw upon the 1962 version of her translation. For Jung's commentary on *The Secret of the Golden Flower*, see CW13 – EDITORS.]

2 [Wilhelm's translation of the Chinese classic was published in Jena, 1924. Translated into English by Cary F. Baynes as *The I Ching, or Book of Changes* (1950), with a Foreword by Jung (see CW11) – EDITORS.]

3 *The Yi King*, trans. by James Legge (Sacred Books of the East, Vol. 16; 1882).

4 For the details and history of the method, see the *I Ching* (1967 edn), pp. xlixff. and 356ff.

5 [See Hellmut Wilhelm, 'The Concept of Time in the Book of Changes', pp. 216ff. – EDITORS.]

3 In search of Indian spiritual values

From: 'The Holy Men of India'[1]

950   Heinrich Zimmer had been interested for years in the Maharshi of Tiruvannamalai, and the first question he asked me on my return from India concerned this latest holy and wise man from southern India. I do not know whether my friend found it an unforgivable or an incomprehensible sin on my part that I had not sought out Shri Ramana. I had the feeling that *he* would certainly not have neglected to pay him a visit, so warm was his interest in the life and thought of the holy man. This was scarcely surprising, as I know how deeply Zimmer had penetrated into the spirit of India. His most ardent wish to see India in reality was unfortunately never fulfilled, and the one chance he had of doing so fell through in the last hours before the outbreak of the Second World War. As if in compensation, his vision of the spiritual India was all the more magnificent. In our work together he gave me invaluable insights into the Oriental psyche, not only through his immense technical knowledge, but above all through his brilliant grasp of the meaning and content of Indian mythology. Unhappily, the early death of those beloved of the gods was fulfilled in him, and it remains for us to mourn the loss of a spirit that overcame the limitations of the specialist and, turning towards humanity, bestowed upon it the joyous gift of 'immortal fruit'.

951   The carrier of mythological and philosophical wisdom in India has been since time immemorial the 'holy man' – a Western title which does not quite render the essence and outward appearance of the parallel figure in the East. This figure is the embodiment of the spiritual India, and we meet him again and again in the literature. No wonder, then, that Zimmer was passionately interested in the latest and best incarnation of this type in the phenomenal personage of Shri Ramana. He saw in this yogi the true avatar of the figure of the *rishi*, seer and philosopher, which strides, as legendary as it is historical, down centuries and the ages.

952   Perhaps I should have visited Shri Ramana. Yet I fear that if I journeyed to India a second time to make up for my omission, it would fare with me just the same: I simply could not, despite the uniqueness of the occasion, bring myself to visit this undoubtedly distinguished man personally. For the fact is, I doubt his uniqueness; he is of a type which always was and

will be. Therefore it was not necessary to seek him out. I saw him all over India, in the pictures of Ramakrishna, in Ramakrishna's disciples, in Buddhist monks, in innumerable other figures of the daily Indian scene, and the words of his wisdom are the *sous-entendu* of India's spiritual life. Shri Ramana is, in a sense, a *hominum homo*, a true 'son of man' of the Indian earth. He is 'genuine', and on top of that he is a 'phenomenon' which, seen through European eyes, has claims to uniqueness. But in India he is merely the whitest spot on a white surface (whose whiteness is mentioned only because there are so many surfaces that are just as black). Altogether, one sees so much in India that in the end one only wishes one could see less: the enormous variety of countries and human beings creates a longing for complete simplicity. This simplicity is there too; it pervades the spiritual life of India like a pleasant fragrance or a melody. It is everywhere the same, but never monotonous, endlessly varied. To get to know it, it is sufficient to read an Upanishad or any discourse of the Buddha. What is heard there is heard everywhere; it speaks out of a million eyes, it expresses itself in countless gestures, and there is no village or country road where that broad-branched tree cannot be found in whose shade the ego struggles for its own abolition, drowning the world of multiplicity in the All and All-Oneness of Universal Being. This note rang so insistently in my ears that soon I was no longer able to shake off its spell. I was then absolutely certain that no one could ever get beyond this, least of all the Indian holy man himself; and should Shri Ramana say anything that did not chime in with this melody, or claim to know anything that transcended it, his illumination would assuredly be false. The holy man is right when he intones India's ancient chants, but wrong when he pipes any other tune. This effortless drone of argumentation, so suited to the heat of southern India, made me refrain, without regret, from a visit to Tiruvannamalai.

953   Nevertheless, the unfathomableness of India saw to it that I should encounter the holy man after all, and in a form that was more congenial to me, without my seeking him out: in Trivandrum, the capital of Travancore, I ran across a disciple of the Maharshi. He was an unassuming little man, of a social status which we would describe as that of a primary-school teacher, and he reminded me most vividly of the shoemaker of Alexandria who (in Anatole France's story) was presented to St Anthony by the angel as an example of an even greater saint than he. Like the shoemaker, my little holy man had innumerable children to feed and was making special sacrifices in order that his eldest son might be educated. (I will not enter here into the closely allied question as to whether holy men are always wise, and conversely, whether all wise men are unconditionally holy. In this respect there is room for doubt.) Be that as it may, in this modest, kindly, devout and childlike spirit I encountered a man who had absorbed the wisdom of the Maharshi with utter devotion, and at the same time had surpassed his master because, notwithstanding his cleverness and

holiness, he had 'eaten' the world. I acknowledge with deep gratitude this meeting with him; nothing better could have happened to me. The man who is only wise and only holy interests me about as much as the skeleton of a rare saurian, which would not move me to tears. The insane contradiction, on the other hand, between existence beyond *māyā* in the cosmic Self, and that amiable human weakness which fruitfully sinks many roots into the black earth, repeating for all eternity the weaving and rending of the veil as the ageless melody of India – this contradiction fascinates me; for how else can one perceive the light without the shadow, hear the silence without the noise, attain wisdom without foolishness? The experience of holiness may well be the most painful of all. My man – thank God – was only a little holy man; no radiant peak above the dark abysses, no shattering sport of nature, but an example of how wisdom, holiness *and* humanity can dwell together in harmony, richly, pleasantly, sweetly, peacefully and patiently, without limiting one another, without being peculiar, causing no surprise, in no way sensational, necessitating no special post-office, yet embodying an age-old culture amid the gentle murmur of the coconut palms fanning themselves in the light sea wind. He has found a meaning in the rushing phantasmagoria of Being, freedom in bondage, victory in defeat.

954   Unadulterated wisdom and unadulterated holiness, I fear, are seen to best advantage in literature, where their reputation remains undisputed. Lao-tzu reads exquisitely, unsurpassably well, in the *Tao Teh Ching*; Lao-tzu with his dancing girl on the western slope of the mountain, celebrating the evening of life, is rather less edifying. But even less can one approve of the neglected body of the 'unadulterated' holy man, especially if one believes that beauty is one of the most excellent of God's creations.

955   Shri Ramana's thoughts are beautiful to read. What we find here is purest India, the breath of eternity, scorning and scorned by the world. It is the song of the ages, resounding like the shrilling of crickets on a summer's night, from a million beings. This melody is built up on the one great theme, which, veiling its monotony under a thousand colourful reflections, tirelessly and everlastingly rejuvenates itself in the Indian spirit, whose youngest incarnation is Shri Ramana himself. It is the drama of *ahamkāra*, the 'I-maker' or ego-consciousness, in opposition and indissoluble bondage to the *atman*, the self or non-ego. The Maharshi also calls the *atman* the 'ego-ego' – significantly enough, for the self is indeed experienced as the subject of the subject, as the true source and controller of the ego, whose (mistaken) strivings are continually directed towards appropriating the very autonomy which is intimated to it by the self.

956   This conflict is not unknown to the Westerner: for him it is the relationship of man to God. The modern Indian, as I can testify from my own experience, has largely adopted European habits of language, 'self' or *atman* being essentially synonymous with 'God'. But, in contradistinction to the Western 'man and God', the Indian posits the opposition (or

correspondence) between 'ego' and 'self'. 'Ego', as contrasted with 'man', is a distinctly psychological concept, and so is 'self' – to *our* way of thinking. We might therefore be inclined to assume that in India the metaphysical problem 'man and God' has been shifted on to the psychological plane. On closer inspection it is clear that this is not so, for the Indian concept of 'ego' and 'self' is not really psychological but – one could well say – just as metaphysical as our 'man and God'. The Indian lacks the epistemological standpoint just as much as our own religious language does. He is still 'pre-Kantian'. This complication is unknown in India and it is still largely unknown with us. In India there is no psychology in our sense of the word. India is 'pre-psychological': when it speaks of the 'self', it *posits* such a thing as existing. Psychology does not do this. It does not in any sense deny the existence of the dramatic conflict, but reserves the right to the poverty, or the riches, of *not* knowing about the self. Though very well acquainted with the self's peculiar and paradoxical phenomenology, we remain conscious of the fact that we are discerning, with the limited means at our disposal, something essentially unknown and expressing it in terms of psychic structures which may not be adequate to the nature of what is to be known.

957   This epistemological limitation keeps us at a remove from what we term 'self' or 'God'. The equation self = God is shocking to the Europeans. As Shri Ramana's statements and many others show, it is a specifically Eastern insight, to which psychology has nothing further to say except that it is not within its competence to differentiate between the two. Psychology can only establish that the empiricism of the 'self' exhibits a religious symptomatology, just as does that category of assertions associated with the term 'God'. Although the phenomenon of religious exaltation transcends epistemological criticism – a feature it shares with all manifestations of emotion – yet the human urge to knowledge asserts itself again and again with 'ungodly' or 'Luciferian' obstinacy and wilfulness, indeed with necessity, whether it be to the loss or gain of the thinking man. Sooner or later he will place his reason in opposition to the emotion that grips him and seek to withdraw from its entangling grasp in order to give an account of what has happened. If he proceeds prudently and conscientiously, he will continually discover that at least a part of his experience is a humanly limited *interpretation*, as was the case with Ignatius Loyola and his vision of the snake with multiple eyes, which he at first regarded as of divine, and later as of diabolical, origin. (Compare the exhortation in I John 4:1: 'Do not believe every spirit, but test the spirits to see whether they are of God.') To the Indian it is clear that the self as the originating ground of the psyche is not different from God, and that, so far as a man is *in* the self, he is not only contained in God but actually is God. Shri Ramana is quite explicit on this point. No doubt this equation, too, is an 'interpretation'. Equally, it is an interpretation to regard the self as the highest good or as the goal of all desire and

fulfilment, although the phenomenology of such an experience leaves no doubt that these characteristics exist *a priori* and are indispensable components of religious exaltation. But that will not prevent the critical intellect from questioning the validity of these characteristics. It is difficult to see how this question could be answered, as the intellect lacks the necessary criteria. Anything that might serve as a criterion is subject in turn to the critical question of validity. The only thing that can decide here is the preponderance of psychic facts.

958   The goal of Eastern religious practice is the same as that of Western mysticism: the shifting of the centre of gravity from the ego to the self, from man to God. This means that the ego disappears in the self, and man in God. It is evident that Shri Ramana has either really been more or less absorbed by the self, or has at least struggled earnestly all his life to extinguish his ego in it. The *Exercitia spiritualia* reveal a similar striving: they subordinate 'self-possession' (possession of an ego) as much as possible to possession by Christ. Shri Ramana's elder contemporary, Ramakrishna, had the same attitude concerning the relation to the self, only in his case the dilemma between ego and self seems to emerge more distinctly. Whereas Shri Ramana displays a 'sympathetic' tolerance towards the worldly callings of his disciples, while yet exalting the extinction of the ego as the real goal of spiritual exertion, Ramakrishna shows a rather more hesitant attitude in this respect. He says: 'So long as ego-seeking exists, neither knowledge (*jñāna*) nor liberation (*mukti*) is possible, and to births and deaths there is no end.'[2] All the same, he has to admit the fatal tenacity of *ahamkāra* (the 'I-maker'): 'Very few can get rid of the sense of "I" through *samādhi* . . .. We may discriminate a thousand times, but the sense of "I" is bound to return again and again. You may cut down the branches of a fig-tree today, but tomorrow you will see that new twigs are sprouting.'[3] He goes so far as to suggest the indestructibility of the ego with the words: 'If this sense of "I" will not leave, then let it stay on as the servant of God.'[4] Compared with this concession to the ego, Shri Ramana is definitely the more radical or, in the sense of Indian tradition, the more conservative. Though the elder, Ramakrishna is the more modern of the two, and this is probably to be attributed to the fact that he was affected by the Western attitude of mind far more profoundly than was Shri Ramana.

959   If we conceive of the self as the essence of psychic wholeness, i.e. as the totality of conscious and unconscious, we do so because it does *in fact* represent something like a goal of psychic development, and this irrespective of all conscious opinions and expectations. The self is the subject-matter of a process that generally runs its course outside consciousness and makes its presence felt only by a kind of long-range effect. A critical attitude towards this natural process allows us to raise questions which are excluded at the outset by the formula self = God. This formula shows the dissolution of the ego in the *atman* to be the unequivocal goal of religion

and ethics, as exemplified in the life and thought of Shri Ramana. The same is obviously true of Christian mysticism, which differs from Oriental philosophy only through having a different terminology. The inevitable consequence is the depreciation and abolition of the physical and psychic man (i.e. of the living body and *ahamkāra*) in favour of the pneumatic man. Shri Ramana speaks of his body as 'this clod'. As against this, and taking into consideration the complex nature of human experience (emotion plus interpretation), the critical standpoint admits the importance of ego-consciousness, well knowing that without *ahamkāra* there would be absolutely no one there to register what was happening. Without the Maharshi's personal ego, which, as a matter of brute experience, only exists in conjunction with the said 'clod' (= body), there would be no Shri Ramana at all. Even if we agreed with him that it is no longer his ego, but the *atman* speaking, it is still the psychic structure of consciousness in association with the body that makes speech communication possible. Without this admittedly very troublesome physical and psychic man, the self would be entirely without substance, as Angelus Silesius has already said:

> I know that without me
> God can no moment live;
> Were I to die, then he
> No longer could survive.

960   The intrinsically goal-like quality of the self and the urge to realize this goal are, as we have said, not dependent on the participation of consciousness. They cannot be denied any more than one can deny one's ego-consciousness. It, too, puts forward its claims peremptorily, and very often in overt or covert opposition to the needs of the evolving self. In reality, i.e. with few exceptions, the entelechy of the self consists in a succession of endless compromises, ego and self laboriously keeping the scales balanced if all is to go well. Too great a swing to one side or the other is often no more than an example of how not to set about it. This certainly does not mean that extremes, when they occur in a natural way, are in themselves evil. We make the right use of them when we examine their meaning, and they give us ample opportunity to do this in a manner deserving our gratitude. Exceptional human beings, carefully hedged about and secluded, are invariably a gift of nature, enriching and widening the scope of our consciousness – but only if our capacity for reflection does not suffer shipwreck. Enthusiasm can be a veritable gift of the gods or a monster from hell. With the hybris which attends it, corruption sets in, even if the resultant clouding of consciousness seems to put the attainment of the highest goals almost within one's grasp. The only true and lasting gain is heightened and broadened reflection.

961   Banalities apart, there is unfortunately no philosophical or psychological proposition that does not immediately have to be reversed. Thus

reflection as an end in itself is nothing but a limitation if it cannot stand firm in the turmoil of chaotic extremes, just as mere dynamism for its own sake leads to inanity. Everything requires for its existence its own opposite, or else it fades into nothingness. The ego needs the self and vice versa. The changing relations between these two entities constitute a field of experience which Eastern introspection has exploited to a degree almost unattainable to Western man. The philosophy of the East, although so vastly different from ours, could be an inestimable treasure for us too; but, in order to possess it, we must first earn it. Shri Ramana's words, which Heinrich Zimmer has bequeathed to us, in excellent translation, as the last gift of his pen, bring together once again the loftiest insights that the spirit of India has garnered in the course of the ages, and the individual life and work of the Maharshi illustrate once again the passionate striving of the Indian for the liberating 'Ground'. I say 'once again', because India is about to take the fateful step of becoming a State and entering into a community of nations whose guiding principles have anything and everything on the programme except detachment and peace of the soul.

962   The Eastern peoples are threatened with a rapid collapse of their spiritual values, and what replaces them cannot always be counted among the best that Western civilization has produced. From this point of view, one could regard Ramakrishna and Shri Ramana as modern prophets, who play the same compensatory role in relation to their people as that of the Old Testament prophets in relation to the 'unfaithful' children of Israel. Not only do they exhort their compatriots to remember their thousand-year-old spiritual culture, they actually embody it and thus serve as an impressive warning, lest the demands of the soul be forgotten amid the novelties of Western civilization with its materialistic technology and commercial acquisitiveness. The breathless drive for power and aggrandizement in the political, social and intellectual sphere, gnawing at the soul of the Westerner with apparently insatiable greed, is spreading irresistibly in the East and threatens to have incalculable consequences. Not only in India but in China, too, much has already perished where once the soul lived and throve. The externalization of culture may do away with a great many evils whose removal seems most desirable and beneficial, yet this step forward, as experience shows, is all too dearly paid for with a loss of spiritual culture. It is undeniably much more comfortable to live in a well-planned and hygienically equipped house, but this still does not answer the question of *who* is the dweller in this house and whether his soul rejoices in the same order and cleanliness as the house which ministers to his outer life. The man whose interests are all outside is never satisfied with what is necessary, but is perpetually hankering after something more and better, which, true to his bias, he always seeks outside himself. He forgets completely that, for all his outward successes, he himself remains the same inwardly, and he therefore laments his poverty if he possesses only one automobile when the majority have two. Obviously the outward

lives of men could do with a lot more bettering and beautifying, but these things lose their meaning when the inner man does not keep pace with them. To be satiated with 'necessities' is no doubt an inestimable source of happiness, yet the inner man continues to raise his claim, and this can be satisfied by no outward possessions. And the less this voice is heard in the chase after the brilliant things of this world, the more the inner man becomes the source of inexplicable misfortune and uncomprehended unhappiness in the midst of living conditions whose outcome was expected to be entirely different. The externalization of life turns to incurable suffering, because no one can understand why he should suffer from himself. No one wonders at his insatiability, but regards it as his lawful right, never thinking that the one-sidedness of this psychic diet leads in the end to the gravest disturbances of equilibrium. That is the sickness of Western man, and he will not rest until he has infected the whole world with his own greedy restlessness.

963   The wisdom and mysticism of the East have, therefore, very much to say to us, even when they speak their own inimitable language. They serve to remind us that we in our culture possess something similar, which we have already forgotten, and to direct our attention to the fate of the inner man, which we set aside as trifling. The life and teaching of Shri Ramana are of significance not only for India, but for the West too. They are more than a *document humain*: they are a warning message to a humanity which threatens to lose itself in unconsciousness and anarchy. It is perhaps, in the deeper sense, no accident that Heinrich Zimmer's last book should leave us, as a testament, the life-work of a modern Indian prophet who exemplifies so impressively the problem of psychic transformation.

NOTES

1 [Introduction to Heinrich Zimmer, *Der Weg zum Selbst: Lehre und Leben des indischen Heiligen Shri Ramana Maharshi aus Tiruvannamalai* (Zürich, 1944), edited by C. G. Jung. The work consists of 167 pages translated by Zimmer from English publications of the Shri Ramanasramam Book Depot, Tiruvannamalai, India, preceded by a brief (non-significant) foreword and this introduction, both by Jung, an obituary notice by Emil Abegg of Zimmer's death in New York in 1944, and an introduction to the Shri Ramana Maharshi texts by Zimmer – EDITORS.]

2 *Worte des Ramakrishna*, ed. by Emma von Pelet, p. 77.

3 *The Gospel of Ramakrishna*, p. 56.

4 ibid.

4 East–West psychological comparisons

From: 'What India Can Teach Us'[1]

1002   India lies between the Asiatic north and the Pacific south, between Tibet and Ceylon. India ends abruptly at the foothills of the Himalayas, and at Adam's Bridge. At one end, a Mongolian world begins, at the other, the 'paradise' of a South Sea island. Ceylon is as strangely different from India as is Tibet. Curiously enough, at either end one finds the 'spoor of the elephant', as the Pali Canon[2] calls the teaching of the Lord Buddha.

1003   Why has India lost her greatest light, Buddha's path of redemption, that glorious synthesis of philosophy and *opus divinum*? It is common knowledge that mankind can never remain on an apex of illumination and spiritual endeavour. Buddha was an untimely intruder, upsetting the historical process, which afterwards got the better of him. Indian religion is like a *vimana*, or pagoda. The gods climb over one another like ants, from the elephants carved on the base to the abstract lotus which crowns the top of the building. In the long run, the gods become philosophical concepts. Buddha, a spiritual pioneer for the whole world, said, and tried to make it true, that the enlightened man is even the teacher and redeemer of his gods (not their stupid denier, as Western 'enlightenment' will have it). This was obviously too much, because the Indian mind was not at all ready to integrate the gods to such an extent as to make them psychologically dependent upon man's mental condition. How Buddha himself could obtain such insight without losing himself in a complete mental inflation borders on a miracle. (But any genius is a miracle.)

1004   Buddha disturbed the historical process by interfering with the slow transformation of the gods into ideas. The true genius nearly always intrudes and disturbs. He speaks to a temporal world out of a world eternal. Thus he says the wrong things at the right time. Eternal truths are never true at any given moment in history. The process of transformation has to make a halt in order to digest and assimilate the utterly impractical things that the genius has produced from the storehouse of eternity. Yet the genius is the healer of his time, because anything he reveals of eternal truth is healing.

1005   The remote goal of the transformation process, however, is very much what Buddha intended. But to get there is possible neither in one generation nor in ten. It obviously takes much longer, thousands of years at all events, since the intended transformation cannot be realized without an enormous development of human consciousness. It can only be 'believed', which is what Buddha's, as well as Christ's, followers obviously did, assuming – as 'believers' always do – that belief is the whole thing. Belief is a great thing, to be sure, but it is a substitute for a conscious reality, which the Christians wisely relegate to a life in the hereafter. This 'hereafter' is really the intended future of mankind, anticipated by religious intuition.

1006   Buddha has disappeared from Indian life and religion more than we could ever imagine Christ disappearing in the aftermath of some future catastrophe to Christianity, more even than the Graeco-Roman religions have disappeared from present-day Christianity. India is not ungrateful to her master minds. There is a considerable revival of interest in classical philosophy. Universities like Calcutta and Benares have important philosophy departments. Yet the main emphasis is laid on classical Hindu philosophy and its vast Sanskrit literature. The Pali Canon is not precisely within their scope. Buddha does not represent a proper philosophy. He challenges man! This is not exactly what philosophy wants. It, like any other science, needs a good deal of intellectual free play, undisturbed by moral and human entanglements. But also, small and fragmentary people must be able to 'do something about it' without getting fatally involved in big issues far beyond their powers of endurance and accomplishment. This is on the right road after all, although it is indeed a *longissima via*. The divine impatience of a genius may disturb or even upset the small man. But after a few generations he will reassert himself by sheer force of numbers, and this too seems to be right.

1007   I am now going to say something which may offend my Indian friends, but actually no offence is intended. I have, so it seems to me, observed the peculiar fact that an Indian, inasmuch as he is really Indian, does not think, at least not what we call 'think'. *He rather perceives the thought.* He resembles the primitive in this respect. I do not say that he *is* primitive, but that the process of his thinking reminds me of the primitive way of thought production. The primitive's reasoning is mainly an unconscious function, and he perceives its results. We should expect such a peculiarity in any civilization which has enjoyed an almost unbroken continuity from primitive times.

1008   Our Western evolution from a primitive level was suddenly interrupted by the invasion of a psychology and spirituality belonging to a much higher level of civilization. Our case was not so bad as that of the Negroes or the Polynesians, who found themselves suddenly confronted with the infinitely higher civilization of the white man, but in essence it was the same. We were stopped in the midst of a still barbarous polytheism, which was eradicated or suppressed in the course of centuries and not so very long ago. I suppose that this fact has given a peculiar twist to the Western mind. Our mental existence was transformed into something which it had not yet reached and which it could not yet truly be. And this could only be brought about by a dissociation between the conscious part of the mind and the unconscious. It was a liberation of consciousness from the burden of irrationality and instinctive impulsiveness at the expense of the totality of the individual. Man became split into a conscious and an unconscious personality. The conscious personality could be domesticated, because it was separated from the natural and primitive man. Thus we became highly disciplined, organized and rational on one side, but the other side remained a suppressed primitive, cut off from education and civilization.

1009　　This explains our many relapses into the most appalling barbarity, and it also explains the really terrible fact that, the higher we climb the mountain of scientific and technical achievement, the more dangerous and diabolical becomes the misuse of our inventions. Think of the great triumph of the human mind, the power to fly: we have accomplished the age-old dream of humanity! And think of the bombing raids of modern warfare! Is this what civilization means? Is it not rather a convincing demonstration of the fact that, when our mind went up to conquer the skies, our other man, that suppressed barbarous individual, went down to hell? Certainly our civilization can be proud of its achievements, yet we have to be ashamed of ourselves.

1010　　This surely is not the only way in which man can become civilized, at all events it is not an ideal way. One could think of another more satisfactory possibility. Instead of differentiating only one side of man, one could differentiate the whole man. By burdening the conscious man with the earthbound weight of his primitive side one could avoid that fatal dissociation between an upper and a lower half. Of course it would be no mean *tour de force* to experiment with the white man of today along these lines. It would obviously lead to devilishly intricate moral and intellectual problems. But, if the white man does not succeed in destroying his own race with his brilliant inventions, he will eventually have to settle down to a desperately serious course of self-education.

1011　　Whatever the ultimate fate of the white man may be, we can at least behold one example of a civilization which has brought every essential trace of primitivity with it, embracing the whole man from top to bottom. India's civilization and psychology resemble her temples, which represent the universe in their sculptures, including man and all his aspects and activities, whether as saint or brute. That is presumably the reason why India seems so dreamlike: one gets pushed back into the unconscious, into that unredeemed, uncivilized, aboriginal world, of which we only dream, since our consciousness denies it. India represents the other way of civilizing man, the way without suppression, without violence, without rationalism. You see them there side by side, in the same town, in the same street, in the same temple, within the same square mile: the most highly cultivated mind and the primitive. In the mental make-up of the most spiritual you discern the traits of the living primitive, and in the melancholy eyes of the illiterate half-naked villager you divine an unconscious knowledge of mysterious truths.

1012   I say all this in order to explain what I mean by not thinking. I could just as well say: Thank heaven there is a man left who has not learned to think, but is still able to perceive his thoughts, as if they were visions or living things; a man who has transformed, or is still going to transform, his gods into visible thoughts based upon the reality of the instincts. He has rescued his gods, and they live with him. It is true that it is an irrational life, full of crudeness, gruesomeness, misery, disease and death, yet somehow complete, satisfactory and of an unfathomable emotional beauty. It is true that the logical processes of India are funny, and it is bewildering to see how fragments of Western science live peacefully side by side with what we, shortsightedly, would call superstitions. Indians do not mind seemingly intolerable contradictions. If they exist, they are the peculiarity of such thinking, and man is not responsible for them. He does not make them, since thoughts appear by themselves. The Indian does not fish out infinitesimal details from the universe. His ambition is to have a vision of the whole. He does not yet know that you can screw the living world up tightly between two concepts. Did you ever stop to think how much of the conqueror (not to say thief or robber) lies in that very term 'concept'? It comes from the Latin *concipere*, 'to take something by grasping it thoroughly'. That is how we get at the world. But Indian 'thinking' is an increase of vision and not a predatory raid into the yet unconquered realms of nature.

1013   If you want to learn the greatest lesson India can teach you, wrap yourself in the cloak of your moral superiority, go to the Black Pagoda of Konarak, sit down in the shadow of the mighty ruin that is still covered with the most amazing collection of obscenities, read Murray's cunning old *Handbook for India*, which tells you how to be properly shocked by this lamentable state of affairs, and how you should go into the temples in the evening, because in the lamplight they look if possible 'more [and how beautifully!] wicked'; and then analyse carefully and with the utmost honesty all your reactions, feelings and thoughts. It will take you quite a while, but in the end, if you have done good work, you will have learned something about yourself, and about the white man in general, which you have probably never heard from anyone else. I think, if you can afford it, a trip to India is on the whole most edifying and, from a psychological point of view, most advisable, although it may give you considerable headaches.

From: 'Foreword to Lily Abegg, *The Mind of East Asia*'[3]

1483   The author of this book, the entire text of which unfortunately I have not seen, has talked to me about her project and about her ideas with regard to the difference between Eastern and Western psychology. Thus I was able to note many points of agreement between us, and also a competence on her part to make judgements which is possible only to one who is a European and at the same time possesses the invaluable advantage of having spent more than half a lifetime in the Far East, in close contact with the mind of Asia. Without such first-hand experience it would be a hopeless task to approach the problem of Eastern psychology. One must be deeply and directly moved by the strangeness, one might almost say by the incomprehensibility, of the Eastern psyche. Decisive experiences of this kind cannot be transmitted through books; they come only from living in immediate daily relationship with the people. Having had unusual advantages in this respect, the author is in a position to discuss what is perhaps the basic, and is in any case an extremely important, question of the difference between Eastern and Western psychology. I have often found myself in situations where I had to take account of this difference, as in the study of Chinese and East Indian literary texts and in the psychological treatment of Asiatics. Among my patients, I am sorry to say, I have never had a Chinese or a Japanese, nor have I had the privilege of visiting either China or Japan. But at least I have had the opportunity to experience with painful clarity the insufficiency of my knowledge. In this field we still have everything to learn, and whatever we learn will be to our immense advantage. Knowedge of Eastern psychology provides the indispensable basis for a critique of Western psychology, as indeed for any objective understanding of it. And in view of the truly lamentable psychic situation of the West, the importance of a deeper understanding of our Occidental prejudices can hardly be overestimated.

1484   Long experience with the products of the unconscious has taught me that there is a very remarkable parallelism between the specific character of the Western unconscious psyche and the 'manifest' psyche of the East. Since our experience shows that the biological role which the unconscious plays in the psychic economy is compensatory to consciousness, one can venture the hypothesis that the mind of the Far East is related to our Western consciousness as the unconscious is, that is, as the left hand to the right.

1485   Our unconscious has, fundamentally, a tendency towards wholeness, as I believe I have been able to prove. One would be quite justified in saying the same thing about the Eastern psyche, but with this difference: that in the East it is consciousness that is characterized by an apperception of totality, while the west has developed a differentiated and therefore necessarily one-sided attention or awareness. With it goes the Western concept of causality, a principle of cognition irreconcilably opposed to the principle of synchronicity which forms the basis and the source of Eastern 'incomprehensibility', and explains as well the 'strangeness' of the unconscious with which we in the West are confronted. The understanding of synchronicity is the key which unlocks the door to the Eastern apperception of totality that we find so mysterious. The author seems to have devoted particular attention to just this point. I do not hesitate to say that I look forward to the publication of her book with the greatest interest.

NOTES

1　[Written in English and first published in *Asia* (New York), XXXIX (1939):2, 97–8. – EDITORS.]

2　[The body of Southern Buddhist Sacred Writings. – EDITORS.]

3　[Zürich, 1950 ('East Asia Thinks Otherwise'). The foreword was not included in the English-language edition of the book, by Lily Abegg, *The Mind of East Asia* (London and New York, 1952). It is reproduced here, in a translation by Hildegard Nagel and Ellen Thayer, titled 'The Mind of East and West', from the *Inward Light* (Washington, D.C.), no. 49, (autumn 1955), having previously appeared in the *Bulletin of the Analytical Psychology Club of New York*, 15:3 (March 1953).]

5   The allures of the East

From: 'Archetypes of the Collective Unconscious'[1]

11   Though the Christian view of the world has paled for many people, the symbolic treasure-rooms of the East are still full of marvels that can nourish for a long time to come the passion for show and new clothes. What is more, these images – be they Christian or Buddhist or what you will – are lovely, mysterious, richly intuitive. Naturally, the more familiar we are with them the more does constant usage polish them smooth, so that what remains is only banal superficiality and meaningless paradox. The mystery of the Virgin Birth, or the *homoousia* of the Son with the Father, or the Trinity which is nevertheless not a triad – these no longer lend wings to any philosophical fancy. They have stiffened into mere objects of belief. So it is not surprising if the religious need, the believing mind and the philo-sophical speculations of the educated European are attracted by the symbols of the East – those grandiose conceptions of divinity in India and the abysms of Taoist philosophy in China – just as once before the heart and mind of the men of antiquity were gripped by Christian ideas. There are many Europeans who began by surrendering completely to the influence of the Christian symbol until they landed themselves in a Kierkegaardian neurosis, or whose relation to God, owing to the progressive impoverish-ment of symbolism, developed into an unbearably sophisticated I–You relationship – only to fall victims in their turn to the magic and novelty of Eastern symbols. This surrender is not necessarily a defeat; rather it proves the receptiveness and vitality of the religious sense. We can observe much the same thing in the educated Oriental, who not infrequently feels drawn to the Christian symbol or to the science that is so unsuited to the Oriental mind, and even develops an enviable understanding of them. That people should succumb to these eternal images is entirely normal, in fact it is what these images are for. They are meant to attract, to convince, to fascinate and to overpower. They are created out of the primal stuff of revelation and reflect the ever-unique experience of divinity. That is why they always give man a premonition of the divine while at the same time safeguarding him from immediate experience of it. Thanks to the labours of the human spirit over the centuries, these images have become embedded in a com-prehensive system of thought that ascribes an order to the world, and are

at the same time represented by a mighty, far-spread and venerable institution called the Church.

21   Dogma takes the place of the collective unconscious by formulating its contents on a grand scale. The Catholic way of life is completely unaware of psychological problems in this sense. Almost the entire life of the collective unconscious has been channelled into the dogmatic archetypal ideas and flows along like a well-controlled stream in the symbolism of creed and ritual. It manifests itself in the inwardness of the Catholic psyche. The collective unconscious, as we understand it today, was never a matter of 'psychology', for before the Christian Church existed there were the antique mysteries, and these reach back into the grey mists of neolithic prehistory. Mankind has never lacked powerful images to lend magical aid against all the uncanny things that live in the depths of the psyche. Always the figures of the unconscious were expressed in protecting and healing images and in this way were expelled from the psyche into cosmic space.

22   The iconoclasm of the Reformation, however, quite literally made a breach in the protective wall of sacred images, and since then one image after another has crumbled away. They became dubious, for they conflicted with awakening reason. Besides, people had long since forgotten what they meant. Or had they really forgotten? Could it be that men had never really known what they meant, and that only in recent times did it occur to the Protestant part of mankind that actually we haven't the remotest conception of what is meant by the Virgin Birth, the divinity of Christ and the complexities of the Trinity? It almost seems as if these images had just lived, and as if their living existence had simply been accepted without question and without reflection, much as everyone decorates Christmas trees or hides Easter eggs without ever knowing what these customs mean. The fact is that archetypal images are so packed with meaning in themselves that people never think of asking what they really do mean. That the gods die from time to time is due to man's sudden discovery that they do not mean anything, that they are made by human hands, useless idols of wood and stone. In reality, however, he has merely discovered that up till then he has never thought about his images at all. And when he starts thinking about them, he does so with the help of what he calls 'reason' – which in point of fact is nothing more than the sumtotal of all his prejudices and myopic views.

23   The history of Protestantism has been one of chronic iconoclasm. One wall after another fell. And the work of destruction was not too difficult once the authority of the Church had been shattered. We all know how, in large things as in small, in general as well as in particular, piece after piece collapsed, and how the alarming poverty of symbols that is now the condition of our life came about. With that the power of the Church has vanished too – a fortress robbed of its bastions and casemates, a house whose walls have been plucked away, exposed to all the winds of the world and to all dangers.

24   Although this is, properly speaking, a lamentable collapse that offends our sense of history, the disintegration of Protestantism into nearly four hundred denominations is yet a sure sign that the restlessness continues. The Protestant is cast out into a state of defencelessness that might well make the natural man shudder. His enlightened consciousness, of course, refuses to take cognizance of this fact, and is quietly looking elsewhere for what has been lost to Europe. We seek the effective images, the thought-forms that satisfy the restlessness of heart and mind, and we find the treasures of the East.

25   There is no objection to this, in and for itself. Nobody forced the Romans to import Asiatic cults in bulk. If Christianity had really been – as so often described – 'alien' to the Germanic tribes, they could easily have rejected it when the prestige of the Roman legions began to wane. But Christianity had come to stay, because it fits in with the existing archetypal pattern. In the course of the centuries, however, it turned into something its founder might well have wondered at had he lived to see it; and the Christianity of Negroes and other dark-skinned converts is certainly an occasion for historical reflections. Why, then, should the West not assimilate Eastern forms? The Romans too went to Eleusis, Samothrace and Egypt in order to get themselves initiated. In Egypt there even seems to have been a regular tourist trade in this commodity.

26   The gods of Greece and Rome perished from the same disease as did our Christian symbols: people discovered then, as today, that they had no thoughts whatever on the subject. On the other hand, the gods of the strangers still had unexhausted *mana*. Their names were weird and incomprehensible and their deeds portentously dark–something altogether different from the hackneyed *chronique scandaleuse* of Olympus. At least one couldn't understand the Asiatic symbols, and for this reason they were not banal like the conventional gods. The fact that people accepted the new as unthinkingly as they had rejected the old did not become a problem at that time.

27   Is it becoming a problem today? Shall we be able to put on, like a new suit of clothes, ready-made symbols grown on foreign soil, saturated with foreign blood, spoken in a foreign tongue, nourished by a foreign culture, interwoven with foreign history, and so resemble a beggar who wraps himself in kingly raiment, a king who disguises himself as a beggar? No doubt this is possible. Or is there something in ourselves that commands us to go in for no mummeries, but perhaps even to sew our garment ourselves?

28   I am convinced that the growing impoverishment of symbols has a meaning. It is a development that has an inner consistency. Everything that we have not thought about, and that has therefore been deprived of a meaningful connection with our developing consciousness, has got lost. If we now try to cover our nakedness with the gorgeous trappings of the East, as the theosophists do, we would be playing our own history false. A man

does not sink down to beggary only to pose afterwards as an Indian potentate. It seems to me that it would be far better stoutly to avow our spiritual poverty, our symbol-lessness, instead of feigning a legacy to which we are not the legitimate heirs at all. We are, surely, the rightful heirs of Christian symbolism, but somehow we have squandered this heritage. We have let the house our fathers built fall into decay, and now we try to break into Oriental palaces that our fathers never knew. Anyone who has lost the historical symbols and cannot be satisfied with substitutes is certainly in a very difficult position today: before him yawns the void, and he turns away from it in horror. What is worse, the vacuum gets filled with absurd political and social ideas, which one and all are distinguished by their spiritual bleakness. But if he cannot get along with these pedantic dogmatisms, he sees himself forced to be serious for once with his alleged trust in God, though it usually turns out that his fear of things going wrong if he did so is even more persuasive. This fear is far from unjustified, for where God is closest the danger seems greatest. It is dangerous to avow spiritual poverty, for the poor man has desires, and whoever has desires calls down some fatality on himself. A Swiss proverb puts it drastically: 'Behind every rich man stands a devil, and behind every poor man two.'

29   Just as in Christianity the vow of worldly poverty turned the mind away from the riches of this earth, so spiritual poverty seeks to renounce the false riches of the spirit in order to withdraw not only from the sorry remnants – which today call themselves the Protestant Church – of a great past, but also from all the allurements of the odorous East; in order, finally, to dwell with itself alone, where, in the cold light of consciousness, the blank barrenness of the world reaches to the very stars.

From: 'The Spiritual Problems of Modern Man'

188   We have not yet realized that Western theosophy is an amateurish, indeed barbarous imitation of the East. We are just beginning to take up astrology again, which to the Oriental is his daily bread. Our studies of sexual life, originating in Vienna and England, are matched or surpassed by Hindu teachings on this subject. Oriental texts ten centuries old introduce us to philosophical relativism, while the idea of indeterminacy, newly broached in the West, is the very basis of Chinese science. As to our discoveries in psychology, Richard Wilhelm has shown me that certain complicated psychic processes are recognizably described in ancient Chinese texts. Psychoanalysis itself and the lines of thought to which it gives rise – a development which we consider specifically Western – are only a beginner's attempt compared with what is an immemorial art in the East. It may not perhaps be known that parallels between psychoanalysis and yoga have already been drawn by Oscar Schmitz.[2]

189   Another thing we have not realized is that while we are turning the

material world of the East upside-down with our technical proficiency, the East with its superior psychic proficiency is throwing our spiritual world into confusion. We have never yet hit upon the thought that while we are overpowering the Orient from without, it may be fastening its hold on us from within. Such an idea strikes us as almost insane, because we have eyes only for obvious causal connections and fail to see that we must lay the blame for the confusion of our intellectual middle class at the doors of Max Müller, Oldenberg, Deussen, Wilhelm and others like them. What does the example of the Roman Empire teach us? After the conquest of Asia Minor, Rome became Asiatic; Europe was infected by Asia and remains so today. Out of Cilicia came the Mithraic cult, the religion of the Roman legions, and it spread from Egypt to fog-bound Britain. Need I point out the Asiatic origin of Christianity?

190   The theosophists have an amusing idea that certain Mahatmas, seated somewhere in the Himalayas or Tibet, inspire and direct every mind in the world. So strong, in fact, can be the influence of the Eastern belief in magic that Europeans of sound mind have assured me that every good thing I say is unwittingly inspired in me by the Mahatmas, my own inspiration being of no account whatever. This myth of the Mahatmas, widely circulated in the West and firmly believed, far from being nonsense, is – like every myth – an important psychological truth. It seems to be quite true that the East is at the bottom of the spiritual change we are passing through today. Only, this East is not a Tibetan monastery full of Mahatmas, but lies essentially within us. It is our own psyche, constantly at work creating new spiritual forms and spiritual forces which may help us to subdue the boundless lust for prey of Aryan man. We shall perhaps come to know something of that narrowing of horizons which has grown in the East into a dubious quietism, and also something of that stability which human existence acquires when the claims of the spirit become as imperative as the necessities of social life. Yet in this age of Americanization we are still far from anything of the sort; it seems to me that we are only at the threshold of a new spiritual epoch. I do not wish to pass myself off as a prophet, but one can hardly attempt to sketch the spiritual problem of modern man without mentioning the longing for rest in a period of unrest, the longing for security in an age of insecurity. It is from need and distress that new forms of existence arise, and not from idealistic requirements or mere wishes.

NOTES

1 [First published in the *Eranos-Jahrbuch* (1934), and later revised and published in *Von den Wurzeln des Bewusstseins* (Zürich, 1954), from which version the present translation is made. The translation of the original version, by Stanley Dell, in *The Integration of the Personality* (New York, 1939; London, 1940), has been freely consulted. – EDITORS.]

2 [*Psychoanalyse und Yoga.*]

Part II

China and the Taoist way

6   The Chinese world-view

From: 'Synchronicity: An Acausal
Connecting Principle'

916   The causality principle asserts that the connection between cause and effect is a necessary one. The synchronicity principle asserts that the terms of a meaningful coincidence are connected by *simultaneity* and *meaning*. So if we assume that the ESP experiments and numerous other observations are established facts, we must conclude that besides the connection between cause and effect there is another factor in nature which expresses itself in the arrangment of events and appears to us as meaning. Although meaning is an anthropomorphic interpretation it nevertheless forms the indispensable criterion of synchronicity. What that factor which appears to us as 'meaning' may be in itself we have no possibility of knowing. As a hypothesis, however, it is not quite so impossible as may appear at first sight. We must remember that the rationalistic attitude of the West is not the only possible one and is not all-embracing, but is in many ways a prejudice and a bias that ought perhaps to be corrected. The very much older civilization of the Chinese has always thought differently from us in this respect, and we have to go back to Heraclitus if we want to find something similar in our civilization, at least where philosophy is concerned. Only in astrology, alchemy and the mantic procedures do we find no differences of principle between our attitude and the Chinese. That is why alchemy developed along parallel lines in East and West and why in both spheres it strove towards the same goal with more or less identical ideas.[1]

917   In Chinese philosophy one of the oldest and most central ideas is that of Tao, which the Jesuits translated as 'God'. But that is correct only for the Western way of thinking. Other translations, such as 'Providence' and the like, are mere makeshifts. Richard Wilhelm brilliantly interprets it as 'meaning'.[2] The concept of Tao pervades the whole philosophical thought of China. Causality occupies this paramount position with us, but it acquired its importance only in the course of the last two centuries, thanks to the levelling influence of the statistical method on the one hand and the unparalleled success of the natural sciences on the other, which brought the metaphysical view of the world into disrepute.

918   Lao-tzu gives the following description of Tao in his celebrated *Tao Teh Ching*:[3]

> There is something formless yet complete
> That existed before heaven and earth.
>   How still! How empty!
> Dependent on nothing, unchanging,
> All pervading, unfailing.
> One may think of it as the mother of all things under heaven.
> I do not know its name,
> But I call it 'Meaning'.
> If I had to give it a name, I should call it 'The Great'.
>
> (ch. XXV)

919   Tao 'covers the ten thousand things like a garment but does not claim to be master over them' (ch. *XXXIV*). Lao-tzu describes it as 'Nothing',[4] by which he means, says Wilhelm, only its 'contrast with the world of reality'. Lao-tzu describes its nature as follows:

> We put thirty spokes together and call it a wheel;
> But it is on the space where there is nothing that the utility of
>   the wheel depends.
> We turn clay to make a vessel;
> But it is on the space where there is nothing that the utility of
>   the vessel depends.
> We pierce doors and windows to make a house;
> And it is on these spaces where there is nothing that the utility of
>   the house depends.
> Therefore just as we take advantage of what is, we should recognize
>   the utility of what is not.
>
> (ch. XI)

920   'Nothing' is evidently 'meaning' or 'purpose', and it is only called Nothing because it does not appear in the world of the senses, but is only its organizer.[5] Lao-tzu says:

> Because the eye gazes but can catch no glimpse of it,
> It is called elusive.
> Because the ear listens but cannot hear it,
> It is called the rarefied.
> Because the hand feels for it but cannot find it,
> It is called the infinitesimal . . ..
> These are called the shapeless shapes,
> Forms without form,
> Vague semblances.
> Go towards them, and you can see no front;
> Go after them, and you see no rear.
>
> (ch. XIV)

921 Wilhelm describes it as 'a borderline conception lying at the extreme
edge of the world of appearances'. In it, the opposites 'cancel out in non-
discrimination', but are still potentially present. 'These seeds', he continues,
'point to something that corresponds firstly to *the visible*, i.e., something
in the nature of an image; secondly to *the audible*, i.e., something in the
nature of words; thirdly to *extension in space*, i.e., something with a form.
But these three things are not clearly distinguished and definable, they are
a non-spatial and non-temporal unity, having no above and below or front
and back.' As the *Tao Teh Ching* says:

> Incommensurable, impalpable,
> Yet latent in it are forms;
> Impalpable, incommensurable,
> Yet within it are entities.
> Shadowy it is and dim.
>
> (ch. XXI)

922 Reality, thinks Wilhelm, is conceptually knowable because according
to the Chinese view there is in all things a latent 'rationality'.[6] This is the
basic idea underlying meaningful coincidence: it is possible because both
sides have the same meaning. Where meaning prevails, order results:

> Tao is eternal, but has no name;
> The Uncarved Block, though seemingly of small account,
> Is greater than anything under heaven.
> If the kings and barons would but possess themselves of it,
> The ten thousand creatures would flock to do them homage;
> Heaven and earth would conspire
> To send Sweet Dew;
> Without law or compulsion men would dwell in harmony.
>
> (ch. *XXXII*)

> Tao never does;
> Yet through it all things are done.
>
> (ch. *XXXVII*)

> Heaven's net is wide;
> Coarse are the meshes, yet nothing slips through.
>
> (ch. *LXXIII*)

923 Chuang-tzu (a contemporary of Plato's) says of the psychological
premises on which Tao is based: 'The state in which ego and non-ego are
no longer opposed is called the pivot of Tao.'[7] It sounds almost like a
criticism of our scientific view of the world when he remarks that 'Tao is
obscured when you fix your eye on little segments of existence only',[8] or
'Limitations are not originally grounded in the meaning of life. Originally
words had no fixed meanings. Differences only arose through looking at
things subjectively.'[9] The sages of old, says Chuang-tzu, 'took as their

starting-point a state when the existence of things had not yet begun. That is indeed the extreme limit beyond which you cannot go. The next assumption was that though things existed they had not yet begun to be separated. The next, that though things were separated in a sense, affirmation and negation had not yet begun. When affirmation and negation came into being, Tao faded. After Tao faded, then came one-sided attachments.'[10] 'Outward hearing should not penetrate further than the ear; the intellect should not seek to lead a separate existence, thus the soul can become empty and absorb the whole world. It is Tao that fills this emptiness.' If you have insight, says Chuang-tzu, 'you use your inner eye, your inner ear, to pierce to the heart of things, and have no need of intellectual knowledge'.[11] This is obviously an allusion to the absolute knowledge of the unconscious, and to the presence in the microcosm of macrocosmic events.

924   This Taoistic view is typical of Chinese thinking. It is, whenever possible, *a thinking in terms of the whole*, a point also brought out by Marcel Granet,[12] the eminent authority on Chinese psychology. This peculiarity can be seen in ordinary conversation with the Chinese: what seems to us a perfectly straightforward, precise question about some detail evokes from the Chinese thinker an unexpectedly elaborate answer, as though one had asked him for a blade of grass and got a whole meadow in return. With us details are important for their own sakes; for the Oriental mind they always complete a total picture. In this totality, as in primitive or in our own mediaeval, pre-scientific psychology (still very much alive!), are included things which seem to be connected with one another only 'by chance', by a coincidence whose meaningfulness appears altogether arbitrary. This is where the theory of *correspondentia*[13] comes in, which was propounded by the natural philosophers of the Middle Ages, and particularly the classical idea of the *sympathy of all things*.[14]

From: 'On the Theory and Practice of Analytical Psychology'

141   A former President of the British Anthropological Society asked me: 'Can you understand that such a highly intelligent people as the Chinese have no science?' I replied: 'They have a science, but you do not understand it. It is not based on the principle of causality. The principle of causality is not the only principle; it is only relative.'

142   People may say: What a fool to say causality is only relative! But look at modern physics! The East bases its thinking and its evaluation of facts on another principle. We have not even a word for that principle. The East naturally has a word for it, but we do not understand it. The Eastern word is Tao. My friend McDougall[15] has a Chinese student, and he asked him: 'What exactly do you mean by Tao?' Typically Western! The Chinese

explained what Tao is and he replied: 'I do not understand yet.' The Chinese went out to the balcony and said: 'What do you see?' 'I see a street and houses and people walking and tramcars passing.' 'What more?' 'There is a hill.' 'What more?' 'Trees.' 'What more?' 'The wind is blowing.' The Chinese threw up his arms and said: 'That is Tao.'

143   There you are. Tao can be anything. I use another word to designate it, but it is poor enough. I call it *synchronicity*. The Eastern mind, when it looks at an ensemble of facts, accepts that ensemble as it is, but the Western mind divides it into entities, small quantities. You look, for instance, at this present gathering of people, and you say: 'Where do they come from? Why should they come together?' The Eastern mind is not at all interested in that. It says: 'What does it *mean* that these people are together?' That is not a problem for the Western mind. You are interested in what you come here for and what you are doing here. Not so the Eastern mind; it is interested in being together.

144   It is like this: you are standing on the seashore and the waves wash up an old hat, an old box, a shoe, a dead fish, and there they lie on the shore. You say: 'Chance, nonsense!' The Chinese mind asks: 'What does it mean that these things are together?' The Chinese mind experiments with that *being together* and *coming together at the right moment*, and it has an experimental method which is not known in the West, but which plays a large role in the philosophy of the East. It is a method of forecasting possibilities, and it is still used by the Japanese government about political situations; it was used, for instance, in the Great War. This method was formulated in 1143 BC.[16]

NOTES

1 Cf. *Psychology and Alchemy*, par. 453, and 'The Spirit Mercurius', par. 273. Also the doctrine of *chên-yên* in Wei Po-yang ['Phil. Tree', pars. 432ff., and *Mysterium*, pars. 490, 711n] and in Chuang-tzu.

2 Jung, 'Commentary on *The Secret of the Golden Flower*', par. 28, and Wilhelm, *Chinesische Lebensweisheit*.

3 [Quotations from Arthur Waley's *The Way and its Power*, with occasional slight changes to fit Wilhelm's reading. – TRANS.]

4 Tao is the contingent, which Andreas Speiser defines as 'pure nothing' ('Über die Freiheit').

5 Wilhelm, *Chinesische Lebensweisheit*, p. 15: 'The relation between meaning (Tao) and reality cannot be conceived under the category of cause and effect.'

6 ibid., p. 19.

7 *Das wahre Buch vom südlichen Blütenland*, trans. by R. Wilhelm, II, 3.

8 ibid., II, 3.

9 ibid., II, 7.

10 ibid., II, 5.

11 ibid., IV, 1.

12 *La Pensée chinoise*; also Lily Abegg, *The Mind of East Asia*. The latter gives an excellent account of the synchronistic mentality of the Chinese.

13 Professor W. Pauli kindly calls my attention to the fact that Niels Bohr used

'correspondence' as a mediating term between the representation of the discontinuum (particle) and the continuum (wave). Originally (1913–18) he called it the 'principle of correspondence', but later (1927) it was formulated as the 'argument of correspondence'.

14 'συμπάθεια τῶν ὅλων'.

15 [William McDougall (1871–1938), American psychiatrist. Cf. Jung's 'On the Psychogenesis of Schizophrenia' (CW 3), par. 504, and 'The Therapeutic Value of Abreaction' (CW 16), par. 255.]

16 [Cf. *The I Ching, or Book of Changes*, trans. by Wilhelm/Baynes, 3rd edn, introduction, p. liii.]

7 *Yin* and *yang*: the unity of opposites

From: *Psychological Types*

358   The idea of a middle way between the opposites is to be found also in China, in the form of Tao. The concept of Tao is usually associated with the name of the philosopher Lao-tzu, born 604 BC. But this concept is older than the philosophy of Lao-tzu. It is bound up with the ancient folk religion of Taoism, the 'way of Heaven', a concept corresponding to the Vedic *rta*. The meanings of Tao are as follows: way, method, principle, natural force or life force, the regulated processes of nature, the idea of the world, the prime cause of all phenomena, the right, the good, the moral order. Some translators even translate it as God, not without some justification, it seems to me, since Tao, like *rta*, has a tinge of substantiality.

359   I will first give a number of passages from the *Tao Teh Ching*, Lao-tzu's classic:

> Was Tao the child of something else? We cannot tell.
> But as a substanceless image it existed before the Ancestor.[1]

> There was something formless yet complete,
> That existed before heaven and earth;
> Without sound, without substance,
> Dependent on nothing, unchanging,
> All pervading, unfailing,
> One may think of it as the mother of all things under heaven.
> Its true name we do not know;
> 'Way' is the name that we give it.[2]

360   In order to characterize its essential quality, Lao-tzu likens it to water:

> The highest good is like that of water. The goodness of water is that it benefits the ten thousand creatures; yet itself does not scramble, but is content with the [low] places that all men disdain. It is this that makes water so near to the Way.[3]

The idea of a 'potential' could not be better expressed.

> He that is without desire sees its essence,
> He that clings to desire sees only its outward form.[4]

361   The affinity with the fundamental Brahmanic ideas is unmistakable, though this does not necessarily imply direct contact. Lao-tzu was an entirely original thinker, and the primordial image underlying *rta–brahman–atman* and Tao is as universal as man, appearing in every age and among all peoples as a primitive conception of energy, or 'soul force', or however else it may be called.

> He who knows the Always-so has room in him for everything;
> He who has room in him for everything is without prejudice.
> To be without prejudice is to be kingly;
> To be kingly is to be of heaven;
> To be of heaven is to be in Tao.
> Tao is forever, and he that possesses it,
> Though his body ceases, is not destroyed.[5]

362   Knowledge of Tao therefore has the same redeeming and uplifting effect as the knowledge of *brahman*. Man becomes one with Tao, with the unending *durée créatrice* (if we may compare this concept of Bergson's with its older congener), for Tao is also the stream of time. It is irrational, inconceivable:

> *Tao* is a thing impalpable, incommensurable.[6]

> For though all creatures under heaven are the products
>   of [Tao as] Being,
> Being itself is the product of [Tao as] Not-Being.[7]

> Tao is hidden and nameless.[8]

It is obviously an irrational union of opposites, a symbol of what is and is not.

> The Valley Spirit never dies;
> It is named the mysterious Female.
> And the door of the mysterious Female
> Is the base from which heaven and earth sprang.[9]

363   Tao is the creative process, begetting as the father and bringing forth as the mother. It is the beginning and end of all creatures.

> He whose actions are in harmony with *Tao* becomes one with *Tao*.[10]

Therefore the perfected sage liberates himself from the opposites, having seen through their connection with one another and their alternation. Therefore it is said:

> When your work is done, then withdraw.
> Such is heaven's way.[11]

> He [the perfected sage] cannot either be drawn into
>   friendship or repelled,

Cannot be benefited, cannot be harmed,
Cannot be either raised or humbled.[12]

364   Being one with Tao resembles the state of infancy:

Can you keep the unquiet physical soul from straying, hold fast
   to the Unity, and never quit it?
Can you, when concentrating your breath, make it soft like that
   of a little child?[13]

He who knows the male, yet cleaves to what is female,
Becomes like a ravine, receiving all things under heaven;
And being such a ravine,
He knows all the time a power that he never calls upon in vain.
This is returning to the state of infancy.[14]

The impunity of that which is fraught with this power
May be likened to that of an infant.[15]

365   This psychological attitude is, as we know, an essential condition for
obtaining the kingdom of heaven, and this in its turn – all rational
interpretations notwithstanding – is the central, irrational symbol whence
the redeeming effect comes. The Christian symbol merely has a more
social character than the related conceptions of the East. These are directly
connected with age-old dynamistic ideas of a magical power emanating
from people and things or – at a higher level of development – from gods
or a divine principle.

366   According to the central concepts of Taoism, Tao is divided into a
fundamental pair of opposites, *yang* and *yin*. *Yang* signifies warmth, light,
maleness; *yin* is cold, darkness, femaleness. *Yang* is also heaven, *yin* earth.
From the *yang* force arises *shen*, the celestial portion of the human soul,
and from the *yin* force comes *kwei*, the earthly part. As a microcosm, man
is a reconciler of the opposites. Heaven, man and earth form the three chief
elements of the world, the *san-tsai*.

367   The picture thus presented is an altogether primitive idea which we find
in similar forms elsewhere, as for instance in the West African myth where
Obatala and Odudua, the first parents (heaven and earth), lie together in a
calabash until a son, man, arises between them. Hence man as a microcosm
uniting the world opposites is the equivalent of an irrational symbol that
unites the psychological opposites. This primordial image of man is in
keeping with Schiller's definition of the symbol as 'living form'.

368   The division of the psyche into a *shen* (or *hwan*) soul and a *kwei* (or
p'o) soul is a great psychological truth. This Chinese conception is echoed
in the well-known passage from *Faust*:

Two souls, alas, are housed within my breast,
   And each will wrestle for the mastery there.
The one has passion's craving crude for love,

And hugs a world where sweet the senses rage;
The other longs for pastures fair above,
Leaving the murk for lofty heritage.[16]

369   The existence of two mutually antagonistic tendencies, both striving to drag man into extreme attitudes and entangle him in the world, whether on the material or spiritual level, sets him at variance with himself and accordingly demands the existence of a counterweight. This is the 'irrational third', Tao. Hence the sage's anxious endeavour to live in harmony with Tao, lest he fall into the conflict of opposites. Since Tao is irrational, it is not something that can be got by the will, as Lao-tzu repeatedly emphasizes. This lends particular significance to another specifically Chinese concept, *wu-wei*. *Wu-wei* means 'not-doing' (which is not to be confused with 'doing nothing'). Our rationalistic 'doing', which is the greatness as well as the evil of our time, does not lead to Tao.

370   The aim of Taoist ethics, then, is to find deliverance from the cosmic tension of opposites by a return to Tao. In this connection we must also remember the 'sage of Omi', Nakae Toju,[17] an outstanding Japanese philosopher of the seventeenth century. Basing himself on the teaching of the Chu-hi school, which had migrated from China, he established two principles, *ri* and *ki*. *Ri* is the world soul, *ki* is the world stuff. *Ri* and *ki* are, however, the same because they are both attributes of God and therefore exist only in him and through him. God is their union. Equally, the soul embraces both *ri* and *ki*. Toju says of God: 'As the essence of the world, God embraces the world, but at the same time he is in our midst and even in our bodies.' For him God is a universal self, while the individual self is the 'heaven' within us, something supra-sensible and divine called *ryochi*. *Ryochi* is 'God within us' and dwells in every individual. It is the true self. Toju distinguishes a true from a false self. The false self is an acquired personality compounded of perverted beliefs. We might define this false self as the *persona*, that general idea of ourselves which we have built up from experiencing our effect upon the world around us and its effect upon us. The persona is, in Schopenhauer's words, how one *appears* to oneself and the world, but not what one *is*. What one is, is one's individual self, Toju's 'true self' or *ryochi*. *Ryochi* is also called 'being alone' or 'knowing alone', clearly because it is a condition related to the essence of the self, beyond all personal judgements conditioned by external experience. Toju conceives *ryochi* as the *summum bonum*, as 'bliss' (*brahman* is bliss, *ananda*). It is the light which pervades the world – a further parallel with *brahman*, according to Inouye. It is love for mankind, immortal, all-knowing, good. Evil comes from the will (shades of Schopenhauer!). *Ryochi* is the self-regulating function, the mediator and uniter of the opposites *ri* and *ki*; it is in fullest accord with the Indian idea of the 'wise old man who dwells in the heart'. Or as Wang Yang-ming, the Chinese father of Japanese philosophy, says: 'In every

heart there dwells a *sejin* (sage). Only, we do not believe it firmly enough, and therefore the whole has remained buried.'[18]

NOTES

1 Waley, trans., *The Way and its Power*, p. 146. [This and the next quotation, unfortunately, contradict Jung's statement that Tao has a tinge of substantiality. – TRANSLATOR.]
2 ibid., p. 174.
3 ibid., p. 151.
4 [Trans. from author's German. Cf. Waley, p. 141.]
5 P. 162.
6 P. 170.
7 P. 192.
8 P. 193.
9 P. 149.
10 [Trans. from author's German. Cf. Waley, p. 172.]
11 P. 153.
12 P. 210.
13 P. 153.
14 P. 178.
15 P. 209.
16 *Faust, Part One*, trans. by Wayne, p. 67.
17 Inouye, 'Die japanische Philosophie', in *Aallg. Geschichte der Phil.*, pp. 84f.
18 ibid., p. 85. [Cf. Wang Yang-ming, *Instructions for Practical Living*, trans. Chan, sec. 207, pp. 193f.]

8 Chinese alchemy and psychological individuation

From: 'Commentary on
The Secret of the Golden Flower'

DIFFICULTIES ENCOUNTERED BY A EUROPEAN IN TRYING TO UNDERSTAND THE EAST

1   A thorough Westerner in feeling, I cannot but be profoundly impressed by the strangeness of this Chinese text. It is true that some knowledge of Eastern religions and philosophies helps my intellect and my intuition to understand these things up to a point, just as I can understand the paradoxes of primitive beliefs in terms of 'ethnology' or 'comparative religion'. This is of course the Western way of hiding one's heart under the cloak of so-called scientific understanding. We do it partly because the *misérable vanité des savants* fears and rejects with horror any sign of living sympathy, and partly because sympathetic understanding might transform contact with an alien spirit into an experience that has to be taken seriously. Our so-called scientific objectivity would have reserved this text for the philological acumen of sinologists, and would have guarded it jealously from any other interpretation. But Richard Wilhelm penetrated too deeply into the secret and mysterious vitality of Chinese wisdom to allow such a pearl of intuitive insight to disappear into the pigeon-holes of specialists. I am greatly honoured that his choice of a psychological commentator has fallen upon me.

2   This, however, involves the risk that this precious example of more-than-specialist insight will be swallowed by still another specialism. Nevertheless, anyone who belittles the merits of Western science is undermining the foundations of the Western mind. Science is not indeed a perfect instrument, but it is a superb and invaluable tool that works harm only when it is taken as an end in itself. Science must serve; it errs when it usurps the throne. It must be ready to serve all its branches, for each, because of its insufficiency, has need of support from the others. Science is the tool of the Western mind, and with it one can open more doors than with bare hands. It is part and parcel of our understanding, and it obscures our insight only when it claims that the understanding it conveys is the only kind there is. The East teaches us another, broader, more profound and higher understanding – understanding through life. We know this only

by hearsay, as a shadowy sentiment expressing a vague religiosity, and we are fond of putting 'Oriental wisdom' in quotation-marks and banishing it to the dim region of faith and superstition. But that is wholly to misunderstand the realism of the East. Texts of this kind do not consist of the sentimental, overwrought mystical intuitions of pathological cranks and recluses, but are based on the practical insights of highly evolved Chinese minds, which we have not the slightest justification for undervaluing.

3   This assertion may seem bold, perhaps, and is likely to cause a good deal of head-shaking. Nor is that surprising, considering how little people know about the material. Its strangeness is indeed so arresting that our puzzlement as to how and where the Chinese world of thought might be joined to ours is quite understandable. The usual mistake of Western man when faced with this problem of grasping the ideas of the East is like that of the student in *Faust*. Misled by the devil, he contemptuously turns his back on science and, carried away by Eastern occultism, takes over yoga practices word for word and becomes a pitiable imitator. (Theosophy is our best example of this.) Thus he abandons the one sure foundation of the Western mind and loses himself in a mist of words and ideas that could never have originated in European brains and can never be profitably grafted upon them.

4   An ancient adept has said: 'If the wrong man uses the right means, the right means work in the wrong way.'[1] This Chinese saying, unfortunately only too true, stands in sharp contrast to our belief in the 'right' method irrespective of the man who applies it. In reality, everything depends on the man and little or nothing on the method. The method is merely the path, the direction taken by a man; the way he acts is the true expression of his nature. If it ceases to be this, the method is nothing more than an affectation, something artificially pieced on, rootless and sapless, serving only the illegitimate goal of self-deception. It becomes a means of fooling oneself and of evading what may perhaps be the implacable law of one's being. This is far removed from the earthiness and self-reliance of Chinese thought. It is a denial of one's own nature, a self-betrayal to strange and unclean gods, a cowardly trick for the purpose of feigning mental superiority, everything in fact that is profoundly contrary to the spirit of the Chinese 'method'. For these insights spring from a way of life that is complete, genuine, and true to itself; from that ancient, cultural life of China which grew logically and organically from the deepest instincts, and which, for us, is forever inaccessible and impossible to imitate.

5   Western imitation is a tragic misunderstanding of the psychology of the East, every bit as sterile as the modern escapades to New Mexico, the blissful South Sea islands and central Africa, where 'the primitive life' is played at in deadly earnest while Western man secretly evades his menacing duties, his *Hic Rhodus hic salta*. It is not for us to imitate what is foreign to our organism or to play the missionary; our task is to build up our Western civilization, which sickens with a thousand ills. This has

to be done on the spot, and by the European just as he is, with all his Western ordinariness, his marriage problems, his neuroses, his social and political delusions, and his whole philosophical disorientation.

6   We should do well to confess at once that, fundamentally, we do not understand the utter unworldliness of a text like this – that actually we do not want to understand it. Have we, perhaps, a dim suspicion that a mental attitude which can direct the glance inward to that extent is detached from the world only because these people have so completely fulfilled the instinctive demands of their natures that there is nothing to prevent them from glimpsing the invisible essence of things? Can it be that the precondition for such a vision is liberation from the ambitions and passions that bind us to the visible world, and does not this liberation come from the sensible fulfilment of instinctive demands rather than from the premature and fear-ridden repression of them? Are our eyes opened to the spirit only when the laws of the earth are obeyed? Anyone who knows the history of Chinese culture and has carefully studied the *I Ching*, that book of wisdom which for thousands of years has permeated all Chinese thought, will not lightly wave these doubts aside. He will be aware that the views set forth in our text are nothing extraordinary to the Chinese, but are actually inescapable psychological conclusions.

7   For a long time the spirit, and the sufferings of the spirit, were positive values and the things most worth striving for in our peculiar Christian culture. Only in the course of the nineteenth century, when spirit began to degenerate into intellect, did a reaction set in against the unbearable dominance of intellectualism, and this led to the unpardonable mistake of confusing intellect with spirit and blaming the latter for the misdeeds of the former. The intellect does indeed do harm to the soul when it dares to possess itself of the heritage of the spirit. It is in no way fitted to do this, for spirit is something higher than intellect since it embraces the latter and includes the feelings as well. It is a guiding principle of life that strives towards superhuman, shining heights. Opposed to this *yang* principle is the dark, feminine, earthbound *yin*, whose emotionality and instinctuality reach back into the depths of time and down into the labyrinth of the physiological continuum. No doubt these are purely intuitive ideas, but one can hardly dispense with them if one is trying to understand the nature of the human psyche. The Chinese could not do without them because, as the history of Chinese philosophy shows, they never strayed so far from the central psychic facts as to lose themselves in a one-sided over-development and over-valuation of a single psychic function. They never failed to acknowledge the paradoxicality and polarity of all life. The opposites always balanced one another – a sign of high culture. One-sidedness, though it lends momentum, is a mark of barbarism. The reaction that is now beginning in the West against the intellect in favour of feeling, or in favour of intuition, seems to me a

sign of cultural advance, a widening of consciousness beyond the narrow confines of a tyrannical intellect.

8   I have no wish to depreciate the tremendous differentiation of the Western intellect; compared with it the Eastern intellect must be described as childish. (Naturally this has nothing to do with intelligence.) If we should succeed in elevating another, and possibly even a third psychic function to the dignified position accorded to the intellect, then the West might expect to surpass the East by a very great margin. Therefore it is sad indeed when the European departs from his own nature and imitates the East or 'affects' it in any way. The possibilities open to him would be so much greater if he would remain true to himself and evolve out of his own nature all that the East has brought forth in the course of the millennia.

9   In general, and looked at from the incurably externalistic standpoint of the intellect, it would seem as if the things the East values so highly were not worth striving for. Certainly the intellect alone cannot comprehend the practical importance Eastern ideas might have for us, and that is why it can classify them as philosophical and ethnological curiosities and nothing more. The lack of comprehension goes so far that even learned sinologists have not understood the practical use of the *I Ching*, and consider the book to be no more than a collection of abstruse magic spells.

MODERN PSYCHOLOGY OFFERS A POSSIBILITY OF UNDERSTANDING

10   Observations made in my practical work have opened out to me a quite new and unexpected approach to Eastern wisdom. In saying this I should like to emphasize that I did not have any knowledge, however inadequate, of Chinese philosophy as a starting-point. On the contrary, when I began my career as a psychiatrist and psychotherapist, I was completely ignorant of Chinese philosophy, and only later did my professional experience show me that in my technique I had been unconsciously following that secret way which for centuries had been the preoccupation of the best minds of the East. This could be taken for a subjective fancy – which was one reason for my previous reluctance to publish anything on the subject – but Richard Wilhelm, that great interpreter of the soul of China, enthusiastically confirmed the parallel and thus gave me the courage to write about a Chinese text that belongs entirely to the mysterious shadowland of the Eastern mind. At the same time – and this is the extraordinary thing – its content forms a living parallel to what takes place in the psychic development of my patients, none of whom is Chinese.

11   In order to make this strange fact more intelligible to the reader, it must be pointed out that just as the human body shows a common anatomy over and above all racial differences, so, too, the human psyche possesses a common substratum transcending all differences in culture and consciousness. I have called this substratum the collective unconscious. This

unconscious psyche, common to all mankind, does not consist merely of contents capable of becoming conscious, but of latent predispositions towards identical reactions. The collective unconscious is simply the psychic expression of the identity of brain structure irrespective of all racial differences. This explains the analogy, sometimes even identity, between the various myth motifs and symbols, and the possibility of human communication in general. The various lines of psychic development start from one common stock whose roots reach back into the most distant past. This also accounts for the psychological parallelisms with animals.

12   In purely psychological terms this means that mankind has common instincts of ideation and action. All conscious ideation and action have developed on the basis of these unconscious archetypal patterns and always remain dependent on them. This is especially the case when consciousness has not attained any high degree of clarity, when in all its functions it is more dependent on the instincts than on the conscious will, more governed by affect than by rational judgement. This ensures a primitive state of psychic health, but it immediately becomes lack of adaptation when circumstances arise that call for a higher moral effort. Instincts suffice only for a nature that remains more or less constant. An individual who is guided more by the unconscious than by conscious choice therefore tends towards marked psychic conservatism. This is the reason why the primitive does not change in the course of thousands of years, and also why he fears anything strange and unusual. It might easily lead to maladaptation, and thus to the greatest psychic dangers – to a kind of neurosis, in fact. A higher and wider consciousness resulting from the assimilation of the unfamiliar tends, on the other hand, towards autonomy, and rebels against the old gods who are nothing other than those mighty, primordial images that hitherto have held our consciousness in thrall.

13   The stronger and more independent our consciousness becomes, and with it the conscious will, the more the unconscious is thrust into the background, and the easier it is for the evolving consciousness to emancipate itself from the unconscious, archetypal pattern. Gaining in freedom, it bursts the bonds of mere instinctuality and finally reaches a condition of instinctual atrophy. This uprooted consciousness can no longer appeal to the authority of the primordial images; it has Promethean freedom, but it also suffers from godless hybris. It soars above the earth and above mankind, but the danger of its sudden collapse is there, not of course in the case of every individual, but for the weaker members of the community, who then, again like Prometheus, are chained to the Caucasus of the unconscious. The wise Chinese would say in the words of the *I Ching*: When *yang* has reached its greatest strength, the dark power of *yin* is born within its depths, for night begins at midday when *yang* breaks up and begins to change into *yin*.

14   The doctor is in a position to see this cycle of changes translated literally

into life. He sees, for instance, a successful businessman attaining all his desires regardless of death and the devil, and then, having retired at the height of his success, speedily falling into a neurosis, which turns him into a querulous old woman, fastens him to his bed and finally destroys him. The picture is complete even to the change from masculine to feminine. An exact parallel to this is the story of Nebuchadnezzar in the Book of Daniel, and Caesarean madness in general. Similar cases of one-sided exaggeration of the conscious standpoint, and the resultant *yin*-reaction from the unconscious, form no small part of the psychiatrist's clientele in our time, which so over-values the conscious will as to believe that 'where there's a will there's a way'. Not that I wish to detract in the least from the high moral value of the will. Consciousness and the will may well continue to be considered the highest cultural achievements of humanity. But of what use is a morality that destroys the man? To bring the will and the capacity to achieve it into harmony seems to me to require more than morality. Morality *à tout prix* can be a sign of barbarism – more often wisdom is better. But perhaps I look at this with the eyes of a physician who has to mend the ills following in the wake of one-sided cultural achievements.

15   Be that as it may, the fact remains that a consciousness heightened by an inevitable one-sidedness gets so far out of touch with the primordial images that a breakdown ensues. Long before the actual catastrophe, the signs of error announce themselves in atrophy of instinct, nervousness, disorientation, entanglement in impossible situations and problems. Medical investigation then discovers an unconscious that is in full revolt against the conscious values, and that therefore cannot possibly be assimilated to consciousness, while the reverse is altogether out of the question. We are confronted with an apparently irreconcilable conflict before which human reason stands helpless, with nothing to offer except sham solutions or dubious compromises. If these evasions are rejected, we are faced with the question as to what has become of the much needed unity of the personality, and with the necessity of seeking it. At this point begins the path travelled by the East since the beginning of things. Quite obviously, the Chinese were able to follow this path because they never succeeded in forcing the opposites in man's nature so far apart that all conscious connection between them was lost. The Chinese owe this all-inclusive consciousness to the fact that, as in the case of the primitive mentality, the yea and the nay have remained in their original proximity. Nonetheless, it was impossible not to feel the clash of opposites, so they sought a way of life in which they would be what the Indians call *nirdvandva*, free of opposites.

16   Our text is concerned with this way, and the same problem comes up with my patients also. There could be no greater mistake than for a Westerner to take up the direct practice of Chinese yoga, for that would merely strengthen his will and consciousness against the unconscious and

bring about the very effect to be avoided. The neurosis would then simply be intensified. It cannot be emphasized enough that we are not Orientals, and that we have an entirely different point of departure in these matters. It would also be a great mistake to suppose that this is the path every neurotic must travel, or that it is the solution at every stage of the neurotic problem. It is appropriate only in those cases where consciousness has reached an abnormal degree of development and has diverged too far from the unconscious. This is the *sine qua non* of the process. Nothing would be more wrong than to open this way to neurotics who are ill on account of an excessive predominance of the unconscious. For the same reason, this way of development has scarcely any meaning before the middle of life (normally between the ages of thirty-five and forty), and if entered upon too soon can be decidedly injurious.

17   As I have said, the essential reason which prompted me to look for a new way was the fact that the fundamental problem of the patient seemed to me insoluble unless violence was done to one or the other side of his nature. I had always worked with the temperamental conviction that at bottom there are no insoluble problems, and experience justified me in so far as I have often seen patients simply outgrow a problem that had destroyed others. This 'outgrowing', as I formerly called it, proved on further investigation to be a new level of consciousness. Some higher or wider interest appeared on the patient's horizon, and through this broadening of his outlook the insoluble problem lost its urgency. It was not solved logically in its own terms, but faded out when confronted with a new and stronger life urge. It was not repressed and made unconscious, but merely appeared in a different light, and so really did become different. What, on a lower level, had led to the wildest conflicts and to panicky outbursts of emotion, from the higher level of personality now looked like a storm in the valley seen from the mountain top. This does not mean that the storm is robbed of its reality, but instead of being in it one is above it. But since, in a psychic sense, we are both valley and mountain, it might seem a vain illusion to deem oneself beyond what is human. One certainly does feel the affect and is shaken and tormented by it, yet at the same time one is aware of a higher consciousness looking on which prevents one from becoming identical with the affect, a consciousness which regards the affect as an object, and can say, 'I *know* that I suffer.' What our text says of indolence, 'Indolence of which a man is conscious, and indolence of which he is unconscious, are a thousand miles apart',[2] holds true in the highest degree of affect.

18   Now and then it happened in my practice that a patient grew beyond himself because of unknown potentialities, and this became an experience of prime importance to me. In the meantime, I had learned that all the greatest and most important problems of life are fundamentally insoluble. They must be so, for they express the necessary polarity inherent in every self-regulating system. They can never be solved, but only outgrown. I

therefore ask myself whether this outgrowing, this possibility of further psychic development, was not the normal thing, and whether getting stuck in a conflict was pathological. Everyone must possess that higher level, at least in embryonic form, and must under favourable circumstances be able to develop this potentiality. When I examined the course of development in patients who quietly, and as if unconsciously, outgrew themselves, I saw that their fates had something in common. The new thing came to them from obscure possibilities either outside or inside themselves; they accepted it and grew with its help. It seemed to me typical that some took the new thing from outside themselves, others from inside; or rather, that it grew into some persons from without, and into others from within. But the new thing never came exclusively either from within or from without. If it came from outside, it became a profound inner experience; if it came from inside, it became an outer happening. In no case was it conjured into existence intentionally or by conscious willing, but rather seemed to be borne along on the stream of time.

19   We are so greatly tempted to turn everything into a purpose and a method that I deliberately express myself in very abstract terms in order to avoid prejudicing the reader in one way or the other. The new thing must not be pigeon-holed under any heading, for then it becomes a recipe to be used mechanically, and it would again be a case of the 'right means in the hands of the wrong man'. I have been deeply impressed by the fact that the new thing prepared by fate seldom or never comes up to conscious expectations. And still more remarkable, though the new thing goes against deeply rooted instincts as we have known them, it is a strangely appropriate expression of the total personality, an expression which one could not imagine in a more complete form.

20   What did these people do in order to bring about the development that set them free? As far as I could see they did nothing (*wu-wei*)[3] but let things happen. As Master Lao-tzu teaches in our text, the light circulates according to its own law if one does not give up one's ordinary occupation. The art of letting things happen, action through non-action, letting go of oneself as taught by Meister Eckhart, became for me the key that opens the door to the way. We must be able to let things happen in the psyche. For us, this is an art of which most people know nothing. Consciousness is forever interfering, helping, correcting and negating, never leaving the psychic processes to grow in peace. It would be simple enough, if only simplicity were not the most difficult of all things. To begin with, the task consists solely in observing objectively how a fragment of fantasy develops. Nothing could be simpler, and yet right here the difficulties begin. Apparently one has no fantasy fragments – or yes, there's one, but it is too stupid! Dozens of good reasons are brought against it. One cannot concentrate on it – it is too boring – what would come of it anyway – it is 'nothing but' this or that, and so on. The conscious mind raises in-numerable objections, in fact it often seems bent on blotting out the

spontaneous fantasy activity in spite of real insight and in spite of the firm determination to allow the psychic process to go forward without interference. Occasionally there is a veritable cramp of consciousness.

21   If one is successful in overcoming the initial difficulties, criticism is still likely to start in afterwards in the attempt to interpret the fantasy, to classify it, to aestheticize it, or to devalue it. The temptation to do this is almost irresistible. After it has been faithfully observed, free rein can be given to the impatience of the conscious mind; in fact it must be given, or obstructive resistances will develop. But each time the fantasy material is to be produced, the activity of consciousness must be switched off again.

22   In most cases the results of these efforts are not very encouraging at first. Usually they consist of tenuous webs of fantasy that give no clear indication of their origin or their goal. Also, the way of getting at the fantasies varies with individuals. For many people, it is easiest to write them down; others visualize them, and others again draw or paint them with or without visualization. If there is a high degree of conscious cramp, often only the hands are capable of fantasy; they model or draw figures that are sometimes quite foreign to the conscious mind.

23   These exercises must be continued until the cramp in the conscious mind is relaxed, in other words, until one can let things happen, which is the next goal of the exercise. In this way a new attitude is created, an attitude that accepts the irrational and the incomprehensible simply because it is happening. This attitude would be poison for a person who is already overwhelmed by the things that happen to him, but it is of the greatest value for one who selects, from among the things that happen, only those that are acceptable to his conscious judgement, and is gradually drawn out of the stream of life into a stagnant backwater.

24   At this point, the way travelled by the two types mentioned earlier seems to divide. Both have learned to accept what comes to them. (As Master Lao-tzu teaches: 'When occupations come to us, we must accept them; when things come to us, we must understand them from the ground up.')[4] One man will now take chiefly what comes to him from outside, and the other what comes from inside. Moreover, the law of life demands that what they take from outside and inside will be the very things that were always excluded before. This reversal of one's nature brings an enlargement, a heightening and enrichment of the personality, if the previous values are retained alongside the change – provided that these values are not mere illusions. If they are not held fast, the individual will swing too far to the other side, slipping from fitness into unfitness, from adaptedness into unadaptedness, and even from rationality into insanity. The way is not without danger. Everything good is costly, and the development of personality is one of the most costly of all things. It is a matter of saying yea to oneself, of taking oneself as the most serious of tasks, of being conscious of everything one does, and keeping it constantly before one's eyes in all its dubious aspects – truly a task that taxes us to the utmost.

25   A Chinese can always fall back on the authority of his whole civilization. If he starts on the long way, he is doing what is recognized as
being the best thing he could possibly do. But the Westerner who wishes
to set out on this way, if he is really serious about it, has all authority
against him – intellectual, moral and religious. That is why it is infinitely
easier for him to imitate the Chinese way and leave the troublesome
European behind him, or else to seek the way back to the mediaevalism
of the Christian Church and barricade himself behind the wall separating
true Christians from the poor heathen and other ethnographic curiosities
encamped outside. Aesthetic or intellectual flirtations with life and fate
come to an abrupt halt here: the step to higher consciousness leaves us
without a rearguard and without shelter. The individual must devote
himself to the way with all his energy, for it is only by means of his
integrity that he can go further, and his integrity alone can guarantee that
his way will not turn out to be an absurd misadventure.

26   Whether his fate comes to him from without or from within, the
experiences and happenings on the way remain the same. Therefore I need
say nothing about the manifold outer and inner events, the endless variety
of which I could never exhaust in any case. Nor would this be relevant to
the text under discussion. On the other hand, there is much to be said about
the psychic states that accompany the process of development. These
states are expressed symbolically in our text, and in the very same symbols
that for many years have been familiar to me from my practice.

THE FUNDAMENTAL CONCEPTS

Tao

27   The great difficulty in interpreting this and similar texts[5] for the
European is that the author always starts from the central point, from the
point we would call the goal, the highest and ultimate insight he has
attained. Thus our Chinese author begins with ideas that demand such a
comprehensive understanding that a person of discriminating mind has the
feeling he would be guilty of ridiculous pretension, or even of talking utter
nonsense, if he should embark on an intellectual discourse on the subtle
psychic experiences of the greatest minds of the East. Our text, for
example, begins: 'That which exists through itself is called the Way.' The
Hui Ming Ching begins with the words: 'The subtlest secret of the Tao is
human nature and life.'

28   It is characteristic of the Western mind that it has no word for Tao. The
Chinese character is made up of the sign for 'head' and the sign for
'going'. Wilhelm translates Tao by *Sinn* (meaning). Others translate it as
'way', 'Providence', or even as 'God', as the Jesuits do. This illustrates
our difficulty. 'Head' can be taken as consciousness,[6] and 'going' as
travelling a way, and the idea would then be: to go consciously, or the

conscious way. This is borne out by the fact that the 'light of heaven' which 'dwells between the eyes' as the 'heart of heaven' is used synonymously with Tao. Human nature and life are contained in the 'light of heaven' and, according to the *Hui Ming Ching*, are the most important secrets of the Tao. 'Light' is the symbolical equivalent of consciousness, and the nature of consciousness is expressed by analogies with light. The *Hui Ming Ching* is introduced with the verses:

> If thou wouldst complete the diamond body with no outflowing,
> Diligently heat the roots of consciousness[7] and life.
> Kindle light in the blessed country ever close at hand,
> And there hidden, let thy true self always dwell.

29   These verses contain a sort of alchemical instruction as to the method or way of producing the 'diamond body', which is also mentioned in our text. 'Heating' is necessary; that is, there must be an intensification of consciousness in order that light may be kindled in the dwelling place of the true self. Not only consciousness, but life itself must be intensified: the union of these two produces conscious life. According to *Hui Ming Ching*, the ancient sages knew how to bridge the gap between consciousness and life because they cultivated both. In this way the *sheli*, the immortal body, is 'melted out' and the 'great Tao is completed'.[8]

30   If we take the Tao to be the method or conscious way by which to unite what is separated, we have probably come close to the psychological meaning of the concept. At all events, the separation of consciousness and life cannot very well be understood as anything else than what I described earlier as an aberration or uprooting of consciousness. There can be no doubt, either, that the realization of the opposite hidden in the unconscious – the process of 'reversal' – signifies reunion with the unconscious laws of our being, and the purpose of this reunion is the attainment of conscious life or, expressed in Chinese terms, the realization of the Tao.

The circular movement and the centre

31   As I have pointed out, the union of opposites[9] on a higher level of consciousness is not a rational thing, nor is it a matter of will; it is a process of psychic development that expresses itself in symbols. Historically, this process has always been represented in symbols, and today the development of personality is still depicted in symbolic form. I discovered this fact in the following way. The spontaneous fantasy products I discussed earlier become more profound and gradually concentrate into abstract structures that apparently represent 'principles' in the sense of Gnostic *archai*. When the fantasies take the form chiefly of thoughts, intuitive formulations of dimly felt laws or principles emerge, which at first tend to be dramatized or personified. (We shall come back to these again later.) If the fantasies are drawn, symbols appear that are chiefly of

the *mandala*[10] type. *Mandala* means 'circle', more especially a magic circle. Mandalas are found not only throughout the East but also among us. The early Middle Ages are especially rich in Christian mandalas; most of them show Christ in the centre, with the four evangelists, or their symbols, at the cardinal points. This conception must be a very ancient one, because Horus and his four sons were represented in the same way by the Egyptians.[11] It is known that Horus with his four sons has close connections with Christ and the four evangelists. An unmistakable and very interesting mandala can be found in Jakob Böhme's book *XL Questions Concerning the Soule*.[12] It is clear that this mandala represents a psychocosmic system strongly coloured by Christian ideas. Böhme calls it the 'Philosophical Eye'[13] or the 'Mirror of Wisdom', by which is obviously meant a *summa* of secret knowledge. Most mandalas take the form of a flower, cross or wheel, and show a distinct tendency towards a quaternary structure reminiscent of the Pythagorean *tetraktys*, the basic number. Mandalas of this sort also occur as sand paintings in the religious ceremonies of the Pueblo and Navaho Indians.[14] But the most beautiful mandalas are, of course, those of the East, especially the ones found in Tibetan Buddhism, which also contain the symbols mentioned in our text. Mandala drawings are often produced by the mentally ill, among them persons who certainly did not have the least idea of the connections we have discussed.[15]

32   Among my patients I have come across cases of women who did not draw mandalas but danced them instead. In India there is a special name for this: *mandala nrithya*, the mandala dance. The dance figures express the same meanings as the drawings. My patients can say very little about the meaning of the symbols but are fascinated by them and find that they somehow express and have an effect on their subjective psychic state.

33   Our text promises to 'reveal the secret of the Golden Flower of the great *One*'. The golden flower is the light, and the light of heaven is the Tao. The golden flower is a mandala symbol I have often met with in the material brought me by my patients. It is drawn either seen from above as a regular geometric pattern, or in profile as a blossom growing from a plant. The plant is frequently a structure in brilliant fiery colours growing out of a bed of darkness, and carrying the blossom of light at the top, a symbol recalling the Christmas tree. Such drawings also suggest the origin of the golden flower, for according to the *Hui Ming Ching* the 'germinal vesicle' is the 'dragon castle at the bottom of the sea'.[16] Other synonyms are the 'yellow castle', the 'heavenly heart', the 'terrace of living', the 'square inch field of the square foot house', the 'purple hall of the city of jade', the 'dark pass', the 'space of former heaven'.[17] It is also called the 'boundary region of the snow mountains', the 'primordial pass', the 'kingdom of greatest joy', the 'boundless country', the 'altar upon which consciousness and life are made'. 'If a dying man does not know this

germinal vesicle', says the *Hui Ming Ching*, 'he will not find the unity of consciousness and life in a thousand births, nor in ten thousand aeons.'[18]

34   The beginning, where everything is still one, and which therefore appears as the highest goal, lies at the bottom of the sea, in the darkness of the unconscious. In the germinal vesicle, consciousness and life (or human nature and life, *hsing-ming*) are still a 'unity, inseparably mixed like the sparks in the refining furnace'. 'Within the germinal vesicle is the fire of the ruler.' 'All the sages began their work at the germinal vesicle.'[19] Note the fire analogies. I know a series of European mandala drawings in which something like a plant seed surrounded by membranes is shown floating in the water. Then, from the depths below, fire penetrates the seed and makes it grow, causing a great golden flower to unfold from the germinal vesicle.[19]

35   This symbolism refers to a quasi-alchemical process of refining and ennobling. Darkness gives birth to light; out of the 'lead of the water region' grows the noble gold; what is unconscious becomes conscious in the form of a living process of growth. (Indian *kundalini* yoga offers a perfect analogy.)[20] In this way the union of consciousness and life takes place.

36   When my patients produce these mandala pictures, it is naturally not the result of suggestion; similar pictures were being made long before I knew their meaning or their connection with the practices of the East, which, at that time, were wholly unknown to me. The pictures arise quite spontaneously, and from two sources. One source is the unconscious, which spontaneously produces fantasies of this kind; the other is life, which, if lived with utter devotion, brings an intuition of the self, of one's own individual being. When the self finds expression in such drawings, the unconscious reacts by enforcing an attitude of devotion to life. For in complete agreement with the Eastern view, the mandala is not only a means of expression, but also produces an effect. It reacts upon its maker. Age-old magical effects lie hidden in this symbol, for it is derived from the 'protective circle' or 'charmed cirle', whose magic has been preserved in countless folk customs.[21] It has the obvious purpose of drawing a *sulcus primigenius*, a magical furrow around the centre, the temple or *temenos* (sacred precinct), of the innermost personality, in order to prevent an 'outflowing' or to guard by apotropaic means against distracting influences from outside. Magical practices are nothing but projections of psychic events, which then exert a counter-influence on the psyche and put a kind of spell upon the personality. Through the ritual action, attention and interest are led back to the inner, sacred precinct, which is the source and goal of the psyche and contains the unity of life and consciousness. The unity once possessed has been lost, and must now be found again.

37   The unity of the two, life and consciousness, is the Tao, whose symbol would be the central white light, also mentioned in the *Bardo Thödol*.[22] This light dwells in the 'square inch' or in the 'face', that is, between the eyes. It is a visualization of the 'creative point', of that which has intensity

without extension, in conjunction with the 'field of the square inch', the symbol for that which has extension. The two together make the Tao. Human nature (*hsing*) and consciousness (*hui*) are expressed in light symbolism, and therefore have the quality of intensity, while life (*ming*) would coincide with extensity. The one is *yang*-like, the other *yin*-like. The aforementioned mandala of a somnambulist girl, aged fifteen and a half, whom I had under observation some thirty years ago, shows in its centre a spring of 'Primary Force', or life energy without extension, whose emanations clash with a contrary spatial principle – in complete analogy with the basic idea of our Chinese text.

38   The 'enclosure', or *circumambulatio*, is expressed in our text by the idea of 'circulation'. The circulation is not merely movement in a circle, but means, on the one hand, the marking-off of the sacred precinct and, on the other, fixation and concentration. The sun-wheel begins to turn; the sun is activated and begins its course – in other words, the Tao begins to work and takes the lead. Action is reversed into non-action; everything peripheral is subordinated to the command of the centre. Therefore it is said: 'Movement is only another name for mastery.' Psychologically, this circulation would be the 'movement in a circle around oneself', so that all sides of the personality become involved. 'The poles of light and darkness are made to rotate', that is, there as an alternation of day and night.

39   The circular movement thus has the moral significance of activating the light and dark forces of human nature, and together with them all psychological opposites of whatever kind they may be. It is nothing less than self-knowledge by means of self-brooding (Sanskrit *tapas*). A similar archetypal concept of a perfect being is that of the Platonic man, round on all sides and uniting within himself the two sexes.

40   One of the best modern parallels is the description which Edward Maitland, the biographer of Anna Kingsford,[23] gave of his central experience. He had discovered that when reflecting on an idea, related ideas became visible, so to speak, in a long series apparently reaching back to their source, which to him was the divine spirit. By concentrating on this series, he tried to penetrate to their origin. He writes:

> I was absolutely without knowledge or expectation when I yielded to the impulse to make the attempt. I simply experimented on a faculty . . . being seated at my writing-table the while in order to record the results as they came, and resolved to retain my hold on my outer and circumferential consciousness, no matter how far towards my inner and central consciousness I might go. For I knew not whether I should be able to regain the former if I once quitted my hold of it, or to recollect the facts of the experience. At length I achieved my object, though only by a strong effort, the tension occasioned by the endeavour to keep both extremes of the consciousness in view at once being very great.
>
> Once well started on my quest, I found myself traversing a succession

of spheres or belts . . . the impression produced being that of mounting a vast ladder stretching from the circumference towards the centre of a system, which was at once my own system, the solar system, the universal system, the three systems being at once diverse and identical . . .. Presently, by a supreme, and what I felt must be a final effort . . . I succeeded in polarizing the whole of the convergent rays of my consciousness into the desired focus. And at the same instant, as if through the sudden ignition of the rays thus fused into a unity, I found myself confronted with a glory of unspeakable whiteness and brightness, and of a lustre so intense as well-nigh to beat me back . . .. But though feeling that I had to explore further, I resolved to make assurance doubly sure by piercing if I could the almost blinding lustre, and seeing what it enshrined. With a great effort I succeeded, and the glance revealed to me that which I had felt must be there . . .. It was the dual form of the Son . . . the unmanifest made manifest, the unformulate formulate, the unindividuate individuate, God as the Lord, proving through His duality that God is Substance as well as Force, Love as well as Will, Feminine as well as Masculine, Mother as well as Father.

41   He found that God is two in one, like man. Besides this he noticed something that our text also emphasizes, namely 'suspension of breathing'. He says ordinary breathing stopped and was replaced by an internal respiration, 'as if by breathing of a distinct personality within and other than the physical organism'. He took this being to be the 'entelechy' of Aristotle and the 'inner Christ' of the apostle Paul, the 'spiritual and substantial individuality engendered within the physical and phenomenal personality, and representing, therefore, the rebirth of man on a plane transcending the material'.

42   This genuine[24] experience contains all the essential symbols of our text. The phenomenon itself, the vision of light, is an experience common to many mystics, and one that is undoubtedly of the greatest significance, because at all times and places it proves to be something unconditioned and absolute, a combination of supreme power and profound meaning. Hildegard of Bingen, an outstanding personality quite apart from her mysticism, writes in much the same way about her central vision:

> Since my childhood I have always seen a light in my soul, but not with the outer eyes, nor through the thoughts of my heart; neither do the five outer senses take part in this vision . . .. The light I perceive is not of a local kind, but is much brighter than the cloud which supports the sun. I cannot distinguish height, breadth or length in it . . .. What I see or learn in such a vision stays long in my memory. I see, hear, and know in the same moment . . .. I cannot recognize any sort of form in this light, although I sometimes see in it another light that is known to me as the living light . . .. While I am enjoying the spectacle of this light, all sadness and sorrow vanish from my memory.[25]

43   I myself know a few individuals who have had personal experience of this phenomenon. So far as I have been able to understand it, it seems to have to do with an acute state of consciousness, as intense as it is abstract, a 'detached' consciousness (see *infra*, pars. 64ff.), which, as Hildegard implies, brings into awareness areas of psychic happenings ordinarily covered in darkness. The fact that the general bodily sensations disappear during the experience suggests that their specific energy has been withdrawn and has apparently gone towards heightening the clarity of consciousness. As a rule, the phenomenon is spontaneous, coming and going on its own initiative. Its effect is astonishing in that it almost always brings about a solution of psychic complications and frees the inner personality from emotional and intellectual entanglements, thus creating a unity of being which is universally felt as 'liberation'.

44   Such a symbolic unity cannot be attained by the conscious will because consciousness is always partisan. Its opponent is the collective unconscious, which does not understand the language of the conscious mind. Therefore it is necessary to have the magic of the symbol which contains those primitive analogies that speak to the unconscious. The unconscious can be reached and expressed only by symbols, and for this reason the process of individuation can never do without the symbol. The symbol is the primitive exponent of the unconscious, but at the same time an idea that corresponds to the highest intuitions of the conscious mind.

45   The oldest mandala drawing known to me is a palaeolithic 'sun-wheel', recently discovered in Rhodesia. It, too, is based on the quaternary principle. Things reaching so far back into human history naturally touch upon the deepest layers of the unconscious, and can have a powerful effect on it even when our conscious language proves itself to be quite impotent. Such things cannot be thought up but must grow again from the forgotten depths if they are to express the supreme insights of consciousness and the loftiest intuitions of the spirit, and in this way fuse the uniqueness of present-day consciousness with the age-old past of life.

PHENOMENA OF THE WAY

The disintegration of consciousness

46   The meeting between the narrowly delimited, but intensely clear, individual consciousness and the vast expanse of the collective unconscious is dangerous, because the unconscious has a decidedly disintegrating effect on consciousness. According to the *Hui Ming Ching*, this effect belongs to the peculiar phenomena of Chinese yoga. It says: 'Every separate thought takes shape and becomes visible in colour and form. The total spiritual power unfolds its traces . . .'[26] The relevant illustration in the text [Figure 8.4; Stage 4] shows a sage sunk in contemplation, his head surrounded by tongues of fire, out of which five human figures emerge; these five again

Figure 8.1 Four stages of meditation. Stage 1: gathering the light.
Source: From the *Hui Ming Ching*; reproduced in Jung's *Collected Works*, Vol. 13.

Figure 8.2 Four stages of meditation. Stage 2: origin of a new being in the place of power.
Source: From the *Hui Ming Ching*; reproduced in Jung's *Collected Works*, Vol. 13.

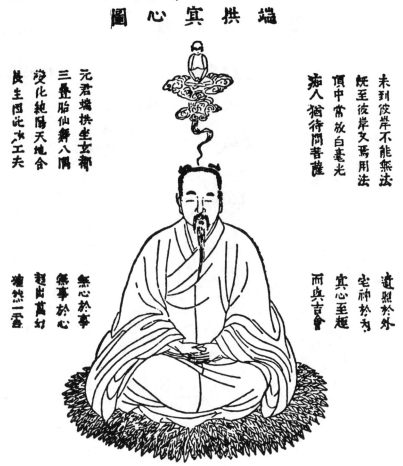

Figure 8.3 Four stages of meditation. Stage 3: separation of the spirit-body for independent existence.
Source: From the *Hui Ming Ching*; reproduced in Jung's *Collected Works*, Vol. 13.

Figure 8.4 Four stages of meditation. Stage 4: the centre in the midst of conditions.
Source: From the *Hui Ming Ching*; reproduced in Jung's *Collected Works*, Vol. 13.

split up into twenty-five smaller figures.[27] This would be a schizophrenic process if it were to become a permanent state. Therefore the *Hui Ming Ching*, as though warning the adept, continues: 'The shapes formed by the spirit fire are only empty colours and forms. The light of human nature (*hsing*) shines back on the primordial, the true.'

47   So we can understand why the figure of the protecting circle was seized upon. It is intended to prevent the 'outflowing' and to protect the unity of consciousness from being burst asunder by the unconscious. The text seeks to mitigate the disintegrating effect of the unconscious by describing the thought-figures as 'empty colours and forms', thus depotentiating them as much as possible. This idea runs through the whole of Buddhism (especially the Mahāyāna form) and, in the instructions to the dead in *The Tibetan Book of the Dead*, it is even pushed to the point of explaining the favourable as well as the unfavourable gods as illusions still to be overcome. It is certainly not within the competence of the psychologist to establish the metaphysical truth or untruth of this idea; he must be content to determine so far as possible its psychic effect. He need not bother himself whether the shape in question is a transcendental illusion or not, since faith, not science, has to decide this point. In any case we are moving on ground that for a long time has seemed to be outside the domain of science and was looked upon as wholly illusory. But there is no scientific justification for such an assumption; the substantiality of these things is not a scientific problem since it lies beyond the range of human perception and judgement and thus beyond any possibility of proof. The psychologist is concerned not with the substantiality of these complexes, but with psychic experience. Without a doubt they are psychic contents that can be experienced, and their autonomy is equally indubitable. They are fragmentary psychic systems that either appear spontaneously in ecstatic states and evoke powerful impressions and effects, or else, in mental disturbances, become fixed in the form of delusions and hallucinations and consequently destroy the unity of the personality.

48   Psychiatrists are always ready to believe in toxins and the like, and even to explain schizophrenia in these terms, putting next to no emphasis on the psychic contents as such. On the other hand, in psychogenic disturbances (hysteria, obsessional neurosis, etc.), where toxic effects and cell degeneration are out of the question, split-off complexes are to be found similar to those occurring in somnambulistic states. Freud would like to explain these spontaneous split-offs as due to unconscious repression of sexuality, but this explanation is by no means valid in all cases, because contents that the conscious mind cannot assimilate can emerge just as spontaneously out of the unconscious, and in these cases the repression theory is inadequate. Moreover, their autonomy can be observed in daily life, in affects that obstinately obtrude themselves against our will and, in spite of the most strenuous efforts to repress them, overwhelm the ego and force it under their control. No wonder the primitive sees in these

moods a state of possession or sets them down to a loss of soul. Our colloquial speech reflects the same thing when we say: 'I don't know what has got into him today', 'he is possessed of the devil', 'he is beside himself', etc. Even legal practice recognizes a degree of diminished responsibility in a state of affect. Autonomous psychic contents are thus quite common experiences for us. Such contents have a disintegrating effect upon consciousness.

49   But besides the ordinary, familiar affects there are subtler, more complex emotional states that can no longer be described as affects pure and simple but are fragmentary psychic systems. The more complicated they are, the more they have the character of personalities. As constituents of the psychic personality, they necessarily have the character of 'persons'. Such fragmentary systems are to be found especially in mental diseases, in cases of psychogenic splitting of the personality (double personality), and of course in mediumistic phenomena. They are also encountered in the phenomenology of religion. Many of the earlier gods developed from 'persons' into personified ideas, and finally into abstract ideas. Activated unconscious contents always appear at first as projections upon the outside world, but in the course of mental development they are gradually assimilated by consciousness and reshaped into conscious ideas that then forfeit their originally autonomous and personal character. As we know, some of the old gods have become, via astrology, nothing more than descriptive attributes (martial, jovial, saturnine, erotic, logical, lunatic, and so on).

50   The instructions of *The Tibetan Book of the Dead* in particular help us to see how great is the danger that consciousness will be disintegrated by these figures. Again and again the dead are instructed not to take these shapes for truth, not to confuse their murky appearance with the pure white light of *dharma-kaya* (the divine body of truth). That is to say, they are not to project the *one* light of highest consciousness into concretized figures and dissolve it into a plurality of autonomous fragmentary systems. If there were no danger of this, and if these systems did not represent menacingly autonomous and disintegrative tendencies, such urgent instructions would not be necessary. Allowing for the simpler, polytheistic attitude of the Eastern mind, these instructions would be almost the equivalent of warning a Christian not to let himself be blinded by the illusion of a personal God, let alone by the Trinity and the host of angels and saints.

51   If tendencies towards dissociation were not inherent in the human psyche, fragmentary psychic systems would never have been split off; in other words, neither spirits nor gods would ever have come into existence. That is also the reason why our time has become so utterly godless and profane: we lack all knowledge of the unconscious psyche and pursue the cult of consciousness to the exclusion of all else. Our true religion is a monotheism of consciousness, a possession by it, coupled with a fanatical denial of the existence of fragmentary autonomous systems. But we differ from the Buddhist yoga doctrines in that we even deny that these systems

are experienceable. This entails a great psychic danger, because the autonomous systems then behave like any other repressed contents: they necessarily induce wrong attitudes, since the repressed material reappears in consciousness in a spurious form. This is strikingly evident in every case of neurosis and also holds true for the collective psychic phenomena. Our time has committed a fatal error; we believe we can criticize the facts of religion intellectually. Like Laplace, we think God is a hypothesis that can be subjected to intellectual treatment, to be affirmed or denied. We completely forget that the reason mankind believes in the 'daemon' has nothing whatever to do with external factors, but is simply due to a naive awareness of the tremendous inner effect of autonomous fragmentary systems. This effect is not abolished by criticizing it – or rather, the name we have given it – or by describing the name as false. The effect is collectively present all the time; the autonomous systems are always at work, for the fundamental structure of the unconscious is not affected by the deviations of our ephemeral consciousness.

52   If we deny the existence of the autonomous systems, imagining that we have got rid of them by a mere critique of the name, then the effect which they still continue to exert can no longer be understood, nor can they be assimilated to consciousness. They become an inexplicable source of disturbance which we finally assume must exist somewhere outside ourselves. The resultant projection creates a dangerous situation in that the disturbing effects are now attributed to a wicked will outside ourselves, which is naturally not to be found anywhere but with our neighbour *de l'autre côté de la rivière*. This leads to collective delusions, 'incidents', revolutions, war – in a word, to destructive mass psychoses.

53   Insanity is possession by an unconscious content that, as such, is not assimilated to consciousness, nor can it be assimilated, since the very existence of such contents is denied. This attitude is equivalent to saying: 'We no longer have any fear of God and believe that everything is to be judged by human standards.' This hybris or narrowness of consciousness is always the shortest way to the insane asylum. I recommend the excellent account of this problem in H. G. Wells's novel *Christina Alberta's Father*, and Schreber's *Memoirs of My Nervous Illness*.

54   It must stir a sympathetic chord in the enlightened European when it is said in the *Hui Ming Ching* that the 'shapes formed by the spirit-fire are only empty colours and forms'. That sounds thoroughly European and seems to suit our reason to a T. We think we can congratulate ourselves on having already reached such a pinnacle of clarity, imagining that we have left all these phantasmal gods far behind. But what we have left behind are only verbal spectres, not the psychic facts that were responsible for the birth of the gods. We are still as much possessed by autonomous psychic contents as if they were Olympians. Today they are called phobias, obsessions, and so forth; in a word, neurotic symptoms. The gods have become diseases; Zeus no longer rules Olympus but rather the solar plexus,

and produces curious specimens for the doctor's consulting room, or disorders the brains of politicians and journalists, who unwittingly let loose psychic epidemics on the world.

55   So it is better for Western man if he does not know too much about the secret insights of the Oriental sages to begin with, for, as I have said, it would be a case of the 'right means in the hands of the wrong man'. Instead of allowing himself to be convinced once more that the daemon is an illusion, he ought to experience once more the reality of this illusion. He should learn to acknowledge these psychic forces anew, and not wait until his moods, nervous states and delusions make it clear in the most painful way that he is not the only master in his house. His dissociative tendencies are actual psychic personalities possessing a differential reality. They are 'real' when they are not recognized as real and consequently projected; they are relatively real when they are brought into relationship with consciousness (in religious terms, when a cult exists); but they are unreal to the extent that consciousness detaches itself from its contents. This last stage, however, is reached only when life has been lived so exhaustively and with such devotion that no obligations remain unfulfilled, when no desires that cannot safely be sacrificed stand in the way of inner detachment from the world. It is futile to lie to ourselves about this. Wherever we are still attached, we are still possessed; and when we are possessed, there is one stronger than us who possesses us. ('Verily I say unto thee, thou shalt by no means come out thence, until thou hast paid the uttermost farthing.') It is not a matter of indifference whether one calls something a 'mania' or a 'god'. To serve a mania is detestable and undignified, but to serve a god is full of meaning and promise because it is an act of submission to a higher, invisible and spiritual being. The personification enables us to see the relative reality of the autonomous system, and not only makes its assimilation possible but also depotentiates the daemonic forces of life. When the god is not acknowledged, egomania develops, and out of this mania comes sickness.

56   Yoga takes acknowledgement of the gods as something self-evident. Its secret instruction is intended only for those whose consciousness is struggling to disentangle itself from the daemonic forces of life in order to enter into the ultimate undivided unity, the 'centre of emptiness', where 'dwells the god of utmost emptiness and life', as our text says.[28] 'To hear such a teaching is difficult to attain in thousands of aeons.' Evidently the veil of *māyā* cannot be lifted by a merely rational resolve; it requires a most thoroughgoing and persevering preparation consisting in the full payment of all debts to life. For as long as unconditional attachment through *cupiditas* exists, the veil is not lifted and the heights of a consciousness free of contents and free of illusion are not attained; nor can any trick nor any deceit bring this about. It is an ideal that can ultimately be realized only in death. Until then there are the real and relatively real figures of the unconscious.

Animus and anima

57   According to our text, among the figures of the unconscious there are not only the gods but also the animus and anima. The word *hun* is translated by Wilhelm as animus. And indeed, the term 'animus' seems appropriate for *hun*, the character for which is made up of the sign for 'clouds' and that for 'demon'. Thus *hun* means 'cloud-demon', a higher breath-soul belonging to the *yang* principle and therefore masculine. After death, *hun* rises upward and becomes *shen*, the 'expanding and self-revealing' spirit or god. 'Anima', called *p'o*, and written with the characters for 'white' and 'demon', that is, 'white ghost', belongs to the lower, earthbound, bodily soul, the *yin* principle, and is therefore feminine. After death, it sinks downward and becomes *kuei* (demon), often explained as 'the one who returns' (i.e. to earth), a revenant, a ghost. The fact that the animus and anima part after death and go their ways independently shows that, for the Chinese consciousness, they are distinguishable psychic factors; originally they were united in 'the one effective, true human nature', but in the 'house of the Creative' they are two. 'The animus is in the heavenly heart.' 'By day it lives in the eyes [i.e. in consciousness]; at night it houses in the liver.' It is 'that which we have received from the great emptiness, that which is identical in form with the primal beginning'. The anima, on the other hand, is the 'energy of the heavy and the turbid'; it clings to the bodily, fleshly heart. Its effects are 'sensuous desires and impulses to anger'. 'Whoever is sombre and moody on waking . . . is fettered to the anima.'[29]

58   Many years ago, before Wilhelm acquainted me with this text, I used the term 'anima'[30] in a way quite analogous to the Chinese definition of *p'o*, and of course entirely apart from any metaphysical premiss. To the psychologist, the anima is not a transcendental being but something quite within the range of experience, as the Chinese definition makes clear: affective states are immediate experiences. Why, then, speak of the anima and not simply of moods? The reason is that affects have an autonomous character, and therefore most people are under their power. But affects are delimitable contents of consciousness, parts of the personality. As such, they partake of its character and can easily be personified – a process that still continues today, as I have shown. The personification is not an idle invention, since a person roused by affect does not show a neutral character but a quite distinct one, entirely different from his ordinary character. Careful investigation has shown that the affective character of a man has feminine traits. From this psychological fact derives the Chinese doctrine of the *p'o* soul as well as my own concept of the anima. Deeper introspection or ecstatic experience reveals the existence of a feminine figure in the unconscious, hence the feminine name: anima, psyche, *Seele*. The anima can be defined as the image or archetype or deposit of all the experiences of man with woman. As we know, the poets have often sung

the anima's praises.[31] The connection of anima with ghost in the Chinese concept is of interest to parapsychologists inasmuch as mediumistic 'controls' are very often of the opposite sex.

59   Although Wilhelm's translation of *hun* as 'animus' seems justified to me, nonetheless I had important reasons for choosing the term 'Logos' for a man's 'spirit', for his clarity of consciousness and his rationality, rather than the otherwise appropriate expression 'animus'. Chinese philosophers are spared certain difficulties that aggravate the task of the Western psychologist. Like all mental and spiritual activity in ancient times, Chinese philosophy was exclusively a component of the masculine world. Its concepts were never understood psychologically, and therefore were never examined as to how far they also apply to the feminine psyche. But the psychologist cannot possibly ignore the existence of woman and her special psychology. For these reasons I would prefer to translate *hun* as it appears in man by 'Logos'. Wilhelm in his translation uses Logos for *hsing*, which can also be translated as 'essence of human nature' or 'creative consciousness'. After death, *hun* becomes *shen*, 'spirit', which is very close, in the philosophical sense, to *hsing*. Since the Chinese concepts are not logical in our sense of the word, but are intuitive ideas, their meanings can only be elicited from the ways in which they are used and from the constitution of the written characters, or from such relationships as obtain between *hun* and *shen*. *Hun*, then, would be the light of consciousness and reason in man, originally coming from the *logos spermatikos* of *hsing*, and returning after death through *shen* to the Tao. Used in this sense the expression 'Logos' would be especially appropriate, since it includes the idea of a universal being, and thus covers the fact that man's clarity of consciousness and rationality are something universal rather than individually unique. The Logos principle is nothing personal, but is in the deepest sense impersonal, and thus in sharp contrast to the anima, which is a personal demon expressing itself in thoroughly personal moods ('animosity'!).

60   In view of these psychological facts, I have reserved the term 'animus' strictly for women, because, to answer a famous question, *mulier non habet animam, sed animum*. Feminine psychology exhibits an element that is the counterpart of a man's anima. Primarily, it is not of an affective nature but is a quasi-intellectual factor best described by the word 'prejudice'. The conscious side of woman corresponds to the emotional side of man, not to his 'mind'. Mind makes up the 'soul', or better, the 'animus' of woman, and just as the anima of a man consists of inferior relatedness, full of affect, so the animus of woman consists of inferior judgements, or better, opinions. As it is made up of a plurality of preconceived opinions, the animus is far less susceptible of personification by a single figure, but appears more often as a group or crowd. (A good example of this from parapsychology is the 'Imperator' group in the case of Mrs Piper.)[32] On a low level the animus is an inferior Logos, a caricature of the differentiated

masculine mind, just as on a low level the anima is a caricature of the
feminine Eros. To pursue the parallel further, we could say that just as *hun*
corresponds to *hsing*, translated by Wilhelm as Logos, so the Eros of
woman corresponds to *ming*, 'fate' or 'destiny', interpreted by Wilhelm as
Eros. Eros is an interweaving; Logos is differentiating knowledge, clarify-
ing light. Eros is relatedness, Logos is discrimination and detachment.
Hence the inferior Logos of woman's animus appears as something quite
unrelated, as an inaccessible prejudice, or as an opinion which, irritatingly
enough, has nothing to do with the essential nature of the object.

61   I have often been accused of personifying the anima and animus as
mythology does, but this accusation would be justified only if it could be
proved that I concretize these concepts in a mythological manner for
psychological use. I must declare once and for all that the personification
is not an invention of mine, but is inherent in the nature of the phenomena.
It would be unscientific to overlook the fact that the anima is a psychic,
and therefore a personal, autonomous system. None of the people who
make the charge against me would hesitate for a second to say, 'I dreamed
of Mr X', whereas, strictly speaking, he dreamed only of a representation
of Mr X. The anima is nothing but a representation of the personal nature
of the autonomous system in question. What the nature of this system is
in a transcendental sense, that is, beyond the bounds of experience, we
cannot know.

62   I have defined the anima as a personification of the unconscious in
general, and have taken it as a bridge to the unconscious, in other words,
as a function of relationship to the unconscious. There is an interesting
point in our text in this connection. The text says that consciousness (that
is, the personal consciousness) comes from the anima. Since the Western
mind is based wholly on the standpoint of consciousness, it must define
the anima in the way I have done. But the East, based as it is on the
standpoint of the unconscious, sees consciousness as an effect of the
anima. And there can be no doubt that consciousness does originate in
the unconscious. This is something we are apt to forget, and therefore we
are always attempting to identify the psyche with consciousness, or at least
to represent the unconscious as a derivative or an effect of consciousness
(as in the Freudian repression theory). But, for the reasons given above, it
is essential that we do not detract from the reality of the unconscious, and
that the figures of the unconscious be understood as real and effective
factors. The person who has understood what is meant by psychic reality
need have no fear that he has fallen back into primitive demonology. If
the unconscious figures are not acknowledged as spontaneous agents, we
become victims of a one-sided belief in the power of consciousness,
leading finally to acute tension. A catastrophe is then bound to happen
because, for all our consciousness, the dark powers of the psyche have
been overlooked. It is not we who personify them; they have a personal
nature from the very beginning. Only when this is thoroughly recognized

can we think of depersonalizing them, of 'subjugating the anima', as our text expresses it.

63   Here again we find an enormous difference between Buddhism and the Western attitude of mind, and again there is a dangerous semblance of agreement. Yoga teaching rejects all fantasy products and we do the same, but the East does so for entirely different reasons. In the East there is an abundance of conceptions and teachings that give full expression to the creative fantasy; in fact, protection is needed against an excess of it. We, on the other hand, regard fantasy as worthless subjective day-dreaming. Naturally the figures of the unconscious do not appear in the form of abstractions stripped of all imaginative trappings; on the contrary, they are embedded in a web of fantasies of extraordinary variety and bewildering profusion. The East can reject these fantasies because it has long since extracted their essence and condensed it in profound teachings. But we have never experienced these fantasies, much less extracted their quintessence. We still have a large stretch of experience to catch up with, and only when we have found the sense in apparent nonsense can we separate the valuable from the worthless. We can be sure that the essence we extract from our experience will be quite different from what the East offers us today. The East came to its knowledge of inner things in childlike ignorance of the external world. We, on the other hand, shall explore the psyche and its depths supported by an immense knowledge of history and science. At present our knowledge of the external world is the greatest obstacle to introspection, but the psychological need will overcome all obstructions. We are already building up a psychology, a science that gives us the key to the very things that the East discovered – and discovered only through abnormal psychic states.

THE DETACHMENT OF CONSCIOUSNESS FROM THE OBJECT

64   By understanding the unconscious we free ourselves from its domination. That is really also the purpose of the instructions in our text. The pupil is taught to concentrate on the light of the innermost region and, at the same time, to free himself from all outer and inner entanglements. His vital impulses are guided towards a consciousness void of content, which nevertheless permits all contents to exist. The *Hui Ming Ching*[33] says of this detachment:

> A halo of light surrounds the world of the law.
> We forget one another, quiet and pure, all-powerful and empty.
> The emptiness is irradiated by the light of the heart of heaven.
> The water of the sea is smooth and mirrors the moon in its surface.
> The clouds disappear in blue space; the mountains shine clear.
> Consciousness reverts to contemplation; the moon-disk rests alone.

65   This description of fulfilment depicts a psychic state that can best be characterized as a detachment of consciousness from the world and a withdrawal to a point outside it, so to speak. Thus consciousness is at the same time empty and not empty. It is no longer preoccupied with the images of things but merely contains them. The fullness of the world which hitherto pressed upon it has lost none of its richness and beauty, but it no longer dominates. The magical claim of things has ceased because the interweaving of consciousness with world has come to an end. The unconscious is not projected any more, and so the primordial *participation mystique* with things is abolished. Consciousness is no longer preoccupied with compulsive plans but dissolves in contemplative vision.

66   How did this effect come about? (We assume, of course, that the Chinese author was first of all not a liar; secondly, that he was of sound mind; and thirdly, that he was an unusually intelligent man.) To understand and explain this detachment, we must proceed by a roundabout way. It is an effect that cannot be simulated; nothing would be more childish than to make such a psychic state an object of aesthetic experiment. I know this effect very well from my practice; it is the therapeutic effect *par excellence*, for which I labour with my students and patients, and it consists in the dissolution of *participation mystique*. By a stroke of genius, Lévy-Bruhl singled out what he called *participation mystique* as being the hallmark of the primitive mentality.[34] What he meant by it is simply the indefinitely large remnant of non-differentiation between subject and object, which is still so great among primitives that it cannot fail to strike our European consciousness very forcibly. When there is no consciousness of the difference between subject and object, an unconscious identity prevails. The unconscious is then projected into the object, and the object is introjected into the subject, becoming part of his psychology. Then plants and animals behave like human beings, human beings are at the same time animals, and everything is alive with ghosts and gods. Civilized man naturally thinks he is miles above these things. Instead of that, he is often identified with his parents throughout his life, or with his affects and prejudices, and shamelessly accuses others of the things he will not see in himself. He too has a remnant of primitive unconsciousness, of non-differentiation between subject and object. Because of this, he is magically affected by all manner of people, things and circumstances, he is beset by disturbing influences nearly as much as the primitive and therefore needs just as many apotropaic charms. He no longer works magic with medicine bags, amulets and animal sacrifices, but with tranquillizers, neuroses, rationalism, cult of the will, etc.

67   But if the unconscious can be recognized as a co-determining factor along with consciousness, and if we can live in such a way that conscious and unconscious demands are taken into account as far as possible, then the centre of gravity of the total personality shifts its position. It is then no longer in the ego, which is merely the centre of consciousness, but in the hypothetical point between conscious and unconscious. This new

centre might be called the self. If the transposition is successful, it does away with the *participation mystique* and results in a personality that suffers only in the lower storeys, as it were, but in its upper storeys is singularly detached from painful as well as from joyful happenings.

68   The production and birth of this superior personality is what is meant when our text speaks of the 'holy fruit', the 'diamond body', or any other kind of incorruptible body. Psychologically, these expressions symbolize an attitude that is beyond the reach of emotional entanglements and violent shocks – a consciousness detached from the world. I have reasons for believing that this attitude sets in after middle life and is a natural preparation for death. Death is psychologically as important as birth and, like it, is an integral part of life. What happens to the detached consciousness in the end is a question the psychologist cannot be expected to answer. Whatever his theoretical position he would hopelessly overstep the bounds of his scientific competence. He can only point out that the views of our text in regard to the timelessness of the detached consciousness are in harmony with the religious thought of all ages and with that of the overwhelming majority of mankind. Anyone who thought differently would be standing outside the human order and would, therefore, be suffering from a disturbed psychic equilibrium. As a doctor, I make every effort to strengthen the belief in immortality, especially with older patients, when such questions come threateningly close. For, seen in correct psychological perspective, death is not an end but a goal, and life's inclination towards death begins as soon as the meridian is passed.

69   Chinese yoga philosophy is based upon this instinctive preparation for death as a goal. In analogy with the goal of the first half of life – procreation and reproduction, the means of perpetuating one's physical existence – it takes as the goal of spiritual existence the symbolic begetting and birth of a 'spirit-body', or 'breath-body', which ensures the continuity of detached consciousness. It is the birth of the pneumatic man, known to the European from antiquity, but which he seeks to produce by quite other symbols and magical practices, by faith and a Christian way of life. Here again we stand on a foundation quite different from that of the East. Again the text sounds as though it were not so very far from Christian ascetic morality, but nothing could be more mistaken than to assume that it actually means the same thing. Behind our text is a civilization thousands of years old, one which is built up organically on primitive instincts and knows nothing of that brutal morality so suited to us as recently civilized Teutonic barbarians. For this reason the Chinese are without the impulse towards violent repression of the instincts that poisons our spirituality and makes it hysterically exaggerated. The man who lives with his instincts can also detach from them, and in just as natural a way as he lived with them. Any idea of heroic self-conquest would be entirely foreign to the spirit of our text, but that is what it would infallibly amount to if we followed the instructions literally.

70   We must never forget our historical antecedents. Only a little more than a thousand years ago we stumbled out of the crudest beginnings of polytheism into a highly developed Oriental religion which lifted the imaginative minds of half-savages to a height that in no way corresponded to their spiritual development. In order to keep to this height in some fashion or other, it was inevitable that the instinctual sphere should be largely repressed. Thus religious practice and morality took on a decidedly brutal, almost malignant, character. The repressed elements naturally did not develop, but went on vegetating in the unconscious, in their original barbarism. We would like to scale the heights of a philosophical religion, but in fact are incapable of it. To grow up to it is the most we can hope for. The Amfortas wound and the Faustian split in the Germanic man are still not healed; his unconscious is still loaded with contents that must first be made conscious before he can be free of them. Recently I received a letter from a former patient which describes the necessary transformation in simple but trenchant words. She writes:

Out of evil, much good has come to me. By keeping quiet, repressing nothing, remaining attentive, and by accepting reality – taking things as they are, and not as I wanted them to be – by doing all this, unusual knowledge has come to me, and unusual powers as well, such as I could never have imagined before. I always thought that when we accepted things they overpowered us in some way or other. This turns out not to be true at all, and it is only by accepting them that one can assume an attitude towards them.[35] So now I intend to play the game of life, being receptive to whatever comes to me, good and bad, sun and shadow forever alternating, and, in this way, also accepting my own nature with its positive and negative sides. Thus everything becomes more alive to me. What a fool I was! How I tried to force everything to go according to the way I thought it ought to!

71   Only on the basis of such an attitude, which renounces none of the Christian values won in the course of Christian development, but which, on the contrary, tries with Christian charity and forbearance to accept even the humblest things in one's own nature, will a higher level of consciousness and culture become possible. This attitude is religious in the truest sense, and therefore therapeutic, for all religions are therapies for the sorrows and disorders of the soul. The development of the Western intellect and will has given us an almost fiendish capacity for aping such an attitude, with apparent success, despite the protests of the unconscious. But it is only a matter of time before the counterposition asserts itself all the more harshly. Aping an attitude always produces an unstable situation that can be overthrown by the unconscious at any time. A safe foundation is found only when the instinctive premises of the unconscious win the same respect as the views of the conscious mind. No one should blind himself to the fact that this necessity of giving due consideration to the

unconscious runs violently counter to our Western, and in particular the Protestant, cult of consciousness. Yet, though the new always seems to be the enemy of the old, anyone with a more than superficial desire to understand cannot fail to discover that, without the most serious application of the Christian values we have acquired, the new integration can never take place.

THE FULFILMENT

72   A growing familiarity with the spirit of the East should be taken merely as a sign that we are beginning to relate to the alien elements within ourselves. Denial of our historical foundations would be sheer folly and would be the best way to bring about another uprooting of consciousness. Only by standing firmly on our own soil can we assimilate the spirit of the East.

73   Speaking of those who do not know where the true springs of secret power lie, an ancient adept says, 'Worldly people lose their roots and cling to the treetops.' The spirit of the East has grown out of the yellow earth, and our spirit can, and should, grow only out of our own earth. That is why I approach these problems in a way that has often been charged with 'psychologism'. If 'psychology' were meant, I should indeed be flattered, for my aim as a psychologist is to dismiss without mercy the metaphysical claims of all esoteric teachings. The unavowed purpose of gaining power through words, inherent in all secret doctrines, ill accords with our profound ignorance, which we should have the modesty to admit. I quite deliberately bring everything that purports to be metaphysical into the daylight of psychological understanding, and do my best to prevent people from believing in nebulous power-words. Let the convinced Christian believe, by all means, for that is the duty he has taken upon himself; but whoever is not a Christian has forfeited the charisma of faith. (Perhaps he was cursed from birth with not being able to believe, but merely to know.) Therefore, he has no right to put his faith elsewhere. One cannot grasp anything metaphysically, one only can do so psychologically. Therefore I strip things of their metaphysical wrappings in order to make them objects of psychology. In that way I can at least extract something understandable from them and avail myself of it, and I also discover psychological facts and processes that before were veiled in symbols and beyond my comprehension. In doing so I may perhaps be following in the footsteps of the faithful, and may possibly have similar experiences; and if in the end there should be something ineffably metaphysical behind it all, it would then have the best opportunity of showing itself.

74   My admiration for the great philosophers of the East is as genuine as my attitude towards their metaphysics is irreverent.[36] I suspect them of being symbolical psychologists, to whom no greater wrong could be done than to take them literally. If it were really metaphysics that they mean,

it would be useless to try to understand them. But if it is psychology, we can not only understand them but can profit greatly by them, for then the so-called 'metaphysical' comes within the range of experience. If I assume that God is absolute and beyond all human experience, he leaves me cold. I do not affect him, nor does he affect me. But if I know that he is a powerful impulse of the soul, at once I must concern myself with him, for then he can become important, even unpleasantly so, and can affect me in practical ways – which sounds horribly banal, like everything else that is real.

75   The epithet 'psychologism' applies only to a fool who thinks he has his soul in his pocket. There are certainly more than enough such fools, for although we know how to talk big about the 'soul', the depreciation of everything psychic is a typically Western prejudice. If I make use of the concept 'autonomous psychic complex', my reader immediately comes up with the ready-made prejudice that it is 'nothing but a psychic complex'. How can we be so sure that the soul is 'nothing but'? It is as if we did not know, or else continually forgot, that everything of which we are conscious is an image, and that image *is* psyche. The same people who think that God is depreciated if he is understood as something moved in the psyche, as well as the moving force of the psyche – i.e. as an autonomous complex – can be so plagued by uncontrollable affects and neurotic states that their wills and their whole philosophy of life fail them miserably. Is that a proof of the impotence of the psyche? Should Meister Eckhart be accused of 'psychologism' when he says, 'God must be born in the soul again and again'? I think the accusation of 'psychologism' can be levelled only at an intellect that denies the genuine nature of the autonomous complex and seeks to explain it rationalistically as the consequence of known causes, i.e. as something secondary and unreal. This is just as arrogant as the metaphysical assertion that seeks to make a God outside the range of our experience responsible for our psychic states. Psychologism is simply the counterpart of this metaphysical presumption, and is just as childish. Therefore it seems to me far more reasonable to accord the psyche the same validity as the empirical world, and to admit that the former has just as much 'reality' as the latter. As I see it, the psyche is a world in which the ego is contained. Maybe there are fishes who believe that they contain the sea. We must rid ourselves of this habitual illusion of ours if we wish to consider metaphysical assertions from the standpoint of psychology.

76   A metaphysical assertion of this kind is the idea of the 'diamond body', the incorruptible breath-body which grows in the golden flower or in the 'field of the square inch'.[37] This body is a symbol for a remarkable psychological fact which, precisely because it is objective, first appears in forms dictated by the experience of biological life – that is, as fruit, embryo, child, living body, and so on. This fact could be best expressed by the words, 'It is not I who live, it lives me.' The illusion of the supremacy of consciousness makes us say, 'I live.' Once this illusion is

shattered by a recognition of the unconscious, the unconscious will appear as something objective in which the ego is included. The attitude towards the unconscious is then analogous to the feeling of the primitive to whom the existence of a son guarantees continuation of life – a feeling that can assume grotesque forms, as when the old Negro, angered at his son's disobedience, cries out, 'There he stands with my body, but does not even obey me!'

77   It is, in fact, a change of feeling similar to that experienced by a father to whom a son has been born, a change known to us from the testimony of St Paul: 'Yet not I, but Christ liveth in me.' The symbol 'Christ' as 'son of man' is an analogous psychic experience of a higher spiritual being who is invisibly born in the individual, a pneumatic body which is to serve us as a future dwelling, a body which, as Paul says, is put on like a garment ('For as many of you as have been baptized into Christ have put on Christ'). It is always a difficult thing to express, in intellectual terms, subtle feelings that are nevertheless infinitely important for the individual's life and well-being. It is, in a sense, the feeling that we have been 'replaced', but without the connotation of having been 'deposed'. It is as if the guidance of life had passed over to an invisible centre. Nietzsche's metaphor 'in most loving bondage, free' would be appropriate here. Religious language is full of imagery depicting this feeling of free dependence, of calm acceptance.

78   This remarkable experience seems to me a consequence of the detachment of consciousness, thanks to which the subjective 'I live' becomes the objective 'It lives me.' This state is felt to be higher than the previous one; it is really like a sort of release from the compulsion and impossible responsibility that are the inevitable results of *participation mystique*. This feeling of liberation fills Paul completely; the consciousness of being a child of God delivers one from the bondage of the blood. It is also a feeling of reconciliation with all that happens, for which reason, according to the *Hui Ming Ching*, the gaze of one who has attained fulfilment turns back to the beauty of nature.

79   In the Pauline Christ symbol the supreme religious experiences of West and East confront one another: Christ the sorrow-laden hero, and the Golden Flower that blooms in the purple hall of the city of jade. What a contrast, what an unfathomable difference, what an abyss of history! A problem fit for the crowning work of a future psychologist!

80   Among the great religious problems of the present is one which has received scant attention, but which is in fact the main problem of our day: the evolution of the religious spirit. If we are to discuss it, we must emphasize the difference between East and West in their treatment of the 'jewel', the central symbol. The West lays stress on the human incarnation, and even on the personality and historicity of Christ, whereas the East says: 'Without beginning, without end, without past, without future.'[38] The Christian subordinates himself to the superior divine person in expectation

of his grace; but the Oriental knows that redemption depends on the work he does on himself. The Tao grows out of the individual. The *imitatio Christi* has this disadvantage: in the long run we worship as a divine example a man who embodied the deepest meaning of life, and then, out of sheer imitation, we forget to make real our own deepest meaning – self-realization. As a matter of fact, it is not altogether inconvenient to renounce one's own meaning. Had Jesus done so, he would probably have become a respectable carpenter and not a religious rebel to whom the same thing would naturally happen today as happened then.

81   The imitation of Christ might well be understood in a deeper sense. It could be taken as the duty to realize one's deepest conviction with the same courage and the same self sacrifice shown by Jesus. Happily not everyone has the task of being a leader of humanity, or a great rebel; and so, after all, it might be possible for each to realize himself in his own way. This honesty might even become an ideal. Since great innovations always begin in the most unlikely places, the fact that people today are not nearly as ashamed of their nakedness as they used to be might be the beginning of a recognition of themselves as they really are. Hard upon this will follow an increasing recognition of many things that formerly were strictly taboo, for the reality of the earth will not forever remain veiled like the *virgines velandae* of Tertullian. Moral unmasking is but a step further in the same direction, and behold there stands man as he is, and admits to himself that he is as he is. If he does this in a meaningless way he is just a muddled fool; but if he knows the significance of what he is doing he could belong to a higher order of man who makes real the Christ symbol, regardless of the suffering involved. It has often been observed that purely concrete taboos or magical rites in an early stage of religion become in the next stage something psychic, or even purely spiritual symbols. An outward law becomes in the course of time an inward conviction. Thus it might easily happen to contemporary man, especially Protestants, that the person Jesus, now existing outside in the realm of history, might become the higher man within himself. Then we would have attained, in a European way, the psychological state corresponding to Eastern enlightenment.

82   All this is a step in the evolution of a higher consciousness on its way to unknown goals, and is not metaphysics as ordinarily understood. To that extent it is only 'psychology', but to that extent, too, it is experienceable, understandable and – thank God – real, a reality we can do something with, a living reality full of possibilities. The fact that I am content with what can be experienced psychically, and reject the metaphysical, does not amount, as any intelligent person can see, to a gesture of scepticism or agnosticism aimed at faith and trust in higher powers, but means approximately the same as what Kant meant when he called the thing-in-itself a 'merely negative borderline concept'. Every statement about the transcendental is to be avoided because it is only a laughable presumption on

the part of a human mind unconscious of its limitations. Therefore, when God or the Tao is named an impulse of the soul, or a psychic state, something has been said about the knowable only, but nothing about the unknowable, about which nothing can be determined.

CONCLUSION

83   The purpose of my commentary is to attempt to build a bridge of psychological understanding between East and West. The basis of every real understanding is man, and therefore I had to speak of human beings. This must be my excuse for having dealt only with general aspects, and for not having entered into technical details. Technical directions are valuable for those who know, for example, what a camera is, or a combustion engine, but they are useless for anyone who has no idea of such apparatus. Western man, for whom I write, is in an analogous position. Therefore it seemed to me important above all to emphasize the agreement between the psychic states and symbolisms of East and West. These analogies open a way to the inner chambers of the Eastern mind, a way that does not require the sacrifice of our own nature and does not confront us with the threat of being torn from our roots. Nor is it an intellectual telescope or microscope offering a view of no fundamental concern to us because it does not touch us. It is the way of suffering, seeking and striving common to all civilized peoples; it is the tremendous experiment of becoming conscious, which nature has laid upon mankind, and which unites the most diverse cultures in a common task.

84   Western consciousness is by no means the only kind of consciousness there is; it is historically conditioned and geographically limited, and representative of only one part of mankind. The widening of our consciousness ought not to proceed at the expense of other kinds of consciousness; it should come about through the development of those elements of our psyche which are analogous to those of the alien psyche, just as the East cannot do without our technology, science and industry. The European invasion of the East was an act of violence on a grand scale, and it has left us with the duty – *noblesse oblige* – of understanding the mind of the East. This is perhaps more necessary than we realize at present.

NOTES

1 [*The Secret of the Golden Flower* (1962 edn), p. 63.]
2 [*The Golden Flower* (1962 edn), p. 42.]
3 [The Taoist idea of action through non-action. – C.F.B.]
4 [*The Golden Flower* (1962 edn), p. 51.]
5 Cf. the *Hui Ming Ching* (*Book of Consciouness and Life*) in *The Secret of the Golden Flower* (1962 edn), pp. 69ff.
6 The head is also the 'seat of heavenly light'.

7 In the *Hui Ming Ching*, 'human nature' (*hsing*) and 'consciousness' (*hui*) are used interchangeably.

8 *The Golden Flower* (1962 edn), p. 70.

9 cf. *Psychological Types*, ch. V.

10 [For a fuller discussion of the *mandala*, see 'A Study in the Process of Individuation' and 'Concerning Mandala Symbolism' in *The Archetypes and the Collective Unconscious*. For examples of European mandalas, see the latter work p. 56.–EDITORS.]

11 Cf. Wallis Budge, *The Gods of the Egyptians*.

12 [The mandala is reproduced in 'A Study in the Process of Individuation', p. 297.]

13 Cf. the Chinese concept of the heavenly light between the eyes.

14 Matthews, 'The Mountain Chant: A Navajo Ceremony' (1887), and Stevenson, 'Ceremonial of Hasjelti Dailjis' (1891).

15 The mandala of a somnambulist is reproduced in *Psychiatric Studies*, p. 40.

16 *The Golden Flower* (1962 edn), p. 70.

17 [ibid., p. 22.]

18 [ibid., p. 70.]

19 [ibid., p. 71.]

20 Cf. Avalon, *The Serpent Power*.

21 Cf. the excellent collection in Knuchel, *Die Umwandlung in Kult, Magie und Rechtsbrauch*.

22 Evans-Wentz, *The Tibetan Book of the Dead*.

23 *Anna Kingsford, Her Life, Letters, Diary, and Work*, pp. 129f. I am indebted for this reference to my colleage, Dr Beatrice Hinkle, New York.

24 Such experiences are genuine, but their genuineness does not prove that all the conclusions or convictions forming their content are necessarily sound. Even in cases of lunacy one comes across perfectly valid psychic experiences. [Author's note added in the first (1931) English edition.]

25 [*Acta S. Hildegardis*, in Migne, *PL*, Vol. 197, col. 18.]

26 *The Golden Flower* (1962 edn), pp. 76f. [For elucidation of the four pictures from the *Hui Ming Ching* reproduced here, see ibid., pp. 75–7. – EDITORS.]

27 These are recollections of earlier incarnations that arise during contemplation.

28 [*The Golden Flower*, p. 22.]

29 [*The Golden Flower*, pp. 26 and 28.]

30 Cf. *Two Essays on Analytical Psychology*, paras 296ff.

31 Cf. *Psychological Types*, ch. V.

32 Cf. Hyslop, *Science and a Future Life*, pp. 113ff. [Mrs Leonora Piper, an American psychic medium active about 1890–1910 in the US and England, was studied by William James, Mrs Henry Sidgwick, Hyslop and others. A group of five of her psychic controls had the collective name 'Imperator'. – EDITORS.]

33 [*The Golden Flower* (1962 edn), pp. 77f.]

34 Lévy-Bruhl, *Primitive Mentality*.

35 Dissolution of *participation mystique*.

36 The Chinese philosphers – in contrast to the dogmatists of the West – are only grateful for such an attitude, because they also are masters of their gods. [Note by Richard Wilhelm in original edn.]

37 Our text is somewhat unclear as to whether by 'continuation of life' a survival after death or a prolongation of physical existence is meant. Expressions such as 'elixir of life' and the like are exceedingly ambiguous. In the later additions to the text it is evident that the yoga instructions were also understood in a purely physical sense. To a primitive mind, there is nothing disturbing in this odd mixture of the physical and the spiritual, because life and death are by no means the complete opposites they are for us. (Particularly interesting in this connection,

apart from the ethnological material, are the communications of the English 'rescue circles' with their thoroughly archaic ideas.) The same ambiguity with regard to survival after death is found in early Christianity, where immortality depends on very similar assumptions, i.e. on the idea of a breath-body as the carrier of life. (Geley's paraphysiological theory would be the latest incarnation of this ancient idea.) But since in our text there are warnings about the superstitious use of it – warnings, for example, against the making of gold – we can safely insist on the spiritual purport of the instructions without contradicting their meaning. In the states which the instructions seek to induce the physical body plays an increasingly unimportant part anyway, since it is replaced by the breath-body (hence the importance of breath control in all yoga exercises). The breath-body is not something 'spiritual' in our sense of the word. It is characteristic of Western man that he has split apart the physical and the spiritual for epistemological purposes. But these opposites exist together in the psyche and psychology must recognize this fact. 'Psychic' means physical *and* spiritual. The ideas in our text all deal with this 'intermediate' world which seems unclear and confused because the concept of psychic reality is not yet current among us, although it expresses life as it actually is. Without soul, spirit is as dead as matter, because both are artificial abstractions; whereas man originally regarded spirit as a volatile body, and matter as not lacking in soul.

38 *The Golden Flower* (1962 edn), p. 77.

9 A dialogue with the *I Ching*

From: *Memories, Dreams, Reflections*

I first met Richard Wilhelm at Count Keyserling's during a meeting of the 'School of Wisdom' in Darmstadt. That was in the early twenties. In 1923 we invited him to Zürich and he spoke on the *I Ching*[1] at the Psychology Club.

Even before meeting him I had been interested in Oriental philosophy, and around 1920 had begun experimenting with the *I Ching*. One summer in Bollingen I resolved to make an all-out attack on the riddle of this book. Instead of traditional stalks of yarrow required by the classical method, I cut myself a bunch of reeds. I would sit for hours on the ground beneath the hundred-year-old pear tree, the *I Ching* beside me, practising the technique by referring the resultant oracles to one another in an interplay of questions and answers. All sorts of undeniably remarkable results emerged – meaningful connections with my own thought processes which I could not explain to myself.

The only subjective intervention in this experiment consists in the experimenter's arbitrarily – that is, without counting – dividing up the bundle of forty-nine stalks at a single swoop. He does not know how many stalks are contained in each bundle, and yet the result depends upon their numerical relationship. All other manipulations proceed mechanically and leave no room for interference by the will. If a psychic causal connection is present at all, it can only consist in the chance division of the bundle (or, in the other method, the chance fall of the coins).

During the whole of those summer holidays I was preoccupied with the question: Are the *I Ching*'s answers meaningful or not? If they are, how does the connection between the psychic and the physical sequence of events come about? Time and again I encountered amazing coincidences which seemed to suggest the idea of an acausal parallelism (a synchronicity, as I later called it). So fascinated was I by these experiments that I altogether forgot to take notes, which I afterwards greatly regretted. Later, however, when I often used to carry out the experiment with my patients, it became quite clear that a significant number of answers did indeed hit the mark. I remember, for example, the case of a young man with a strong mother complex. He wanted to marry, and had made the acquaintance of a seemingly suitable girl.

However, he felt uncertain, fearing that under the influence of his complex he might once more find himself in the power of an overwhelming mother. I conducted the experiment with him. The text of his hexagram read: 'The maiden is powerful. One should not marry such a maiden.'

In the mid-thirties I met the Chinese philosopher Hu Shih. I asked him his opinion of the *I Ching*, and received the reply: 'Oh, that's nothing but an old collection of magic spells, without significance.' He had had no experience with it – or so he said. Only once, he remembered, had he come across it in practice. One day on a walk with a friend, the friend had told him about his unhappy love affair. They were just passing by a Taoist temple. As a joke, he had said to his friend: 'Here you can consult the oracle!' No sooner said than done. They went into the temple together and asked the priest for an *I Ching* oracle. But he had not the slightest faith in this nonsense.

I asked him whether the oracle had been correct. Whereupon he replied reluctantly, 'Oh, yes, it was, of course . . .' Remembering the well-known story of the 'good friend' who does everything one does not wish to do oneself, I cautiously asked him whether he had not profited by this opportunity. 'Yes', he replied, 'as a joke I asked a question too.'

'And did the oracle give you a sensible answer?' I asked.

He hesitated. 'Oh well, yes, if you wish to put it that way.' The subject obviously made him uncomfortable.

A few years after my first experiments with the reeds, the *I Ching* was published with Wilhelm's commentary. I instantly obtained the book, and found to my gratification that Wilhelm took much the same view of the meaningful connections as I had. But he knew the entire literature and could therefore fill in the gaps which had been outside my competence. When Wilhelm came to Zürich, I had the opportunity to discuss the matter with him at length, and we talked a great deal about Chinese philosophy and religion. What he told me, out of his wealth of knowledge of the Chinese mentality, clarified some of the most difficult problems that the European unconscious had posed for me. On the other hand, what I had to tell him about the results of my investigations of the unconscious caused him no little surprise; for he recognized in them things he had considered to be the exclusive possession of the Chinese philosophical tradition.

From: 'Foreword to the *I Ching*'[2]

964   Since I am not a sinologue, a foreword to the *Book of Changes* from my hand must be a testimonial of my individual experience with this great and singular book. It also affords me a welcome opportunity to pay tribute again to the memory of my late friend, Richard Wilhelm. He himself was profoundly aware of the cultural significance of his translation of the *I Ching*, a version unrivalled in the West.

965   If the meaning of the *Book of Changes* were easy to grasp, the work

would need no foreword. But this is far from being the case, for there is so much that is obscure about it that Western scholars have tended to dispose of it as a collection of 'magic spells', either too abstruse to be intelligible or of no value whatsoever. Legge's translation of the *I Ching*, up to now the only version available in English, has done little to make the work accessible to Western minds.[3] Wilhelm, however, has made every effort to open the way to an understanding of the symbolism of the text. He was in a position to do this because he himself was taught the philosophy and the use of the *I Ching* by the venerable sage Lao Nai-hsüan; moreover, he had over a period of many years put the peculiar technique of the oracle into practice. His grasp of the living meaning of the text gives his version of the *I Ching* a depth of perspective that an exclusively academic knowledge of Chinese philosophy could never provide.

966   I am greatly indebted to Wilhelm for the light he has thrown upon the complicated problem of the *I Ching*, and for insight into its practical application. For more than thirty years I have interested myself in this oracle technique, for it seemed to me of uncommon significance as a method of exploring the unconscious. I was already fairly familiar with the *I Ching* when I first met Wilhelm in the early 1920s; he confirmed then what I already knew, and taught me many things more.

967   I do not know Chinese and have never been in China. I can assure my reader that it is not altogether easy to find the right approach to this monument of Chinese thought, which departs so completely from our ways of thinking. In order to understand what such a book is all about, it is imperative to cast off certain of our Western prejudices. It is a curious fact that such a gifted and intelligent people as the Chinese has never developed what we call science. Our science, however, is based upon the principle of causality, and causality is considered to be an axiomatic truth. But a great change in our standpoint is setting in. What Kant's *Critique of Pure Reason* failed to do is being accomplished by modern physics. The axioms of causality are being shaken to their foundations: we know now that what we term natural laws are merely statistical truths and thus must necessarily allow for exceptions. We have not sufficiently taken into account as yet that we need the laboratory with its incisive restrictions in order to demonstrate the invariable validity of natural law. If we leave things to nature, we see a very different picture: every process is partially or totally interfered with by chance, so much so that under natural circumstances a course of events conforming to specific laws is almost an exception.

968   The Chinese mind, as I see it at work in the *I Ching*, seems to be exclusively preoccupied with the chance aspect of events. What we call coincidence seems to be the chief concern of this peculiar mind, and what we worship as causality passes almost unnoticed. We must admit that there is something to be said for the immense importance of chance. An incalculable amount of human effort is directed to combating and restricting the nuisance or danger that chance represents. Theoretical

considerations of cause and effect often look pale and dusty in comparison with the practical results of chance. It is all very well to say that the crystal of quartz is a hexagonal prism. The statement is quite true in so far as an ideal crystal is envisaged. But in nature one finds no two crystals exactly alike, although all are unmistakably hexagonal. The actual form, however, seems to appeal more to the Chinese sage than the ideal one. The jumble of natural laws constituting empirical reality holds more significance for him than a causal explanation of events that, in addition, must usually be separated from one another in order to be properly dealt with.

969   The manner in which the *I Ching* tends to look upon reality seems to disfavour our causal procedures. The moment under actual observation appears to the ancient Chinese view more of a chance hit than a clearly defined result of concurrent causal chains. The matter of interest seems to be the configuration formed by chance events at the moment of observation, and not at all the hypothetical reasons that seemingly account for the coincidence. While the Western mind carefully sifts, weighs, selects, classifies, isolates, the Chinese picture of the moment encompasses everything down to the minutest nonsensical detail, because all of the ingredients make up the observed moment.

970   Thus it happens that when one throws the three coins, or counts through the forty-nine yarrow-stalks, these chance details enter into the picture of the moment of observation and form a part of it – a part that is insignificant to us, yet most meaningful to the Chinese mind. With us it would be a banal and almost meaningless statement (at least on the face of it) to say that whatever happens in a given moment has inevitably the quality peculiar to that moment. This is not an abstract argument but a very practical one. There are certain connoisseurs who can tell you merely from the appearance, taste and behaviour of a wine the site of its vineyard and the year of its origin. There are antiquarians who with almost uncanny accuracy will name the time and place of origin and the maker of an *objet d'art* or piece of furniture on merely looking at it. And there are even astrologers who can tell you, without any previous knowledge of your nativity, what the position of sun and moon was and what zodiacal sign rose above the horizon at the moment of your birth. In the face of such facts, it must be admitted that moments can leave long-lasting traces.

971   In other words, whoever invented the *I Ching* was convinced that the hexagram worked out in a certain moment coincided with the latter in quality no less than in time. To him the hexagram was the exponent of the moment in which it was cast – even more so than the hours of the clock or the divisions of the calendar could be – inasmuch as the hexagram was understood to be an indicator of the essential situation prevailing at the moment of its origin.

972   This assumption involves a certain curious principle which I have termed synchronicity,[4] a concept that formulates a point of view diametrically opposed to that of causality. Since the latter is a merely statistical truth

and not absolute, it is a sort of working hypothesis of how events evolve one out of another, whereas synchronicity takes the coincidence of events in space and time as meaning something more than mere chance, namely, a peculiar interdependence of objective events among themselves as well as with the subjective (psychic) states of the observer or observers.

973   The ancient Chinese mind contemplates the cosmos in a way comparable to that of the modern physicist, who cannot deny that his model of the world is a decidedly psychophysical structure. The microphysical event includes the observer just as much as the reality underlying the *I Ching* comprises subjective, i.e. psychic, conditions in the totality of the momentary situation. Just as causality describes the sequence of events, so synchronicity to the Chinese mind deals with the coincidence of events. The causal point of view tells us a dramatic story about how *D* came into existence: it took its origin from *C*, which existed before *D*, and *C* in turn had a father, *B*, etc. The synchronistic view on the other hand tries to produce an equally meaningful picture of coincidence. How does it happen that *A'*, *B'*, *C'*, *D'*, etc., appear all at the same moment and in the same place? It happens in the first place because the physical events *A'* and *B'* are of the same quality as the psychic events *C'* and *D'*, and further because all are the exponents of one and the same momentary situation. The situation is assumed to represent a legible or understandable picture.

974   Now the sixty-four hexagrams of the *I Ching* are the instrument by which the meaning of sixty-four different yet typical situations can be determined. These interpretations are equivalent to causal explanations. Causal connection can be determined statistically and can be subjected to experiment. Inasmuch as situations are unique and cannot be repeated, experimenting with synchronicity seems to be impossible under ordinary conditions.[5] In the *I Ching*, the only criterion of the validity of synchronicity is the observer's opinion that the text of the hexagram amounts to a true rendering of his psychic condition. It is assumed that the fall of the coins or the result of the division of the bundle of yarrow-stalks is what it necessarily must be in a given 'situation', inasmuch as anything happening at that moment belongs to it as an indispensable part of the picture. If a handful of matches is thrown to the floor, they form the pattern characteristic of that moment. But such an obvious truth as this reveals its meaningful nature only if it is possible to read the pattern and to verify its interpretation, partly by the observer's knowledge of the subjective and objective situation, partly by the character of subsequent events. It is obviously not a procedure that appeals to a critical mind used to experimental verification of facts or to factual evidence. But for someone who likes to look at the world at the angle from which ancient China saw it, the *I Ching* may have some attraction.

975   My argument as outlined above has of course never entered a Chinese mind. On the contrary, according to the old tradition, it is 'spiritual agencies', acting in a mysterious way, that make the yarrow-stalks give a

meaningful answer.[6] These powers form, as it were, the living soul of the book. As the latter is thus a sort of animated being, the tradition assumes that one can put questions to the *I Ching* and expect to receive intelligent answers. Thus it occurred to me that it might interest the uninitiated reader to see the *I Ching* at work. For this purpose I made an experiment strictly in accordance with the Chinese conception: I personified the book in a sense, asking its judgement about its present situation, i.e. my intention to introduce it to the English-speaking public.

976   Although this procedure is well within the premises of Taoist philosophy, it appears exceedingly odd to us. However, not even the strangeness of insane delusions or of primitive superstition has ever shocked me. I have always tried to remain unbiased and curious – *rerum novarum cupidus.* Why not venture a dialogue with an ancient book that purports to be animated? There can be no harm in it, and the reader may watch a psychological procedure that has been carried out time and again throughout the millennia of Chinese civilization, representing to a Confucius or a Lao-tzu both a supreme expression of spiritual authority and a philosophical enigma. I made use of the coin method, and the answer obtained was hexagram 50, *ting*, THE CAULDRON.[7]

977   In accordance with the way my question was phrased, the text of the hexagram must be regarded as though the *I Ching* itself were the speaking person. Thus it describes itself as a cauldron, that is, as a ritual vessel containing cooked food. Here the food is to be understood as spiritual nourishment. Wilhelm says about this:

> The *ting*, as a utensil pertaining to a refined civilization, suggests the fostering and nourishing of able men, which redounded to the benefit of the state . . .. Here we see civilization as it reaches its culmination in religion. The *ting* serves in offering sacrifice to God . . .. The supreme revelation of God appears in prophets and holy men. To venerate them is true veneration of God. The will of God, as revealed through them, should be accepted in humility.

978   Keeping to our hypothesis, we must conclude that the *I Ching* is here testifying concerning itself.

979   When any of the lines of a given hexagram have the value of six or nine, it means that they are specially emphasized and hence important in the interpretation.[8] In my hexagram the 'spiritual agencies' have given the emphasis of a nine to the lines in the second and in the third place. The text says:

> Nine in the second place means:

> There is food in the *ting*.
> My comrades are envious,
> But they cannot harm me.
> Good fortune.

980   Thus the *I Ching* says of itself: 'I contain (spiritual) nourishment.' Since a share in something great always arouses envy, the chorus of the envious[9] is part of the picture. The envious want to rob the *I Ching* of its great possession, that is, they seek to rob it of meaning, or to destroy its meaning. But their enmity is in vain. Its richness of meaning is assured; that is, it is convinced of its positive achievements, which no one can take away. The text continues:

Nine in the third place means:

The handle of the *ting* is altered.
One is impeded in his way of life.
The fat of the pheasant is not eaten.
Once rain falls, remorse is spent.
Good fortune comes in the end.

981   The handle [German *Griff*] is the part by which the *ting* can be grasped [*gegriffen*]. Thus it signifies the concept[10] [*Begriff*] one has of the *I Ching* (the *ting*). In the course of time this concept has apparently changed, so that today we can no longer grasp [*begreifen*] the *I Ching*. Thus 'one is impeded in his way of life.' We are no longer supported by the wise counsel and deep insight of the oracle; therefore we no longer find our way through the mazes of fate and the obscurities of our own natures. The fat of the pheasant, that is, the best and richest part of a good dish, is no longer eaten. But when the thirsty earth finally receives rain again, that is, when this state of want has been overcome, 'remorse', that is, sorrow over the loss of wisdom, is ended, and then comes the longed-for opportunity. Wilhelm comments: 'This describes a man who, in a highly evolved civilization, finds himself in a place where no one notices or recognizes him. This is a severe block to his effectiveness.' The *I Ching* is complaining, as it were, that its excellent qualities go unrecognized and hence lie fallow. It comforts itself with the hope that it is about to regain recognition.

982   The answer given in these two salient lines to the question I put to the *I Ching* requires no particular subtlety for its interpretation, no artifices, and no unusual knowledge. Anyone with a little commonsense can understand the meaning of the answer; it is the answer of one who has a good opinion of himself, but whose value is neither generally recognized nor even widely known. The answering subject has an interesting notion of itself: it looks upon itself as a vessel in which sacrificial offerings are brought to the gods, ritual food for their nourishment. It conceives of itself as a cult utensil serving to provide spiritual nourishment for the unconscious elements or forces ('spiritual agencies') that have been projected as gods – in other words, to give these forces the attention they need in order to play their part in the life of the individual. Indeed, this is the original meaning of the word *religio* – a careful observation and taking account of (from *relegare*)[11] the numinous.

983   The method of the *I Ching* does indeed take into account the hidden individual quality in things and men, and in one's own unconscious self as well. I questioned the *I Ching* as one questions a person whom one is about to introduce to friends: one asks whether or not it will be agreeable to him. In answer the *I Ching* tells me of its religious significance, of the fact that at present it is unknown and misjudged, of its hope of being restored to a place of honour – this last obviously with a sidelong glance at my as yet unwritten foreword,[12] and above all at the English translation. This seems a perfectly understandable reaction, such as one could expect also from a person in a similar situation.

984   But how has this reaction come about? Simply because I threw three small coins into the air and let them fall, roll and come to rest, heads up or tails up as the case might be. This peculiar fact – that a reaction that makes sense arises out of a technique which at the outset seemingly excludes all sense – is the great achievement of the *I Ching*. The instance I have just given is not unique; meaningful answers are the rule. Western sinologues and distinguished Chinese scholars have been at pains to inform me that the *I Ching* is a collection of obsolete 'magic spells'. In the course of these conversations my informant has sometimes admitted having consulted the oracle through a fortune-teller, usually a Taoist priest. This could be 'only nonsense' of course. But oddly enough, the answer received apparently coincided with the questioner's psychological blind-spot remarkably well.

985   I agree with Western thinking that any number of answers to my question were possible, and I certainly cannot assert that another answer would not have been equally significant. However, the answer received was the first and only one; we know nothing of other possible answers. It pleased and satisfied me. To ask the same question a second time would have been tactless and so I did not do it: 'the master speaks but once'. The heavy-handed pedagogic approach that attempts to fit irrational phenomena into a preconceived rational pattern is anathema to me. Indeed, such things as this answer should remain as they were when they first emerged to view, for only then do we know what nature does when left to herself undisturbed by the meddlesomeness of man. One ought not to go to dead bodies to study life. Moreover, a repetition of the experiment is impossible, for the simple reason that the original situation cannot be reconstituted. Therefore in each instance there is only a first and single answer.

986   To return to the hexagram itself. There is nothing strange in the fact that all of *ting*, THE CAULDRON, amplifies the themes announced by the two salient lines.[13] The first line of the hexagram says:

A *ting* with legs upturned
Furthers removal of stagnating stuff.
One takes a concubine for the sake of her son.
No blame.

987   A *ting* that is turned upside down is not in use. Hence the *I Ching* is like an unused cauldron. Turning it over serves to remove stagnating matter, as the line says. Just as a man takes a concubine when his wife has no son, so the *I Ching* is called upon when one sees no other way out. Despite the quasi-legal status of the concubine in China, she is in reality only a somewhat awkward makeshift; so likewise the magic procedure of the oracle is an expedient that may be utilized for a higher purpose. There is no blame, although it is an exceptional recourse.

988   The second and third lines have already been discussed. The fourth line says:

> The legs of the *ting* are broken.
> The prince's meal is spilled
> And his person is soiled.
> Misfortune.

989   Here the *ting* has been put to use, but evidently in a very clumsy manner, that is, the oracle has been abused or misinterpreted. In this way the divine food is lost and one puts oneself to shame. Legge translates as follows: 'Its subject will be made to blush for shame.' Abuse of a cult utensil such as the *ting* (i.e. the *I Ching*) is a gross profanation. The *I Ching* is evidently insisting here on its dignity as a ritual vessel and protesting against being profanely used.

990   The fifth line says:

> The *ting* has yellow handles, golden carrying rings.
> Perseverance furthers.

991   The *I Ching* has, it seems, met with a new, correct (yellow) understanding, that is, a new concept [*Begriff*] by which it can be grasped. This concept is valuable (golden). There is indeed a new edition in English, making the book more accessible to the Western world than before.

992   The sixth line says:

> The *ting* has rings of jade.
> Great good fortune.
> Nothing that would not act to further.

993   Jade is distinguished for its beauty and soft sheen. If the carrying rings are of jade, the whole vessel is enhanced in beauty, honour and value. The *I Ching* expresses itself here as being not only well satisfied but indeed very optimistic. One can only await further events and in the meantime remain content with the pleasant conclusion that the *I Ching* approves of the new edition.

994   I have shown in this example as objectively as I can how the oracle proceeds in a given case. Of course the procedure varies somewhat according to the way the question is put. If for instance a person finds himself in a confusing situation, he may himself appear in the oracle as

the speaker. Or, if the question concerns a relationship with another person, that person may appear as the speaker. However, the identity of the speaker does not depend entirely on the manner in which the question is phrased, inasmuch as our relations with our fellow-beings are not always determined by the latter. Very often our relations depend almost exclusively on our own attitudes, though we may be quite unaware of this fact. Hence, if an individual is unconscious of his role in a relationship, there may be a surprise in store for him; contrary to expectation, he himself may appear as the chief agent, as is sometimes unmistakably indicated by the text. It may also happen that we take a situation too seriously and consider it extremely important, whereas the answer we get on consulting the *I Ching* draws attention to some unsuspected other aspect implicit in the question.

995   Such instances might at first lead one to think that the oracle is fallacious. Confucius is said to have received only one inappropriate answer, i.e. hexagram 22, GRACE – a thoroughly aesthetic hexagram. This is reminiscent of the advice given to Socrates by his daemon – 'You ought to make more music' – whereupon Socrates took to playing the flute. Confucius and Socrates compete for first place as far as rationality and a pedagogic attitude to life are concerned; but it is unlikely that either of them occupied himself with 'lending grace to the beard on his chin', as the second line of this hexagram advises. Unfortunately, reason and pedagogy often lack charm and grace, and so the oracle may not have been wrong after all.

996   To come back once more to our hexagram. Though the *I Ching* not only seems to be satisfied with its new edition, but even expresses emphatic optimism, this still does not foretell anything about the effect it will have on the public it is intended to reach. Since we have in our hexagram two *yang* lines stressed by the numerical value nine, we are in a position to find out what sort of prognosis the *I Ching* makes for itself. Lines designated by a six or a nine have, according to the ancient conception, an inner tension so great as to cause them to change into their opposites, that is, *yang* into *yin* and vice versa. Through this change we obtain in the present instance hexagram 35, *chin*, PROGRESS.

997   The subject of this hexagram is someone who meets with all sorts of vicissitudes of fortune in his climb upward, and the text describes how he should behave. The *I Ching* is in this same situation: it rises like the sun and declares itself, but it is rebuffed and finds no confidence – it is 'progressing, but in sorrow'. However, 'one obtains great happiness from one's ancestress'. Psychology can help us to elucidate this obscure passage. In dreams and fairy-tales the grandmother, or ancestress, often represents the unconscious, because the latter in a man contains the feminine component of the psyche. If the *I Ching* is not accepted by the conscious, at least the unconscious meets it halfway, for the *I Ching* is more closely connected with the unconscious than with the rational

attitude of consciousness. Since the unconscious is often represented in dreams by a feminine figure, this may be the explanation here. The feminine person might be the translator, who has given the book her maternal care, and this might easily appear to the *I Ching* a 'great happiness'. It anticipates general understanding, but is afraid of misuse – 'Progress like a hamster.' But it is mindful of the admonition 'Take not gain and loss to heart.' It remains free of 'partisan motives'. It does not thrust itself on anyone.

998   The *I Ching* therefore faces its future on the American book market calmly and expresses itself here just about as any reasonable person would in regard to the fate of so controversial a work. This prediction is so very reasonable and full of commonsense that it would be hard to think of a more fitting answer.

999   All this happened before I had written the foregoing paragraphs. When I reached this point, I wished to know the attitude of the *I Ching* to the new situation. The state of things had been altered by what I had written, inasmuch as I myself had now entered upon the scene, and I therefore expected to hear something referring to my own action. I must confess that I had not been feeling too happy in the course of writing this foreword, for, as a person with a sense of responsibility towards science, I am not in the habit of asserting something I cannot prove or at least present as acceptable to reason. It is a dubious task indeed to try to introduce a collection of archaic 'magic spells' to a critical modern public with the idea of making them more or less acceptable. I have undertaken it because I myself think that there is more to the ancient Chinese way of thinking than meets the eye. But it is embarrassing to me that I must appeal to the goodwill and imagination of the reader, instead of giving him conclusive proofs and scientifically watertight explanations. Unfortunately I am only too well aware of the arguments that can be brought against this age-old oracle technique. We are not even certain that the ship that is to carry us over the unknown seas has not sprung a leak somewhere. May not the old text be corrupt? Is Wilhelm's translation accurate? Are we not self-deluded in our explanations?

1000   The *I Ching* insists upon self-knowledge throughout. The method by which this is to be achieved is open to every kind of misuse, and is therefore not for the frivolous-minded and immature; nor is it for intellectualists and rationalists. It is appropriate only for thoughtful and reflective people who like to think about what they do and what happens to them – a predilection not to be confused with the morbid brooding of the hypochondriac. As I have indicated above, I have no answer to the multitude of problems that arise when we seek to harmonize the oracle of the *I Ching* with our accepted scientific canons. But needless to say, nothing 'occult' is to be inferred. My position in these matters is pragmatic, and the great disciplines that have taught me the practical usefulness of this viewpoint are psychotherapy and medical psychology.

Probably in no other field do we have to reckon with so many unknown quantities, and nowhere else do we become more accustomed to adopting methods that work even though for a long time we may not know why they work. Unexpected cures may arise from questionable therapies, and unexpected failures from allegedly reliable methods. In the exploration of the unconscious we come upon very strange things, from which a rationalist turns away with horror, claiming afterwards that he did not see anything. The irrational fullness of life has taught me never to discard anything, even when it goes against all our theories (so short-lived at best) or otherwise admits of no immediate explanation. It is of course disquieting, and one is not certain whether the compass is pointing true or not; but security, certitude and peace do not lead to discoveries. It is the same with this Chinese mode of divination. Clearly the method aims at self-knowledge, though at all times it has also been put to superstitious use.

1001   I of course am thoroughly convinced of the value of self-knowledge, but is there any use in recommending such insight, when the wisest of men throughout the ages have preached the need of it without success? Even to the most biased eye it is obvious that this book represents one long admonition to careful scrutiny of one's own character, attitude and motives. This attitude appeals to me and has induced me to undertake the foreword. Only once before have I expressed myself in regard to the problem of the *I Ching*: this was in a memorial address in tribute to Richard Wilhelm.[14] For the rest I have maintained a discreet silence. It is by no means easy to feel one's way into such a remote and mysterious mentality as that underlying the *I Ching*. One cannot easily disregard such great minds as Confucius and Lao-tzu, if one is at all able to appreciate the quality of the thoughts they represent; much less can one overlook the fact that the *I Ching* was their main source of inspiration. I know that previously I would not have dared to express myself so explicitly about so uncertain a matter. I can take this risk because I am now in my eighth decade, and the changing opinions of men scarcely impress me any more; the thoughts of the old masters are of greater value to me than the philosophical prejudices of the Western mind.

1002   I do not like to burden the reader with these personal considerations; but, as already indicated, one's own personality is very often implicated in the answer of the oracle. Indeed, in formulating my question I even invited the oracle to comment directly on my action. The answer was hexagram 29, *k'an*, THE ABYSMAL. Special emphasis is given to the third place by the fact that the line is designated by a six. This line says:

> Forward and backward, abyss on abyss.
> In danger like this, pause at first and wait,
> Otherwise you will fall into a pit in the abyss.
> Do not act in this way.

1003   Formerly I would have accepted unconditionally the advice 'Do not act in this way', and would have refused to give my opinion of the *I Ching*, for the sole reason that I had none. But now the counsel may serve as an example of the way in which the *I Ching* functions. It is a fact that if one begins to think about it, the problems of the *I Ching* do represent 'abyss on abyss', and unavoidably one must 'pause at first and wait' in the midst of the dangers of limitless and uncritical speculation; otherwise one really will lose one's way in the darkness. Could there be a more uncomfortable position intellectually than that of floating in the thin air of unproven possibilities, not knowing whether what one sees is truth or illusion? This is the dreamlike atmosphere of the *I Ching*, and in it one has nothing to rely upon except one's own so fallible subjective judgement. I cannot but admit that this line represents very appropriately the feelings with which I wrote the foregoing passages. Equally fitting is the comforting beginning of this hexagram – 'If you are sincere, you have success in your heart' – for it indicates that the decisive thing here is not the outer danger but the subjective condition, that is, whether one believes oneself to be 'sincere' or not.

1004   The hexagram compares the dynamic action in this situation to the behaviour of flowing water, which is not afraid of any dangerous place but plunges over cliffs and fills up the pits that lie in its course (*k'an* also stands for water). This is the way in which the 'superior man' acts and 'carries on the business of teaching'.

1005   *K'an* is definitely one of the less agreeable hexagrams. It describes a situation in which the subject seems in grave danger of being caught up in all sorts of pitfalls. I have found that *k'an* often turned up with patients who were too much under the sway of the unconscious (water) and hence threatened with the possible occurrence of psychotic phenomena. If one were superstitious, one would be inclined to assume that some such meaning attaches intrinsically to this hexagram. But just as, in interpreting a dream, one must follow the dream-text with the utmost exactitude, so in consulting the oracle one must keep in mind the form of the question put, for this sets a definite limit to the interpretation of the answer. When I consulted the oracle the first time, I was thinking above all of the meaning for the *I Ching* of the foreword I had still to write. I thus put the book in the foreground and made it, so to speak, the acting subject. But in my second question, it is I who am the acting subject. So it would be illogical to take the *I Ching* as the subject in this case too, and, in addition, the interpretation would become unintelligible. But if I am the subject, the interpretation is meaningful to me, because it expresses the undeniable feeling of uncertainty and risk present in my mind. If one ventures upon such uncertain ground, it is easy to come dangerously under the influence of the unconscious without knowing it.

1006   The first line of the hexagram notes the presence of the danger: 'In the abyss one falls into a pit.' The second line does the same, then adds the counsel: 'One should strive to attain small things only.' I apparently anticipated this advice by limiting myself in this foreword to a demonstration of how the *I Ching* functions in the Chinese mind, and by renouncing the more ambitious project of writing a psychological commentary on the whole book.

1007   The simplification of my task is expressed in the fourth line which says:

> A jug of wine, a bowl of rice with it;
> Earthen vessels
> Simply handed in through the window.
> There is certainly no blame in this.

1008   Wilhelm makes the following comment here:

> Although as a rule it is customary for an official to present certain introductory gifts and recommendations before he is appointed, here everything is simplified to the utmost. The gifts are insignificant, there is no one to sponsor him, he introduces himself; yet all this need not be humiliating if only there is the honest intention of mutual help in danger.

1009   The fifth line continues the theme of limitation. If one studies the nature of water, one sees that it fills a pit only to the rim and then flows on. It does not stay caught there:

> The abyss is not filled to overflowing,
> It is filled only to the rim.

1010   But if, tempted by the danger, and just because of the uncertainty, one were to insist on forcing conviction by special effots, such as elaborate commentaries and the like, one would only be bogged down in the difficulty, which the top line describes very accurately as a tied-up and caged-in condition. Indeed, the last line often shows the consequences that result when one does not take the meaning of the hexagram to heart.

1011   In our hexagram we have a six in the third place. This *yin* line of mounting tension changes into a *yang* line and thus produces a new hexagram showing a new possibility or tendency. We now have hexagram 48, *ching*, THE WELL. The water-hole no longer means danger, however, but rather something beneficial, a well:

> Thus the superior man encourages the people at their work,
> And exhorts them to help one another.

1012   The image of people helping one another would seem to refer to the reconstruction of the well, for it is broken down and full of mud. Not even animals drink from it. There are fishes living in it, and one can catch these, but the well is not used for drinking, that is, for human needs. This description is reminiscent of the overturned and unused *ting* that is to receive a new handle. Moreover, like the *ting*, 'the well is cleaned, but no one drinks from it':

This is my heart's sorrow,
For one might draw from it.

1013   The dangerous water-hole or abyss pointed to the *I Ching*, and so does
the well, but the latter has a positive meaning: it contains the waters of
life. It should be restored to use. But one has no concept [*Begriff*] of it, no
utensil with which to carry the water; the jug is broken and leaks. The *ting*
needs new handles and carrying rings by which to grasp it, and so also the
well must be newly lined, for it contains 'a clear, cold spring from which
one can drink'. One may draw water from it, because 'it is dependable'.

1014   It is clear that in this prognosis the speaking subject is once more the *I
Ching*, representing itself as a spring of living water. The previous
hexagram described in detail the danger confronting the person who
accidentally falls into the pit within the abyss. He must work his way out
of it, in order to discover that it is an old, ruined well, buried in mud, but
capable of being restored to use again.

1015   I submitted two questions to the method of chance represented by the
coin oracle, the second question being put after I had written my analysis
of the answer to the first. The first question was directed, as it were, to the
I Ching: what had it to say about my intention to write a foreword? The
second question concerning my own action, or rather the situation in which
I was the acting subject who had discussed the first hexagram. To the first
question the *I Ching* replied by comparing itself to a cauldron, a ritual
vessel in need of renovation, a vessel that was finding only doubtful favour
with the public. To the second question the reply was that I had fallen into
a difficulty, for the *I Ching* represented a deep and dangerous water-hole
in which one might easily be bogged down. However, the water-hole
proved to be an old well that needed only to be renovated in order to be
put to useful purposes once more.

1016   These four hexagrams are in the main consistent as regards theme
(vessel, pit, well); and as regards intellectual content, they seem to be
meaningful. Had a human being made such replies, I should, as a
psychiatrist, have had to pronounce him of sound mind, at least on the
basis of the material presented. Indeed, I should not have been able to
discover anything delirious, idiotic or schizophrenic in the four answers.
In view of the *I Ching*'s extreme age and its Chinese origin, I cannot
consider its archaic, symbolic and flowery language abnormal. On the
contrary, I should have had to congratulate this hypothetical person on the
extent of his insight into my unexpressed state of doubt. On the other hand,
any person of clever and versatile mind can turn the whole thing around
and show how I have projected my subjective contents into the symbolism
of the hexagrams. Such a critique, though catastrophic from the standpoint
of Western rationality, does no harm to the function of the *I Ching*. On the
contrary, the Chinese sage would smilingly tell me: 'Don't you see how
useful the *I Ching* is in making you project your hitherto unrealized

thoughts into its abstruse symbolism? You could have written your foreword without ever realizing what an avalanche of misunderstanding might be released by it.'

1017 The Chinese standpoint does not concern itself with the attitude one takes towards the performance of the oracle. It is only we who are puzzled, because we trip time and again over our prejudice, viz. the notion of causality. The ancient wisdom of the East lays stress upon the fact that the intelligent individual realizes his own thoughts, but not in the least upon the way in which he does it. The less one thinks about the theory of *I Ching*, the more soundly one sleeps.

1018 It would seem to me that on the basis of this example an unprejudiced reader should now be in a position to form at least a tentative judgement on the operation of the *I Ching*.[15] More cannot be expected from a simple introduction. If by means of this demonstration I have succeeded in elucidating the psychological phenomenology of the *I Ching*, I shall have carried out my purpose. As to the thousands of questions, doubts and criticisms that this singular book stirs up – I cannot answer these. The *I Ching* does not offer itself with proofs and results; it does not vaunt itself, nor is it easy to approach. Like a part of nature, it waits until it is discovered. It offers neither facts nor power, but for lovers of self-knowledge, of wisdom – if there be such – it seems to be the right book. To one person its spirit appears as clear as day; to another, shadowy as twilight; to a third, dark as night. He who is not pleased by it does not have to use it, and he who is against it is not obliged to find it true. Let it go forth into the world for the benefit of those who can discern its meaning.

NOTES

1 The *I Ching, or Book of Changes*, English trans. by Cary F. Baynes, from the German version of R. Wilhelm (New York and London, 1950). The origins of this ancient Chinese book of wisdom and oracles go back to the fourth millennium BC.

2 [Grateful acknowledgement is made here to Cary F. Baynes for permission to use, with a few minor changes, her translation of this Foreword, which Professor Jung wrote specially for the English edition of the *I Ching, or Book of Changes*, translated by Mrs Baynes from the German translation of Richard Wilhelm (New York and London, 1950); 2nd edn in 1 vol., 1961; 3rd edn in small format, 1967. References are to the 3rd edn – TRANS.]

3 Legge makes the following comment on the explanatory text for the individual lines: 'According to our notions, a framer of emblems should be a good deal of a poet, but those of the *Yi* only make us think of a dryasdust. Out of more than three hundred and fifty, the greater number are only grotesque' (*The Yi King*, p. 22). Of the 'lessons' of the hexagrams, the same author says: 'But why, it may be asked, why should they be conveyed to us by such an array of lineal figures, and in such a farrago of emblematic representations' (p. 25). However, we are nowhere told that Legge ever bothered to put the method to a practical test.

4 [Cf. Jung's 'Synchronicity: An Acausal Connecting Principle'. In that work (pp. 450–53) he is concerned with the synchronistic aspects of the *I Ching* – EDITORS.]

5　Cf. J. B. Rhine, *The Reach of the Mind*.

6　They are *shen*, that is, 'spirit-like'. 'Heaven produced the "spirit-like things"' (Legge, p. 41).

7　[Cf. the *I Ching*, pp. 193ff. – EDITORS.]

8　See the explanation of the method, ibid., pp. 721ff.

9　For example, the *invidi* ('the envious') are a constantly recurring image in the old Latin books on alchemy, especially in the *Turba philosophorum* (11th or 12th cent.).

10　From the Latin *concipere* 'to take together', e.g. in a vessel: *concipere* derives from *capere*, 'to take', 'to grasp'.

11　This is the classical etymology. The derivation of *religio* from *religare*, 're-connect', 'link back', originated with the Church Fathers.

12　I made this experiment before I actually wrote the foreword.

13　The Chinese interpret only the changing lines in the hexagram obtained by the use of the oracle. I have found all the lines of the hexagram to be relevant in most cases.

14　[Cf. Wilhelm and Jung, *The Secret of the Golden Flower* (1931), in which this address appears as an appendix. The book did not appear in English until a year after Wilhelm's death – C. F. B.]

　　[For the address, see CW15 – EDITORS.]

15　The reader will find it helpful to look up all four of these hexagrams in the [Baynes-Wilhelm] text and to read them together with the relevant commentaries.

Part III
Indian yoga and meditation

10 *Brahman* and the uniting of opposites

189   The Indian conception teaches liberation from the opposites, by which are to be understood every sort of affective state and emotional tie to the object. Liberation follows the withdrawal of libido from all contents, resulting in a state of complete introversion. This psychological process is, very characteristically, known as *tapas*, a term which can best be rendered as 'self-brooding'. This expression clearly pictures the state of meditation without content, in which the libido is supplied to one's own self somewhat in the manner of incubating heat. As a result of the complete detachment of all affective ties to the object, there is necessarily formed in the inner self an equivalent of objective reality, or a complete identity of inside and outside, which is technically described as *tat tvam asi* ('that art thou'). The fusion of the self with its relations to the object produces the identity of the self (*atman*) with the essence of the world (i.e. with the relations of subject to object), so that the identity of the inner with the outer *atman* is cognized. The concept of *brahman* differs only slightly from that of *atman*, for in *brahman* the idea of the self is not explicitly given; it is, as it were, a general indefinable state of identity between inside and outside.

190   Parallel in some ways with *tapas* is the concept of yoga, understood not so much as a state of meditation as a conscious technique for attaining the *tapas* state. Yoga is a method by which the libido is systematically 'introverted' and liberated from the bondage of opposites. The aim of *tapas* and yoga alike is to establish a mediatory condition from which the creative and redemptive element will emerge. For the individual, the psychological result is the attainment of *brahman*, the 'supreme light', or *ananda* ('bliss'). This is the whole purpose of the redemptory exercises. At the same time, the process can also be thought of as a cosmogonic one, since *brahman–atman* is the universal Ground from which all creation proceeds. The existence of this myth proves, therefore, that creative processes take place in the unconscious of the yogi which can be interpreted as new adaptations to the object. Schiller says:

As soon as it is light in man, it is no longer night without. As soon as it is hushed within him, the storm in the universe is stilled, and the contending forces of nature find rest between lasting bounds. No wonder, then, that age-old poetry speaks of this great event in the inner man as though it were a revolution in the world outside him.[1]

191   Yoga introverts the relations to the object. Deprived of energic value, they sink into the unconscious, where, as we have shown, they enter into new relations with other unconscious contents, and then reassociate themselves with the object in new form after the completion of the *tapas* exercise. The transformation of the relation to the object has given the object a new face. It is as though newly created; hence the cosmogonic myth is an apt symbol for the outcome of the *tapas* exercise. The trend of Indian religious practice being almost exclusively introverted, the new adaptation to the object has of course little significance; but it still persists in the form of an unconsciously projected, doctrinal cosmogonic myth, though without leading to any practical innovations. In this respect the Indian religious attitude is the diametrical opposite of the Christian, since the Christian principle of love is extraverted and positively demands an object. The Indian principle makes for riches of knowledge, the Christian for fullness of works.

192   The *brahman* concept also contains the concept of *rta*, right order, the orderly course of the world. In *brahman*, the creative universal essence and universal Ground, all things come upon the right way, for in it they are eternally dissolved and recreated; all development in an orderly way proceeds from *brahman*. The concept of *rta* is a stepping-stone to the concept of Tao in Lao-tzu. Tao is the right way, the reign of law, the middle road between the opposites, freed from them and yet uniting them in itself. The purpose of life is to travel this middle road and never to deviate towards the opposites. The ecstatic element is entirely absent in Lao-tzu; its place is taken by sublime philosophic lucidity, an intellectual and intuitive wisdom obscured by no mystical haze – a wisdom that represents what is probably the highest attainable degree of spiritual superiority, as far removed from chaos as the stars from the disorder of the actual world. It tames all that is wild, without denaturing it and turning it into something higher.

a. THE BRAHMANIC CONCEPTION OF THE PROBLEM OF OPPOSITES

327   The Sanskrit term for pairs of opposites in the psychological sense is *dvandva*. It also means pair (particularly man and woman), strife, quarrel, combat, doubt. The pairs of opposites were ordained by the world-creator. The *Laws of Manu* says:[2]

> Moreover, in order to distinguish actions, he separated merit from demerit, and he caused the creatures to be affected by the pairs of opposites, such as pain and pleasure.

As further pairs of opposites, the commentator Kulluka names desire and anger, love and hate, hunger and thirst, care and folly, honour and disgrace. The *Ramayana* says: 'This world must suffer under the pairs of opposites, for ever.'[3] Not to allow oneself to be influenced by the pairs of opposites, but to be *nirdvandva* (free, untouched by the opposites), to raise oneself above them, is an essentially ethical task, because deliverance from the opposites leads to redemption.

328   In the following passages I give a series of examples:

When by the disposition [of his heart] he becomes indifferent to all objects, he obtains eternal happiness both in this world and after death. He who has in this manner gradually given up all attachments and is freed from all pairs of opposites reposes in *brahman* alone.[4]

The Vedas speak of the three *gunas*; but do you, O Arjuna, be indifferent to the three *gunas*, indifferent to the opposites, ever steadfast in courage.[5]

Then [in deepest meditation, *samādhi*] comes the state of being untroubled by the opposites.[6]

There he shakes off his good deeds and his evil deeds. His dear relatives succeed to the good deeds; those not so dear, to the evil deeds. Then, just as one driving a chariot looks down upon the two chariot wheels, so he looks down upon day and night, so upon good deeds and evil deeds, and upon all the pairs of opposites. Being freed from good and from evil, the knower of *brahman* enters into *brahman*.[7]

One entering into meditation must be a master over anger, attachment to the world, and the desires of the senses, free from the pairs of opposites, void of self-seeking, empty of expectation.[8]

Clothed with dust, housed under the open sky, I will make my lodging at the root of a tree, surrendering all things loved as well as unloved, tasting neither grief nor pleasure, forfeiting blame and praise alike, neither cherishing hope, nor offering respect, free from the opposites, with neither fortune nor belongings.[9]

He who remains the same in living as in dying, in fortune as in misfortune, whether gaining or losing, loving or hating, will be liberated. He who covets nothing and despises nothing, who is free from the opposites, whose soul knows no passion, is in every way liberated . . .. He who does neither right nor wrong, renouncing the merit and demerit acquired in former lives, whose soul is tranquil when the bodily elements vanish away, he will be liberated.[10]

A thousand years I have enjoyed the things of sense, while still the craving for them springs up unceasingly. These I will therefore renounce, and direct my mind upon *brahman*; indifferent to the opposites and free from self-seeking, I will roam with the wild.[11]

Through forbearance towards all creatures, through the ascetic life, through self-discipline and freedom from desire, through the vow and the blameless life, through equanimity and endurance of the opposites, man will partake of the bliss of *brahman*, which is without qualities.[12]

Free from pride and delusion, with the evils of attachment conquered, faithful always to the highest *atman*, with desires extinguished, untouched by the opposites of pain and pleasure, they go, undeluded, towards that imperishable place.[13]

329   As is clear from these quotations, it is external opposites, such as heat and cold, that must first be denied participation in the psyche, and then extreme fluctuations of emotion, such as love and hate. Fluctuations of emotion are, of course, the constant concomitants of all psychic opposites, and hence of all conflicts of ideas, whether moral or otherwise. We know from experience that the emotions thus aroused increase in proportion as the exciting factor affects the individual as a whole. The Indian purpose is therefore clear: it wants to free the individual altogether from the opposites inherent in human nature, so that he can attain a new life in *brahman*, which is the state of redemption and at the same time God. It is an irrational union of opposites, their final overcoming. Although *brahman*, the world-ground and world-creator, created the opposites, they must nevertheless be cancelled out in it again, for otherwise it would not amount to a state of redemption. Let me give another series of examples:

> *Brahman* is *sat* and *asat*, being and non-being, *satyam* and *asatyam*, reality and irreality.[14]

> There are two forms of *brahman*: the formed and the formless, the mortal and the immortal, the stationary and the moving, the actual and the transcendental.[15]

> That Person, the maker of all things, the great Self, seated forever in the heart of man, is perceived by the heart, by the thought, by the mind; they who know that become immortal. When there is no darkness [of ignorance] there is neither day nor night, neither being nor not-being.[16]

> In the imperishable, infinite, highest *brahman*, two things are hidden: knowing and not-knowing. Not-knowing perishes, knowing is immortal; but he who controls both knowing and not-knowing is another.[17]

> That Self, smaller than small, greater than great, is hidden in the heart of this creature here. Man becomes free from desire and free from sorrow when by the grace of the Creator he beholds the glory of the Self. Sitting still he walks afar; lying down he goes everywhere. Who but I can know the God who rejoices and rejoices not?[18]

> > Unmoving, the One is swifter than the mind.
> > Speeding ahead, it outruns the gods of the senses.
> > Past others running, it goes standing . . .

It moves. It moves not.
Far, yet near.
Within all,
Outside all.[19]

Just as a falcon or an eagle, after flying to and fro in space, wearies, and folds its wings, and drops down to its eyrie, so this Person (*purusha*) hastens to that state where, asleep, he desires no desires and sees no dream.

This, verily, is that form of his which is beyond desire, free from evil, without fear. As a man in the embrace of a beloved woman knows nothing of a without and within, so this Person, in the embrace of the knowing Self, knows nothing of a without and within. This, verily, is that form of his in which all desire is satisfied, Self his sole desire, which is no desire, without sorrow.

An ocean of seeing, one without a second, he becomes whose world is *brahman* . . .. This is man's highest achievement, his greatest wealth, his utmost joy.[20]

That which moves, that which flies and yet stands still,
That which breathes yet draws no breath,
                              that which closes the eyes,
That, many-formed, sustains the whole earth,
That, uniting, becomes One only.[21]

330   These quotations show that *brahman* is the union and dissolution of all opposites, and at the same time stands outside them as an irrational factor. It is a divine entity, at once the self (though to a lesser degree than the analogous *atman* concept) and a definite psychological state characterized by isolation from the flux of affects. Since suffering is an affect, release from affects means deliverance. Deliverance from the flux of affects, from the tension of opposites, is synonymous with the way of redemption that gradually leads to *brahman*. *Brahman* is thus not only a state but also a process, a *durée créatrice*. It is therefore not surprising that it is expressed in the Upanishads by means of the symbols I have termed libido symbols.[22] In the following section I give some examples of these.

b. THE BRAHMANIC CONCEPTION OF THE UNITING SYMBOL

331   When it is said that *brahman* was first born in the East, it means that each day *brahman* is born in the East like yonder sun.[23]

Yonder man in the sun is *parameshtin, brahman, atman.*[24]

Brahman is a light like the sun.[25]

As to that *brahman*, it is yonder burning disk.[26]

First was brahman born in the East.
From the horizon the Gracious One appears in splendour;
He illumines the forms of this world, the deepest, the highest,
He is the cradle of what is and is not.
Father of the luminaries, *begetter* of the treasure,
He entered many-formed into the spaces of the air.
They glorify him with hymns of praise,
Making the youth that is brahman increase by brahman.[27]

Brahman brought forth the gods, *brahman* created the world.[28]

332   In this last passage, I have italicized certain characteristic points which make it clear that *brahman* is not only the producer but the produced, the ever-becoming. The epithet 'Gracious One' (*vena*), here bestowed on the sun, is elsewhere applied to the seer who is endowed with the divine light, for, like the *brahman*-sun, the mind of the seer traverses 'earth and heaven contemplating *brahman*'.[29] The intimate connection, indeed identity, between the divine being and the self (*atman*) of man is generally known. I give an example from the *Atharva-Veda*:

> The disciple of *brahman* gives life to both worlds.
> In him all the gods are of one mind.
> He contains and sustains earth and heaven,
> His *tapas* is food even for his teacher.
> To the disciple of *brahman* there come, to visit him,
> Fathers and gods, singly and in multitudes,
> And he nourishes all the gods with his *tapas*.[30]

333   The disciple of *brahman* is himself an incarnation of *brahman*, whence it follows that the essence of *brahman* is identical with a definite psychological state.

> The sun, set in motion by the gods, shines unsurpassed yonder.
> From it came the Brahma-power, the supreme *brahman*,
> And all the gods, and what makes them immortal.
> The disciple of *brahman* upholds the splendour of *brahman*,
> Interwoven in him are the hosts of the gods.[31]

334   *Brahman* is also *prana*, the breath of life and the cosmic principle; it is *vayu*, wind, which is described in the *Brihadaran-yaka Upanishad* (3, 7) as 'the thread by which this world and the other world and all things are tied together, the Self, the inner controller, the immortal'.

He who dwells in man, he who dwells in the sun, are the same.[32]

Prayer of the dying:

> The face of the Real
> Is covered with a golden disk.
> Open it, O sun,
> That we may see the nature of the Real . . .

Spread thy rays, and gather them in!
The light which is thy fairest form,
I see it.
That Person who dwells yonder, in the sun, is myself.
May my breath go to the immortal wind
When my body is consumed to ash.[33]

And this light which shines above this heaven, higher than all, on top of everything, in the highest world, beyond which there are no other worlds, this same is the light which is in man. And of this we have tangible proof, when we perceive by touch the heat here in the body.[34]

As a grain of rice, or a grain of barley, or a grain of millet, or the kernel of a grain of millet, is this golden Person in the heart, like a flame without smoke, greater than the earth, greater than the sky, greater than space, greater than all these worlds. That is the soul of all creatures, that is myself. Into that I shall enter on departing hence.[35]

335   *Brahman* is conceived in the *Atharva-Veda* as the vitalistic principle, the life force, which fashions all the organs and their respective instincts:

Who planted the seed within him, that he might spin the thread of generation? Who assembled within him the powers of mind, gave him voice and the play of features?[36]

336   Even man's strength comes from *brahman*. It is clear from these examples, which could be multiplied indefinitely, that the *brahman* concept, by virtue of all its attributes and symbols, coincides with that of a dynamic or creative principle which I have termed libido. The word *brahman* means prayer, incantation, sacred speech, sacred knowledge (*veda*), holy life, the sacred caste (the Brahmans), the Absolute. Deussen stresses the prayer connotation as being especially characteristic.[37] The word derives from *barh* (cf. L. *farcire*), 'to swell',[38] whence 'prayer' is conceived as 'the upward-striving will of man towards the holy, the divine'. This derivation indicates a particular psychological state, a specific concentration of libido, which through overflowing innervations produces a general state of tension associated with the feeling of swelling. Hence, in common speech, one frequently uses images like 'overflowing with emotion', 'unable to restrain oneself', 'bursting' when referring to such a state. ('What filleth the heart, goeth out by the mouth.') The yogi seeks to induce this concentration or accumulation of libido by systematically withdrawing attention (libido) both from external objects and from interior psychic states, in a word, from the opposites. The elimination of sense perception and the blotting out of conscious contents enforce a lowering of consciousness (as in hypnosis) and an activation of the contents of the unconscious, i.e. the primordial images, which, because of their universality and immense antiquity, possess a cosmic and suprahuman character. This accounts for

all those sun, fire, flame, wind, breath similes that from time immemorial have been symbols of the procreative and creative power that moves the world. As I have made a special study of these libido symbols in my book *Symbols of Transformation*, I need not expand on this theme here.

337   The idea of a creative world-principle is a projected perception of the living essence in man himself. In order to avoid all vitalistic misunderstandings, one would do well to regard this essence in the abstract, as simply *energy*. On the other hand, the hypostatizing of the energy concept after the fashion of modern physicists must be rigorously rejected. The concept of energy implies that of polarity, since a current of energy necessarily presupposes two different states, or poles, without which there can be no current. Every energic phenomenon (and there is no phenomenon that is not energic) consists of pairs of opposites: beginning and end, above and below, hot and cold, earlier and later, cause and effect, etc. The inseparability of the energy concept from that of polarity also applies to the concept of the libido. Hence libido symbols, whether mythological or speculative in origin, either present themselves directly as opposites or can be broken down into opposites. I have already referred in my earlier work to this inner splitting of libido, thereby provoking considerable resistance, unjustifiably, it seems to me, because the direct connection between a libido symbol and the concept of polarity is sufficient justification in itself. We find this connection also in the concept or symbol of *brahman*. *Brahman* as a combination of prayer and primordial creative power, the latter resolving itself into the opposition of the sexes, occurs in a remarkable hymn of the *Rig-Veda* (10.31.6):

> And this prayer of the singer, spreading afar,
> Became the bull which existed before the world was.
> The gods are nurslings of the same brood,
> Dwelling together in Asura's mansion.
> What was the wood, what was the tree,
> Out of which heaven and earth were fashioned?
> These two stand fast and never grow old,
> They have sung praises to many a dawn and morning.
> There is no other thing greater than he,
> The bull, supporter of earth and heaven.
> He makes his skin a filter purifying the rays,
> When as Surya his bay horses bear him along.
> As the arrow of the sun he illumines the broad earth,
> As the wind scatters the mist he storms through the world.
> With Mitra and Varuna he comes anointed with ghee,
> As Agni in the firesticks he shoots out splendour.
> Driven to him, the cow once barren brought forth,
> The moveless thing she created moved, pasturing freely.
> She bore the son who was older than the parents.[39]

338   The polarity of the creative world-principle is represented in another form in the *Shatapatha Brahmana* (2.2.4):

> In the beginning, Prajapati[40] was this world alone. He meditated: How can I propagate myself? He travailed, he practised *tapas*; then he begat Agni (fire) out of his mouth,[41] and because he begat him out of his mouth, Agni is a devourer of food.
>
> Prajapati meditated: As a devourer of food I have begotten this Agni out of myself, but there is nothing else beside myself that he may devour. For the earth at that time was quite barren, there were no herbs and no trees, and this thought was heavy upon him.
>
> Then Agni turned upon him with gaping maw. His own greatness spoke to him: Sacrifice! Then Prajapati knew: My own greatness has spoken to me. And he sacrificed.
>
> Thereupon that rose up which shines yonder (the sun); thereupon that rose up which purifies all things here (the wind). Thus Prajapati, by offering sacrifice, propagated himself, and at the same time saved himself from death, who as Agni would have devoured him.

339   Sacrifice always means the renunciation of a valuable part of oneself, and through it the sacrificer escapes being devoured. In other words, there is no transformation into the opposite, but rather equilibrium and union, from which arises a new form of libido: sun and wind. Elsewhere the *Shatapatha Brahmana* says that one half of Prajapati is mortal, the other immortal.[42]

340   In the same way as he divides himself into bull and cow, Prajapati also divides himself into the two principles, *manas* (mind) and *vac* (speech):

> This world was Prajapati alone, *vac* was his self, and *vac* his second self. He meditated: This *vac* I will send forth, and she shall go hence and pervade all things. Then he sent forth *vac*, and she went and filled the universe.[43]

This passage is of especial interest in that speech is conceived as a creative, extraverted movement of libido, a diastole in Goethe's sense. There is a further parallel in the following passage:

> In truth Prajapati was this world, and with him was *vac* his second self. He copulated with her; she conceived; she went forth out of him, and made these creatures, and once again entered into Prajapati.[44]

341   In *Shatapatha Brahmana* 8.1.2, 9 the role attributed to *vac* is a prodigious one: 'Truly *vac* is the wise Vishvakarman, for by *vac* was this whole world made.' But at 1.4.5, 8–11 the question of primacy between *manas* and *vac* is decided differently:

> Now it happened that Mind and Speech strove for priority one with the other. Mind said: I am better than you, for you speak nothing that I have

not first discerned. Then Speech said: I am better than you, for I announce what you have discerned and make it known.

They went to Prajapati for judgement. Prajapati decided in favour of Mind, saying to Speech: Truly, Mind is better than you, for you copy what Mind does and run in his tracks; moreover it is the inferior who is wont to imitate his betters.

342   These passages show that the principles into which the world-creator divides himself are themselves divided. They were at first contained in Prajapati, as is clear from the following:

Prajapati desired: I wish to be many, I will multiply myself. Then he meditated silently in his Mind, and what was in his Mind became *brihat* (song). He bethought himself: This embryo of me is hidden in my body, through Speech I will bring it forth. Then he created Speech.[45]

343   This passage shows the two principles as psychological functions: *manas* an introversion of libido begetting an inner product, *vac* a function of exteriorization or extraversion. This brings us to another passage relating to *brahman*:

When *brahman* had entered into that other world, he bethought himself: How can I extend myself through these worlds? And he extended himself twofold through these worlds, by Form and Name.

These two are the two monsters of *brahman*; whoever knows these two monsters of *brahman*, becomes a mighty monster himself. These are the two mighty manifestations of *brahman*.[46]

344   A little later, 'form' is defined as *manas* ('*manas* is form, for through *manas* one knows it is this form') and 'name' as *vac* ('for through *vac* one grasps the name'). Thus the two 'mighty monsters' of *brahman* turn out to be mind and speech, two psychic functions by which *brahman* can 'extend himself' through both worlds, clearly signifying the function of 'relationship'. The forms of things are 'apprehended' or 'taken in' by introverting through *manas*; names are given to things by extraverting through *vac*. Both involve relationship and adaptation to objects as well as their assimilation. The two 'monsters' are evidently thought of as personifications; this is indicated by their other name, *yaksha* (manifestation) for *yaksha* means much the same as a daemon or superhuman being. Psychologically, personification always denotes the relative autonomy of the content personified, i.e. its splitting-off from the psychic hierarchy. Such contents cannot be voluntarily reproduced; they reproduce themselves spontaneously, or else withdraw themselves from consciousness in the same way.[47] A dissociation of this kind occurs, for instance, when an incompatibility exists between the ego and a particular complex. As we know, it is observed most frequently when the latter is a sexual complex, but other complexes can get split off too, for instance the power-

complex, the sum of all those strivings and ideas aiming at the acquisition of personal power. There is, however, another form of dissociation, and that is the splitting-off of the conscious ego, together with a selected function, from the other components of the personality. This form of dissociation can be defined as an identification of the ego with a particular function or group of functions. It is very common in people who are too deeply immersed in one of their psychic functions and have differentiated it into their sole conscious means of adaptation.

NOTES

1 Cf. CW6, para. 193.
2 *Sacred Books of the East* (*SBE*), XXV, p. 13. [Since the existing English translations of the Sanskrit texts quoted in sections a, b and c often differ widely from one another, and also from the German sources used by the author, both in meaning and in readability, the quotations given here are for the most part composites of the English and German versions, and in general lean towards the latter. For the purpose of comparison, standard translations are cited in the footnotes; full details are given in the bibliography. – TRANS.]
3 [Source in the *Ramayana* untraceable. – EDITORS.]
4 Cf. *The Laws of Manu*, SBE, XXV, p. 212.
5 The famous exhortation of Krishna, *Bhagavad Gita* 2.45. [The three *gunas* are the qualities or constituents of organic matter: *tamas* (darkness, inertia), *rajas* (passion, impurity, activity), *sattva* (purity, clarity, harmony). – TRANSLATOR.]
6 *Yogasutra* of Patanjali. Deussen, *Allgemeine Geschichte der Philosophie*, I, part 3, p. 511.
7 *Kaushitaki Upanishad* 1.4. Cf. Hume, *The Thirteen Principal Upanishads*, pp. 304f.
8 *Tejobindu Upanishad* 3. Cf. *Minor Upanishads*, p. 17.
9 *Mahabharata* 1.119.8f. Cf. Dutt trans., I, p. 168.
10 Ibid. 14.19.4f. Cf. Dutt, XIV, p. 22.
11 *Bhagavata Purana* 9.19.18f. Cf. *Brihadaranyaka Upanishad* 3.5, in Hume, p. 112: 'When he has become disgusted both with the non-ascetic state and with the ascetic state, then he becomes a Brahman.'
12 *Bhagavata Purana* 4.22.24.
13 *Garuda Purana* 16.110. Cf. *Sacred Books of the Hindus*, XXVI, p. 167.
14 Deussen, *Geschichte der Philosophie*, I, part 2, p. 117.
15 *Brihadaranyaka Upanishad* 2.3.1. Cf. Hume, p. 97.
16 *Shvetashvatara Upanishad* 4.17–8. Cf. Hume, p. 405.
17 *Shvetashvatara Upanishad* 5.1. Cf. Hume, p. 406.
18 *Katha Upanishad* 2.20–1. Cf. Hume, pp. 349ff.
19 *Isha Upanishad* 4–5. Cf. Hume, pp. 362f. [Last two lines perhaps: 'immanent, transcendent' – TRANSLATOR.]
20 *Brihadaranyaka Upanishad*. 4.3.19, 21, 32. Cf. Hume, pp. 136ff.
21 *Atharva-Veda* 10.8.11. Cf. Whitney/Lanman trans., VIII, p. 597.
22 *Symbols of Transformation*, pars. 204ff.
23 *Shatapatha Brahmana* 14.1.3, 3. Cf. *SBE*, XLIV, pp. 459f.
24 *Taittiriya Aranyaka* 10.63.15.
25 *Vajasanayi Samhita* 23.48. Cf. Griffith trans., p. 215.
26 *Shatapatha Brahmana* 8.5.3, 7. Cf. *SBE*, XLIII, p. 94.
27 [One meaning of *brahman* is prayer, hymn, sacred knowledge, magic formula. Cf. par. 336 – TRANSLATOR.]

28 *Taittiriya Brahmana* 2.8.8, 8ff.
29 *Atharva-Veda* 10.5.1.
30 ibid. [For *tapas* (self-incubation) see *Symbols of Transformation*, paras 588ff.]
31 *Atharva-Veda* 11.5.23f. Cf. Whitney/Lanman trans., VIII, pp. 639f.
32 *Taittiriya Upanishad* 2.8. Cf. Hume, p. 289.
33 *Brihadaranyaka Upanishad.* 5.15. Cf. Hume, p. 157.
34 *Chhandogya Upanishad* 3.13.7. Cf. Hume, p. 209.
35 *Shatapatha Brahmana* 10.6.3. Cf. *SBE*, XLIII, p. 400. [Cf. *Chhandogya Upanishad* 3.14.3–4; Hume, p. 209. – TRANSLATOR.]
36 *Atharva-Veda* 10.2.17. Cf. Whitney/Lanman trans., VIII, p. 569.
37 Deussen, I, part 1, pp. 240ff.
38 Also confirmed by the reference to *brahman*, or breath (*prana*), as *mata-risvan*, 'he who swells in the mother', in *Atharva-Veda* 11.4.15. Cf. Whitney/Lanman trans., VIII, p. 63.
39 [This rendering is a composite of the Deussen version (Jung, *Gesammelte Werke*, 6, p. 217) translated by Baynes in the 1923 edn (p. 251) of the present volume, and the Griffith version in *The Hymns of the Rig-Veda*, II, p. 426. The interested reader would do well to compare all four versions. – TRANSLATOR.]
40 Prajapati is the cosmic creative principle = libido. *Taittiriya Samhita* 5.5.2,1: 'After he had created them, Prajapati instilled love into all his creatures.' Cf. Keith, trans., II, p. 441.
41 The begetting of fire in the mouth has remarkable connections with speech. Cf. *Symbols of Transformation*, paras 208ff.
42 Cf. the Dioscuri motif in *Symbols of Transformation*, para. 294.
43 *Pañcavimsha Brahmana* 20.14.12. Cf. *Bibliotheca Indica*, Vol. 252, pp. 145f.
44 Weber, *Indische Studien*, IX, p. 477, as in Deussen, I, part 1, p. 206.
45 *Pañcavimsha Brahmana* 7.6.
46 *Shatapatha Brahmana* 11.2.3. Cf. *SBE*, XXVI, pp. 27f.
47 [Jung, 'A Review of the Complex Theory'. – EDITORS.]

11 The psychological symbolism of *kundalini* yoga

From: 'The Realities of Practical Psychotherapy'

561   The fundamental idea of Tantrism is that a feminine creative force in the shape of a serpent, named *kundalini*, rises up from the perineal centre, where she had been sleeping, and ascends through the *chakras*, thereby activating them and constellating their symbols. This 'Serpent Power' is personified as the *mahādevishakti*, the goddess who brings everything into existence by means of *māyā*, the building material of reality.

560   According to this system, there are seven centres, called *chakras* or *padmas* (lotuses), which have been fairly definite localizations in the body. They are, as it were, psychic localizations, and the higher ones correspond to the historical localizations of consciousness. The nethermost *chakra*, called *mulādhāra*, is the perineal lotus and corresponds to the cloacal zone in Freud's sexual theory. This centre, like all the others, is represented in the shape of a flower, with a circle in the middle, and has attributes that express in symbols the psychic qualities of that particular localization. Thus, the perineal *chakra* contains as its main symbol the sacred *white elephant*. The next *chakra*, called *svadhisthāna*, is localized near the bladder and represents the sexual centre. Its main symbol is water or sea, and subsidiary symbols are the sickle moon as the feminine principle, and a devouring water monster called *makara*, which corresponds to the biblical and cabalistic Leviathan. The mythological whale-dragon is, as you know, a symbol for the devouring and birth-giving womb, which in its turn symbolizes certain reciprocal actions between consciousness and the unconscious. The patient's bladder symptoms can be referred to the *svadhisthāna* symbolism, and so can the inflamed spots in the uterus. Soon afterwards she began her drawings of flowers, whose symbolic content relates them quite clearly to the *chakras*. The third centre, called *manipura*, corresponds to the solar plexus. As we have seen, the noises in the abdomen gradually moved up to the small intestine. This third *chakra* is the emotional centre, and is the earliest known localization of consciousness. There are primitives in existence who still think with their bellies. Everyday speech still shows traces of this: something lies heavy on the stomach, the bowels turn to water, etc. The fourth *chakra*, called *anāhata*, is situated in the region of the heart and the diaphragm. In Homer the

diaphragm (*phren, phrenes*) was the seat of feeling and thinking.[1] The fifth and sixth, called *vishuddha* and *ajña*, are situated respectively in the throat and between the eyebrows. The seventh, *sahāsrāra*, is at the top of the skull.

From: 'Psychological Commentary on *Kundalini* Yoga'

[The] *chakras* are symbols. They symbolize highly complex psychic facts which at the present moment we could not possibly express except in images. The *chakras* are therefore of great value to us because they represent a real effort to give a symbolic theory of the psyche. The psyche is something so highly complicated, so vast in extent and so rich in elements unknown to us, and its aspects overlap each other and interweave with one another in such an amazing degree, that we always turn to symbols in order to try to represent what we know about it. Any theory about it would be premature because it would become entangled in particularities and would lose sight of the totality we set out to envisage.

You have seen from my attempt at an analysis of the *chakras* how difficult it is to reach their content, and with what complex conditions we have to deal when we are studying not just consciousness, but the totality of the psyche. The *chakras*, then, become a valuable guide for us in this obscure field because the East, and India especially, has always tried to understand the psyche as a whole. It has an intuition of the Self, and therefore it sees the ego and consciousness as only more or less inessential parts of the Self. All of this seems very strange to us. It appears to us as though India were fascinated by the background of consciousness, because we ourselves are entirely identified with our foreground, with the conscious. But now among us too, the background, or hinterland of the psyche has come to life, and since it is so obscure and so difficult of access, we are at first forced to represent it symbolically. Thus, for example, there comes to our notice the paradoxical situation in which *mulādhāra* is localized in the pelvis, and at the same time represents our world, and this paradox can only be expressed by a symbol. It is the same with the apparent contradiction contained in the fact that we think of consciousness as located in our heads and nonetheless we live in the lowest *chakra*, in *mulādhāra*.

As we have seen, *mulādhāra* is the symbol of our present psychic situation because we live entangled in earthly causalities. It presents the entanglement of our conscious life *as it actually is*. *Mulādhāra* is not just the outer world as we live in it; it is our total consciousness of all outer and inner personal experiences. In our conscious life of every day we are like highly developed animals, tied down by our environment and entangled and conditioned by it. But our Western consciousness does not look at it this way at all. In our world, on the contrary, we are living in the upper centres. Our consciousness is localized in the head. We feel it to be there; we think and will in our heads;

we are the lords of nature, and have command over the environmental conditions and the blind laws that bind the primitive man hand and foot. In our consciousness we sit enthroned on high and look down upon nature and animals. To us archaic man is a Neanderthal man, little better than an animal. We do not see in the very least that God appears as an animal also. To us animal means 'bestial'. What should really seem above us, seems to be below us and is taken as something regressive and degraded. Therefore we 'go down' into *svadhisthāna* or 'fall' into the emotionality of *manipura*. Because we are identified with consciousness, we talk about the *sub*conscious. When we go into the unconscious, we descend to a lower level. Therefore we can say that humanity in general has reached the level of the *anāhata chakra*, in so far as it feels itself bound by the suprapersonal values of *anāhata*. All culture creates suprapersonal values. A thinker whose ideas show an activity that is independent of the events of daily life could say that he is in the *vishuddha*, or almost in the *ajña* centre.

But all of that is only the *sthula* aspect of the problem.

The *sthula* aspect is the personal aspect. To us personally it seems as if we were in the higher centres. We think that because our consciousness and the collective suprapersonal culture in which we live are in the *anāhata* centre, we are there in all respects. Being identified with the conscious, we do not see that there exists something outside it and that this is not above but below.

But by means of psychology or Tantric philosophy we achieve a standpoint from which we can observe that suprapersonal events do take place within our own psyche. To look at things from the suprapersonal standpoint is to arrive at the *suksma* aspect.

We can attain this standpoint because, inasmuch as we create culture, we create suprapersonal values, and when we do this, we begin to see the *suksma* aspect. Through culture we get an intuition of the other-than-personal psychological possibilities, because the suprapersonal appears in it. The *chakra* system manifests itself in culture, and culture can therefore be divided into various levels: such as the belly, heart and head centres. Therefore we can experience and demonstrate the various centres as they appear in the life of the individual, or in the evolution of humanity.

We begin in the head. We identify with our eyes and our consciousness; quite detached and objective, we survey the world. That is *ajña*. But we cannot linger for ever in the pure spheres of detached observation, and must bring our thoughts into reality. We voice them and so trust them to the air. When we clothe our knowledge in words, we are in the region of *visuddha*, or the throat centre. But as soon as we say something that is especially difficult, or that causes us positive or negative feelings, we have a throbbing of the heart and then the *anāhata* centre begins to be activated. And still another step further, when, for example, a dispute with someone starts up, when we have become irritable and angry and get beside ourselves, then we are in *manipura*.

If we go lower still, the situation becomes impossible, because then the *body* begins to speak. For this reason, in England, everything below the diaphragm is taboo. Germans always go a little below it and hence easily become emotional. Russians live altogether below the diaphragm – they consist of emotions. The French and Italians behave as if they were below it, but they know perfectly well, and so does everyone else, that they are not.

It is a rather delicate and painful matter to speak of what happens in *svadhisthāna*. When, for example, an emotion reaches a point of great intensity, it no longer expresses itself in words, but in a physiological way. It does not leave the body by way of the mouth, but in other ways, as for instance, the bladder. *Svadhisthāna* represents the level where psychic life may be said to begin. Only when this level became activated did mankind awaken from the sleep of *mulādhāra*, and learn the first rules of bodily decency. The beginning of moral education consisted in attending to our needs in the places suitable for them, just as still happens in the education of a small child. Dogs, too, have learned this. They are already living in *svadhisthāna*, inasmuch as they deposit their visiting cards at trees and corners. The dogs that come after read the messages and know from them how the land lies, whether the preceding dog was fed or empty, whether it was a large or a small dog – an important difference in the breeding season. Thus dogs can give all sorts of news about one another and can direct themselves accordingly.

The first and lowest means of expressing psychic life is also still used by human beings, for instance, by very primitive criminals. You know what is meant by *grumus merdae*. The thief deposits his excrement in the place he has looted and says in this way: this is my signature. This place belongs to me, and woe to him who crosses my path. Thus it becomes a sort of apotropaic charm – a relic of archaic times. For in primitive conditions this sign language has actually a great, even a vital, importance. A person can tell by it whether dangerous or useful animals have made a given track, and whether the track is fresh or not. Naturally the same thing is true of human tracks. If hostile tribes are in the neighbourhood, fresh human excrement is a signal of alarm. The more primitive the conditions of life, the more valuable the psychic manifestations of this level. We could say it is the first speech of nature. Psychic manifestations belonging to *svadhisthāna* are therefore often present in our dreams, and certain witticisms and the broad jokes of the Middle Ages are full of them.

As to *mulādhāra*, we know nothing about it because at this level psychic life is dormant.

Therefore one is quite correct in saying that *mulādhāra* is the life of animals and primitives who live in complete harmony with nature. Our cultivated life, on the other hand, is to be looked at as the *sthula* aspect of the higher *chakras*. The awakening of Kundalini would then be similar to the conscious understanding of the *suksma* aspect. That is quite true. But what must we do in order to understand consciously the *suksma* aspect of *mulādhāra*, or of the earth?

Here we meet again the great paradox. In consciousness we are in *ajna* and yet actually we live in *mulādhāra*. That is the *sthula* aspect. But can we win another aspect? As we know, we cannot understand a thing if we are still immersed in it and identified with it. Only when we reach a standpoint that is 'outside' the experience in question can we wholly understand what we were experiencing before. Thus, for example, we can form an objective judgement of the nation, race or continent to which we belong only when we have lived for a time in a foreign country and so are able to look at our own country from without.

How then can we put aside our personal standpoint, which represents the *sthula* aspect, and take another, a suprapersonal one, which will show us where we actually are in this world? How can we find out that we are in *mulādhāra*? *Mulādhāra* is a condition of psychic sleep, we have said. We have, then, no consciousness there and can say nothing about it.

I began by saying that by means of culture we create suprapersonal values and that by this means we can get an inkling of other psychological possibilities and can reach another state of mind. In the creation of suprapersonal values we begin with the *suksma* aspect. We see things from the *suksma* aspect when we create symbols. We can also see our psyche under the *suksma* aspect, and this is just what the symbols of the *chakras* are.

Nor can I describe this standpoint to you in any way except by means of a symbol. It is as if we viewed our psychology and the psychology of mankind from the standpoint of a fourth dimension, unlimited by space or time. The *chakra* system is created from this standpoint. It is a standpoint that transcends time and the individual.

The spiritual point of view in India in general is a standpoint of this sort. Hindus do not begin, as we do, to explain the world by taking the hydrogen atom as the starting-point, nor do they describe the evolution of mankind or of the individual from lower to higher, from deep unconsciousness to the highest consciousness. They do not see humanity under the *sthula* aspect. They speak only of the *suksma* aspect and therefore say: 'In the beginning was the one *brahman* without a second. It is the *one* indubitable reality, being and not-being.' They begin in *sahāsrāra*. They speak the language of the gods and think of man from above down, taking him from the *suksma* or *para* aspect. Inner experience is to them revelation. They would never say about this experience: 'I thought it.'

Naturally we see the East quite differently. In comparison with our conscious *anāhata* culture, we can truthfully say that the collective culture of India is in *mulādhāra*. For proof of this we only need to think of the actual conditions of life in India: its poverty, its dirt, its lack of hygiene, its ignorance of scientific and technical achievements. Looked at from the *sthula* aspect, the collective culture of India really is in *mulādhāra*, while ours has reached *anāhata*. But the Indian concept of life understands humanity under the *suksma* aspect, and looked at from that standpoint everything becomes completely reversed. Our personal consciousness can indeed be located in *anāhata* or even in *ajña*, but nonetheless our psychic situation as a whole is undoubtedly in *mulādhāra*.

Suppose we began to explain the world in terms of *sahāsrāra*, and started off a lecture, for instance, with the words of the Vedanta: 'This world in the beginning was *brahman* solely. Since *brahman* was alone it was not unfolded. It knew itself only, and it realized: I am *brahman*. In this way it became the universe.' We would be taken for mad, or it would at least be thought that we were holding a revival meeting. So if we are wise and live in reality, when we want to describe something we always begin with everyday banal events, and with the practical and concrete. In a word, we begin with the *sthula* aspect. To us the things that are real beyond question are our professions, the places where we live, our bank accounts, our families and our social connections. We are forced to take these realities as our premises, if we want to live at all. Without personal life, without the here and now, we cannot attain to the suprapersonal. Personal life must first be fulfilled in order that the process of the suprapersonal side of the psyche can be introduced.

What is suprapersonal in us is shown us again and again in the visions of our seminar; it is an event outside of the ego and of consciousness. In the fantasies of our patient we are always dealing with symbols and experiences which have nothing to do with her as Mrs So-and-So, but which arise from the collective human soul in her and which are therefore collective contents. In analysis the suprapersonal process can begin only when all of personal life has been assimilated to consciousness. In this way psychology opens up a standpoint and types of experience that lie beyond ego-consciousness. (The same thing happens in Tantric philosophy, but with this difference: there the ego plays no role at all.) This standpoint and this experience answer the question as to how we can free ourselves from the overwhelming realities of the world; that is, how to disentangle our consciousness from the world. You remember, for example, the symbol of water and fire, a picture in which the patient stood in flames [*Visions* Seminar]. That represents the diving-down into the unconscious, into the baptismal font of *svadhisthāna*, and the suffering of the fire of *manipura*. We now understand that the diving into the water and the enduring of the flames is not a descent, not a fall into lower levels, but an ascent. It is a development beyond the conscious ego, an experience of the personal way into the suprapersonal – a widening of the psychic horizons of the individual so as to include what is common to all mankind. When we assimilate the collective unconscious, we are not dissolving but creating it.

Only after having reached this standpoint, only after having touched the baptismal waters of *svadhisthāna*, can we realize that our conscious culture, despite all its heights, is still in *mulādhāra*. We may have reached *ajña* in our personal conscious, our race in general can be in *anāhata*, but that is all on the personal side still; it is still the *sthula* aspect, because it is only valid for our consciousness. And as long as the ego is identified with consciousness, it is caught up in this world, the world of the *mulādhāra chakra*. But we only see that it is so when we have an experience and achieve a standpoint that transcends consciousness. Only when we have become acquainted with the wide extent of the psyche, and no longer remain inside the confines of the conscious alone, can we know that our conscious is entangled in *mulādhāra*.

The symbols of the *chakra*, then, afford us a standpoint that extends beyond the conscious. They are intuitions about the psyche as a whole, about its various conditions and possibilities. They symbolize the psyche from a cosmic standpoint. It is as if a superconsciousness, an all-embracing divine consciousness, surveyed the psyche from above. Looked at from the angle of this four-dimensional consciousness, we can recognize the fact that we are still living in *mulādhāra*. That is the *suksma* aspect. Observed from that angle we ascend when we go into the unconscious, because it frees us from everyday consciousness. In the state of ordinary consciousness, we actually are down below, entangled, rooted in the earth under the spell of illusions, dependent, in short, only a little more free than the higher animals. We have culture, it is true, but our culture is not suprapersonal, it is culture in *mulādhāra*. We can indeed develop our consciousness till it reaches the *ajña* centre, but our *ajña* is a personal *ajña*, and therefore it is in *mulādhāra*. Nonetheless, we do not know that we are in *mulādhāra*, any more than the American Indians know that they are living in America. Our *ajña* is caught in this world. It is a spark of light, imprisoned in the world, and when we think, we are merely thinking in terms of this world.

But the Hindu thinks in terms of the great light. His thinking does not start from a personal, but from a cosmic *ajña*. His thinking begins with the *brahman* and ours with the ego. Our thought starts out with the individual and goes out into the general; the Hindu begins with the general and works down to the individual. From the *suksma* aspect everything is reversed: from this aspect we realize that everywhere we are still enclosed within the world of causality, that in terms of the *chakra* we are not 'high up', but absolutely 'down below'. We are sitting in a hole, in the pelvis of the world, and our *anāhata* culture is *anāhata* in *mulādhāra*. Our culture represents the conscious held prisoner in *mulādhāra*. Looked at from the *suksma* aspect everything is still in *mulādhāra*.

Christianity too is based on the *suksma* aspect. To it, too, the world is only a preparation for a higher condition, and the here and now, the state of being involved in this world, is error and sin. The sacraments and rites of the early Church all meant the freeing of man from the merely personal state of mind and allowing him to participate symbolically in a higher condition. In the mystery of baptism – the plunge into *svadhisthāna* – the 'old Adam' dies and the 'spiritual man' is born. The transfiguration and ascension of Christ is the symbolical representation and anticipation of the desired end – that is, being lifted above the personal into the suprapersonal. In the old Church, Christ represents the leader, and hence a promise of what the mystic or initiate could also attain.

But to non-Christians of the West, the here and now is the only reality. The *sthula* aspect, the rootedness in *mulādhāra*, must first be fully lived in order that we can grow beyond it afterwards. Before we get that far, we are not to know that we are caught in *mulādhāra*. In this way only can we develop our personal consciousness to the level of the *ajña* centre, and in this way only can we create culture. It is indeed only a personal culture, as I have said, but behind the culture stands God, the suprapersonal. And so we attain to the *suksma* aspect. Only then do we see that what seemed to us the summit of our endeavour is merely something personal, merely the light-spark of consciousness. Then we realize that taken from the standpoint of the psyche as a whole, it is only our personal consciousness that has attained *ajña*, but that we, from the aspect of the cosmic *chakra* system, are still in *mulādhāra*.

It is best to understand this by a metaphor. You can imagine the cosmic *chakra* system as an immense sky-scraper whose foundations go deep down in the earth and contain six cellars one above the other. One could then go from the first up to the sixth cellar, but one would still find oneself in the depths of the earth. This whole cellar system is the cosmic *mulādhāra*, and we still find ourselves in it even after we have reached the sixth cellar, i.e. our personal *ajña*. This we have to keep in mind always; otherwise we fall into the mistake made by theosophy and confuse the personal with the cosmic, the individual light-spark with the divine light. If we do this we get nowhere, but merely undergo a tremendous inflation.

Taken from the standpoint of the cosmic *chakra* system, then, we can see that we are still very low down, that our culture is a culture in *mulādhāra*, only a personal culture where the gods have not yet awakened from sleep. Therefore we have to awaken *kundalini* in order to make clear to the individual spark of consciousness the light of the gods.

NOTE

1 [As Onians (*The Origins of European Thought*, pp. 26ff.) has demonstrated, *phrenes* in Homer were the lungs – TRANSLATOR.]

12   Yoga and the spiritual crisis of the West

From: 'Yoga and the West'[1]

859   Less than a century has passed since yoga became known to the West. Although all sorts of miraculous tales had come to Europe two thousand years before from the fabled land of India, with its wise men, its gymnosophists and omphalosceptics, yet no real knowledge of Indian philosophy and philosophical practices can be said to have existed until, thanks to the efforts of the Frenchman Anquetil Duperron, the Upanishads were transmitted to the West. A general and more profound knowledge was first made possible by Max Müller, of Oxford, and the *Sacred Books of the East* edited by him. To begin with, this knowledge remained the preserve of Sanskrit scholars and philosophers. But it was not so very long before the theosophical movement inaugurated by Mme Blavatsky possessed itself of the Eastern traditions and promulgated them among the general public. For several decades after that, knowledge of yoga in the West developed along two separate lines. On the one hand it was regarded as a strictly academic science, and on the other it became something very like a religion, though it did not develop into an organized church – despite the endeavours of Annie Besant and Rudolf Steiner. Although he was the founder of the anthroposophical secession, Steiner was originally a follower of Mme Blavatsky.

860   The peculiar product resulting from this Western development can hardly be compared with what yoga means in India. In the West, Eastern teaching encountered a special situation, a condition of mind such as the earlier India, at any rate, had never known. This was the strict line of division between science and philosophy, which had already existed, to a greater or lesser degree, for some three hundred years before yoga teachings began to be known in the West. The beginning of this split – a specifically Western phenomenon – really set in with the Renaissance, in the fifteenth century. At that time, there arose a widespread and passionate interest in antiquity, stimulated by the fall of the Byzantine Empire under the onslaught of Islam. Then, for the first time, knowledge of the Greek language and of Greek literature was carried to every corner of Europe. As a direct result of this invasion of so-called pagan philosophy, there arose the great schism in the Roman Church – Protestantism, which soon

covered the whole of northern Europe. But not even this renewal of Christianity was able to hold the liberated minds in thrall.

861   The period of world discovery in the geographical and scientific sense had begun, and to an ever-increasing degree thought emancipated itself from the shackles of religious tradition. The Churches, of course, continued to exist because they were maintained by the strictly religious needs of the public, but they lost their leadership in the cultural sphere. While the Church of Rome, thanks to her unsurpassed organization, remained a unity, Protestantism split into nearly four hundred denominations. This is a proof on the one hand of its bankruptcy and, on the other, of a religious vitality which refuses to be stifled. Gradually, in the course of the nineteenth century, this led to syncretistic outgrowths and to the importation on a mass scale of exotic religious systems, such as the religion of Abdul Baha, the Sufi sects, the Ramakrishna Mission, Buddhism and so on. Many of these systems, for instance anthroposophy, were syncretized with Christian elements. The resultant picture corresponds roughly to the Hellenistic syncretism of the third and fourth centuries AD, which likewise showed traces of Indian thought. (Cf. Apollonius of Tyana, the Orphic–Pythagorean secret doctrines, the Gnosis, etc.)

862   All these systems moved on the religious plane and recruited the great majority of their adherents from Protestantism. They are thus, fundamentally, Protestant sects. By directing its main attack against the authority of the Roman Church, Protestantism largely destroyed belief in the Church as the indispensable agent of divine salvation. Thus the burden of authority fell to the individual, and with it a religious responsibility that had never existed before. The decline of confession and absolution sharpened the moral conflict of the individual and burdened him with problems which previously the Church had settled for him, since her sacraments, particularly that of the Mass, guaranteed his salvation through the priest's enactment of the sacred rite. The only things the individual had to contribute were confession, repentance and penance. With the collapse of the rite, which did the work for him, he had to do without God's answer to his plans. This dissatisfaction explains the demand for systems that promise an answer – the visible or at least noticeable favour of another (higher, spiritual or divine) power.

863   European science paid no attention to these hopes and expectations. It lived its intellectual life unconcerned with religious needs and convictions. This – historically inevitable – split in the Western mind also affected yoga so far as this had gained a footing in the West, and led to its being made an object of scientific study on the one hand, while on the other it was welcomed as a way of salvation. But inside the religious movement there were any number of attempts to combine science with religious belief and practice, as for instance Christian Science, theosophy and anthroposophy. The last-named, especially, likes to give itself scientific airs and has, therefore, like Christian Science, penetrated into intellectual circles.

864   Since the way of the Protestant is not laid down for him in advance, he gives welcome, one might say, to practically any system which holds out the promise of successful development. He must now do for himself the very thing which had always been done by the Church as intermediary, and he does not know *how* to do it. If he is a man who has taken his religious needs seriously, he has also made untold efforts towards faith, because his doctrine sets exclusive store by faith. But faith is a charisma, a gift of grace, and not a method. The Protestant is so entirely without a method that many of them have seriously interested themselves in the rigorously Catholic exercises of Ignatius Loyola. Yet, do what they will, the thing that disturbs them most is naturally the contradiction between religious and scientific truth, the conflict between faith and knowledge, which reaches far beyond Protestantism into Catholicism itself. This conflict is due solely to the historical split in the European mind. Had it not been for the – psychologically speaking – unnatural compulsion to believe, and an equally unnatural belief in science, this conflict would have had no reason to exist. One can easily imagine a state of mind in which one simply *knows* and in addition *believes* a thing which seems probable for such and such reasons. There are no grounds whatsoever for any conflict between these two things. Both are necessary, for knowledge alone, like faith alone, is always insufficient.

865   When, therefore, a 'religious' method recommends itself at the same time as 'scientific', it can be sure of finding a public in the West. Yoga fulfils this expectation. Quite apart from the charm of the new and the fascination of the half-understood, there is good reason for yoga to have many adherents. It offers not only the much-sought way, but also a philosophy of unrivalled profundity. It holds out the possibility of controllable experience, and thus satisfies the scientist's need for 'facts'. Moreover, by reason of its breadth and depth, its venerable age, its teachings and methods, which cover every sphere of life, it promises undreamed-of possibilities, which the missionaries of yoga seldom omit to emphasize.

866   I will remain silent on the subject of what yoga means for India, because I cannot presume to judge something I do not know from personal experience. I can, however, say something about what it means for the West. Our lack of direction borders on psychic anarchy. Therefore, any religious or philosophical practice amounts to a psychological discipline; in other words, it is a method of psychic hygiene. The numerous purely physical procedures of yoga are a physiological hygiene as well, which is far superior to ordinary gymnastics or breathing exercises in that it is not merely mechanistic and scientific but, at the same time, philosophical. In its training of the parts of the body, it unites them with the whole of the mind and spirit, as is quite clear, for instance, in the *prānayāma* exercises, where *prāna* is both the breath and the universal dynamics of the cosmos. When the doing of the individual is at the same time a cosmic happening, the elation of the body (innervation) becomes one with the elation of the

spirit (the universal idea), and from this there arises a living whole which no technique, however scientific, can hope to produce. Yoga practice is unthinkable, and would also be ineffectual, without the ideas on which it is based. It works the physical and the spiritual into one another in an extraordinarily complete way.

867   In the East, where these ideas and practices originated, and where an uninterrupted tradition extending over some four thousand years has created the necessary spiritual conditions, yoga is, as I can readily believe, the perfect and appropriate method of fusing body and mind together so that they form a unity that can hardly be doubted. They thus create a psychological disposition which makes possible intuitions that transcend consciousness. The Indian mentality has no difficulty in operating intelligently with a concept like *prāna*. The West, on the contrary, with its bad habit of wanting to believe on the one hand, and its highly developed scientific and philosophical critique on the other, finds itself in a real dilemma. Either it falls into the trap of faith and swallows concepts like *prāna, atman, chakra, samādhi,* etc., without giving them a thought, or its scientific critique repudiates them one and all as 'pure mysticism'. The split in the Western mind therefore makes it impossible at the outset for the intentions of yoga to be realized in any adequate way. It becomes either a strictly religious matter, or else a kind of training like Pelmanism, breath-control, eurhythmics, etc., and not a trace is to be found of the unity and wholeness of nature which is characteristic of yoga. The Indian can forget neither the body nor the mind, while the European is always forgetting either the one or the other. With this capacity to forget he has, for the time being, conquered the world. Not so the Indian. He not only knows his own nature, but he knows also how much he himself is nature. The European, on the other hand, has a science of nature and knows astonishingly little of his own nature, the nature within him. For the Indian, it comes as a blessing to know of a method which helps him to control the supreme power of nature within and without. For the European, it is sheer poison to suppress his nature, which is warped enough as it is, and to make out of it a willing robot.

868   It is said of the yogi that he can remove mountains, though it would be difficult to furnish any real proof of this. The power of the yogi operates within limits acceptable to his environment. The European, on the other hand, can blow up mountains, and the World War has given us a bitter foretaste of what he is capable of when free rein is given to an intellect that has grown estranged from human nature. As a European, I cannot wish the European more 'control' and more power over the nature within and around us. Indeed, I must confess to my shame that I owe my best insights (and there are some quite good ones among them) to the circumstances that I have always done just the opposite of what the rules of yoga prescribe. Through his historical development, the European has become so far removed from his roots that his mind was finally split into faith and

knowledge, in the same way that every psychological exaggeration breaks up into its inherent opposites. He needs to return, not to Nature in the manner of Rousseau, but to his own nature. His task is to find the natural man again. Instead of this, there is nothing he likes better than systems and methods by which he can repress the natural man who is everywhere at cross-purposes with him. He will infallibly make a wrong use of yoga because his psychic disposition is quite different from that of the Oriental. I say to whomsoever I can: 'Study yoga – you will learn an infinite amount from it – but do not try to apply it, for we Europeans are not so constituted that we apply these methods correctly, just like that. An Indian guru can explain everything and you can imitate everything. But do you know *who* is applying the yoga? In other words, do you know who you are and how you are constituted?'

869   The power of science and technics in Europe is so enormous and indisputable that there is little point in reckoning up all that can be done and all that has been invented. One shudders at the stupendous possibilities. Quite another question begins to loom up: *Who* is applying this technical skill? In *whose* hands does this power lie? For the present, the state is a provisional means of protection, because, apparently, it safeguards the citizen from the enormous quantities of poison gas and other infernal engines of destruction which can be manufactured by the thousand tons at a moment's notice. Our technical skill has grown to be so dangerous that the most urgent question today is not what *more* can be done in this line, but how the man who is entrusted with the control of this skill should be constituted, or how to alter the mind of Western man so that he would renounce his terrible skill. It is infinitely more important to strip him of the illusion of his power than to strengthen him still further in the mistaken idea that he can do everything he wills. The slogan one hears so often in Germany, 'Where there's a will there's a way', has cost the lives of millions of human beings.

870   Western man has no need of more superiority over nature, whether outside or inside. He has both in almost devilish perfection. What he lacks is conscious recognition of his inferiority to the nature around and within him. He must learn that he may not do exactly as he wills. If he does not learn this, his own nature will destroy him. He does not know that his own soul is rebelling against him in a suicidal way.

871   Since Western man can turn everything into a technique, it is true in principle that everything that looks like a method is either dangerous or condemned to futility. In so far as yoga is a form of hygiene, it is as useful to him as any other system. In the deepest sense, however, yoga does not mean this but, if I understand it correctly, a great deal more, namely the final release and detachment of consciousness from all bondage to object and subject. But since one cannot detach oneself from something of which one is unconscious, the European must first learn to know his subject. This, in the West, is what one calls the unconscious. Yoga technique applies

itself exclusively to the conscious mind and will. Such an undertaking promises success only when the unconscious has no potential worth mentioning, that is to say, when it does not contain large portions of the personality. If it does, then all conscious effort remains futile, and what comes out of this cramped condition of mind is a caricature or even the exact opposite of the intended result.

872   The rich metaphysic and symbolism of the East express the larger and more important part of the unconscious and in this way reduce its potential. When the yogi says '*prāna*', he means very much more than mere breath. For him the word *prāna* brings with it the full weight of its metaphysical components, and it is as if he really knew what *prāna* meant in this respect. He does not know it with his understanding, but with his heart, belly and blood. The European only imitates and learns ideas by rote, and is therefore incapable of expressing his subjective facts through Indian concepts. I am more than doubtful whether the European, if he were capable of the corresponding experiences, would choose to express them through intuitive ideas like *prāna*.

873   Yoga was originally a natural process of introversion, with all manner of individual variations. Introversions of this sort lead to peculiar inner processes which change the personality. In the course of several thousand years these introversions became organized as methods, and along widely differing lines. Indian yoga itself recognizes numerous and extremely diverse forms. The reason for this lies in the original diversity of individual experience. This is not to say that any one of these methods is suited to the peculiar historical structure of the European. It is much more likely that the yoga natural to the European proceeds from historical patterns unknown to the East. As a matter of fact, the two cultural achievements which, in the West, have had to concern themselves most with the psyche in the practical sense, namely medicine and the Catholic cure of souls, have both produced methods comparable to yoga. I have already referred to the exercises of Ignatius Loyola. With respect to medicine, it is the modern psychotherapeutic methods which come closest to yoga. Freud's psychoanalysis leads the conscious mind of the patient back to the inner world of childhood reminiscences on one side, and on the other to wishes and drives which have been repressed from consciousness. The latter technique is a logical development of confession. It aims at an artificial introversion for the purpose of making conscious the unconscious components of the subject.

874   A somewhat different method is the so-called 'autogenic training' of Professor Schultz,[2] which consciously links up with yoga. His chief aim is to break down the conscious cramp and the repression of the unconscious this has caused.

875   My method, like Freud's, is built up on the practice of confession. Like him, I pay close attention to dreams, but when it comes to the unconscious our views part company. For Freud it is essentially an appendage of

consciousness, in which all the individual's incompatibilities are heaped up. For me the unconscious is a collective psychic disposition, creative in character. This fundamental difference of viewpoint naturally produces an entirely different evaluation of the symbolism and the method of interpreting it. Freud's procedure is, in the main, analytical and reductive. To this I add a synthesis which emphasizes the purposiveness of unconscious tendencies with respect to personality development. In this line of research important parallels with yoga have come to light, especially with *kundalini* yoga and the symbolism of Tantric yoga, lamaism, and Taoistic yoga in China. These forms of yoga with their rich symbolism afford me invaluable comparative material for interpreting the collective unconscious. However, I do not apply yoga methods in principle, because, in the West, nothing ought to be forced on the unconscious. Usually, consciousness is characterized by an intensity and narrowness that have a cramping effect, and this ought not to be emphasized still further. On the contrary, everything must be done to help the unconscious to reach the conscious mind and to free it from its rigidity. For this purpose I employ a method of active imagination, which consists in a special training for switching off consciousness, at least to a relative extent, thus giving the unconscious contents a chance to develop.

876   If I remain so critically averse to yoga, it does not mean that I do not regard this spiritual achievement of the East as one of the greatest things the human mind has ever created. I hope my exposition makes it sufficiently clear that my criticism is directed solely against the application of yoga to the people of the West. The spiritual development of the West has been along entirely different lines from that of the East and has therefore produced conditions which are the most unfavourable soil one can think of for the application of yoga. Western civilization is scarcely a thousand years old and must first of all free itself from its barbarous one-sidedness. This means, above all, deeper insight into the nature of man. But no insight is gained by repressing and controlling the unconscious, and least of all by imitating methods which have grown up under totally different psychological conditions. In the course of the centuries the West will produce its own yoga, and it will be on the basis laid down by Christianity.

NOTES

1 [Originally published in *Prabuddha Bharata* (Calcutta), February 1936, Shri Ramakrishna Centenary Number, Sec. III, in a translation by Cary F. Baynes, upon which the present translation is based. – EDITORS.]

2 The German psychiatrist J. H. Schultz. The reference is to his book *Das autogene Training* (Berlin, 1932). – EDITORS.]

13 Meditation and Western psychology

From: 'The Psychology of Eastern Meditation'[1]

908   The profound relationship between yoga and the hieratic architecture of India has already been pointed out by my friend Heinrich Zimmer, whose unfortunate early death is a great loss to indology. Anyone who has visited Borobudur or seen the *stupas* at Bharhut and Sanchi can hardly avoid feeling that an attitude of mind and a vision quite foreign to the European have been at work here – if he has not already been brought to this realization by a thousand other impressions of Indian life. In the overflowing wealth of Indian spirituality there is reflected a vision of the soul which at first appears strange and inaccessible to the Greek-trained European mind. Our minds perceive things, our eyes, as Gottfried Keller says, 'drink what the eyelids hold of the golden abundance of the world', and we draw conclusions about the inner world from our wealth of outward impressions. We even derive its content from outside on the principle that 'nothing is in the mind which was not previously in the senses'. This principle seems to have no validity in India. Indian thought and Indian art merely *appear* in the sense-world, but do not derive from it. Although often expressed with startling sensuality, they are, in their truest essence, unsensual, not to say suprasensual. It is not the world of the senses, of the body, of colours and sounds, not human passions that are born anew in transfigured form, or with realistic pathos, through the creativity of the Indian soul, but rather an underworld or an overworld of a metaphysical nature, out of which strange forms emerge into the familiar earthly scene. For instance, if one carefully observes the tremendously impressive impersonations of the gods performed by the Kathakali dancers of southern India, there is not a single *natural* gesture to be seen. Everything is bizarre, subhuman and superhuman at once. The dancers do not walk like human beings – they glide; they do not think with their heads but with their hands. Even their human faces vanish behind blue-enamelled masks. The world we know offers nothing even remotely comparable to this grotesque splendour. Watching these spectacles one is transported to a world of dreams, for that is the only place where we might conceivably meet with anything similar. But the Kathakali dancers, as we see them in the flesh or in the temple sculptures, are no nocturnal phantoms; they are

intensely dynamic figures, consistent in every detail, or as if they had grown organically. These are no shadows or ghosts of a bygone reality, they are more like realities which have *not yet been*, potential realities which might at any moment step over the threshold.

909   Anyone who wholeheartedly surrenders to these impressions will soon notice that these figures do not strike the Indians themselves as dreamlike but as real. And, indeed, they touch upon something in our own depths, too, with an almost terrifying intensity, though we have no words to express it. At the same time, one notices that the more deeply one is stirred the more our sense-world fades into a dream, and that we seem to wake up in a world of gods, so immediate is their reality.

910   What the European notices at first in India is the outward corporeality he sees everywhere. But that is not India as the Indian sees it; that is not *his* reality. Reality, as the German word 'Wirklichkeit' implies, is that which *works*. For us the essence of that which works is the world of appearance; for the Indian it is the soul. The world for him is a mere show or façade, and his reality comes close to being what we would call a dream.

911   This strange antithesis between East and West is expressed more clearly in religious practice. We speak of religious uplift and exaltation; for us God is the Lord of the universe, we have a religion of brotherly love, and in our heaven-aspiring churches there is a *high altar*. The Indian, on the other hand, speaks of *dhyāna*, of self-immersion, and of *sinking* into meditation; God is within all things and especially man, and one turns away from the outer world to the inner. In the old Indian temples the altar is sunk six to eight feet deep in the earth, and what we hide most shamefacedly is the holiest symbol to the Indian. We believe in *doing*, the Indian in impassive *being*. Our religious exercises consist of prayer, worship and singing hymns. The Indian's most important exercise is yoga, an immersion in what we would call an unconscious state, but which he praises as the highest consciousness. Yoga is the most eloquent expression of the Indian mind and at the same time the instrument continually used to produce this peculiar attitude of mind.

912   What, then, is yoga? The word means literally 'yoking', i.e. the disciplining of the instinctual forces of the psyche, which in Sanskrit are called *kleshas*. The yoking aims at controlling these forces that fetter human beings to the world. The *kleshas* would correspond, in the language of St Augustine, to *superbia* and *concupiscentia*. There are many different forms of yoga, but all of them pursue the same goal. Here I will only mention that besides the purely psychic exercises there is also a form called *hatha* yoga, a sort of gymnastics consisting chiefly of breathing exercises and special body postures. In this lecture I have undertaken to describe a yoga text which allows a deep insight into the psychic processes of yoga. It is a little-known Buddhist text, written in Chinese but translated from the original Sanskrit, and dating from AD 424. It is called the *Amitā-yur-dhyāna Sūtra*, the Sutra of Medication on Amitāyus. This *sutra*, highly

valued in Japan, belongs to the sphere of theistic Buddhism, in which is found the teaching that the Ādi-Buddha or Mahābuddha, the Primordial Buddha, brought forth the five Dhyāni-Buddhas or Dhyāni-Bodhisattvas. One of the five is Amitābha, 'the Buddha of the *setting sun* of immeasurable light', the Lord of Sukhāvati, land of supreme bliss. He is the protector of our present world-period, just as Shākyamuni, the historical Buddha, is its teacher. In the cult of Amitābha there is, oddly enough, a kind of Eucharistic feast with consecrated bread. He is sometimes depicted holding in his hand the vessel of the life-giving food of immortality, or the vessel of holy water.

913   The text[2] begins with an introductory story that need not detain us here. A crown prince seeks to take the life of his parents, and in her extremity the queen calls upon the Buddha for help, praying him to send her his two disciples Maudgalyāyana and Ānanda. The Buddha fulfils her wish, and the two appear at once. At the same time Shākyamuni, the Buddha himself, appears before her eyes. He shows her in a vision all the ten worlds, so that she can choose in which one she wishes to be reborn. She chooses the western realm of Amitābha. He then teaches her the yoga which should enable her to retain rebirth in the Amitābha land, and after giving her various moral instructions he speaks to her as follows:

914   You and all other beings besides ought to make it their only aim, with concentrated thought, to get a perception of the western quarter. You will ask how that perception is to be formed. I will explain it now. All beings, if not blind from birth, are uniformly possessed of sight, and they all see the setting sun. You should sit down properly, looking in the western direction, and prepare your thought for a close meditation on the sun: cause your mind to be firmly fixed on it so as to have an unwavering perception by the exclusive application of your thought, and gaze upon it more particularly when it is about to set and looks like a suspended drum. After you have thus seen the sun, let that image remain clear and fixed, whether your eyes be shut or open. Such is the perception of the sun, which is the First Meditation.

915   As we have already seen, the setting sun is an allegory of the immortality-dispensing Amitābha. The text continues:

Next you should form the perception of water; gaze on the water clear and pure, and let this image also remain clear and fixed afterwards; never allow your thought to be scattered and lost.

916   As already mentioned, Amitābha is also the dispenser of the water of immortality.

917   When you have thus seen the water you should form the perception of ice. As you see the ice shining and transparent, so you should imagine the appearance of lapis lazuli. After that has been done, you will see the

ground consisting of lapis lazuli transparent and shining both within and without. Beneath this ground of lapis lazuli there will be seen a golden banner with the seven jewels, diamonds, and the rest, supporting the ground. It extends to the eight points of the compass, and thus the eight corners of the ground are perfectly filled up. Every side of the eight quarters consists of a hundred jewels, every jewel has a thousand rays, and every ray has eighty-four thousand colours which, when reflected in the ground of lapis lazuli, look like a thousand millions of suns, and it is difficult to see them all one by one. Over the surface of that ground of lapis lazuli there are stretched golden ropes intertwined crosswise; divisions are made by means of [strings of] seven jewels with every part clear and distinct . . ..

When this perception has been formed you should meditate on its constituents one by one and make the images as clear as possible, so that they may never be scattered and lost, whether your eyes be shut or open. Except only during the time of your sleep, you should always keep this in mind. One who has reached this stage of perception is said to have dimly seen the Land of Highest Happiness [Sukhāvati]. One who has obtained *samādhi* [the state of supernatural calm] is able to see the land of that Buddha country clearly and distinctly; this state is too much to be explained fully. Such is the perception of the land, and it is the Third Meditation.

918   *Samādhi* is 'withdrawnness', i.e. a condition in which all connections with the world are absorbed into the inner world. *Samādhi* is the eighth phase of the Eightfold Path.

919   After the above comes a meditation on the Jewel Tree of the Amitābha land, and then follows the meditation on water:

In the Land of Highest Happiness there are waters in eight lakes; the water in every lake consists of seven jewels which are soft and yielding. Its source derives from the king of jewels that fulfils every wish [*cintāmani*, the wishing-pearl] . . .. In the midst of each lake there are sixty millions of lotus-flowers, made of seven jewels; all the flowers are perfectly round and exactly equal in circumference . . .. The water of jewels flows amidst the flowers and . . . the sound of the streaming water is melodious and pleasing. It proclaims all the perfect virtues [*pāramitās*], 'suffering', 'non-existence', 'impermanence' and 'non-self'; it proclaims also the praise of the signs of perfection, and minor marks of excellence, of all Buddhas. From king of jewels that fulfils every wish stream forth the golden-coloured rays excessively beautiful, the radiance of which transforms itself into birds possessing the colours of a hundred jewels, which sing out harmonious notes, sweet and delicious, ever praising the remembrance of the Buddha, the remembrance of the Law, and the remembrance of the Church. Such is the perception of the water of eight good qualities, and it is the Fifth Meditation.

920   Concering the meditation on Amitābha himself, the Buddha instructs the queen in the following manner: 'Form the perception of a lotus-flower on a ground of seven jewels.' The flower has 84,000 petals, each petal 84,000 veins, and each vein possesses 84,000 rays, 'of which each can clearly be seen'.

921   When you have perceived this, you should next perceive the Buddha himself. Do you ask how? Every Buddha Tathāgata is one whose spiritual body is the principle of nature [*Dharmadhātu-kāya*], so that he may enter into the mind of all beings. Consequently, when you have perceived the Buddha, it is indeed that mind of yours that possesses those thirty-two signs of perfection and eighty minor marks of excellence which you see in the Buddha. In fine, it is your mind that becomes the Buddha, nay, it is your mind that is indeed the Buddha. The ocean of true and universal knowledge of all the Buddhas derives its source from one's own mind and thought. Therefore you should apply your thought with undivided attention to a careful meditation on that Buddha Tathāgata, the *Arhat*, the Holy and Fully Enlightened One. In forming the perception of that Buddha, you should first perceive the image of that Buddha; whether your eyes be open or shut, look at him as at an image like to Jambunada[3] gold in colour, sitting on the flower.

When you have seen the seated figure your mental vision will become clear, and you will be able to see clearly and distinctly the adornment of that Buddha-country, the jewelled ground, etc. In seeing these things let them be clear and fixed just as you see the palms of your hands . . ..

If you pass through this experience, you will at the same time see all the Buddhas of the ten quarters . . .. Those who have practised this meditation are said to have contemplated the bodies of all the Buddhas. Since they have meditated on the Buddha's body, they will also see the Buddha's mind. It is great compassion that is called the Buddha's mind. It is by his absolute compassion that he receives all beings. Those who have practised this meditation will, when they die, be born in the presence of the Buddhas in another life, and obtain a spirit of resignation wherewith to face all the consequences which shall hereafter arise. Therefore those who have wisdom should direct their thought to the careful meditation upon that Buddha Amitāyus.

922   Of those who practise this meditation it is said that they no longer live in an embryonic condition but will 'obtain free access to the excellent and admirable countries of Buddhas'.

923   After you have had this perception, you should imagine yourself to be born in the World of Highest Happiness in the western quarter, and to be seated, cross-legged, on a lotus-flower there. Then imagine that the flower has shut you in and has afterwards unfolded; when the flower has thus unfolded, five hundred coloured rays will shine over your body,

your eyes will be opened so as to see the Buddhas and Bodhisattvas who fill the whole sky; you will hear the sounds of waters and trees, the notes of birds, and the voices of many Buddhas . . . .

924   The Buddha then says to Ānanda and Vaidehi (the Queen):

Those who wish, by means of their serene thoughts, to be born in the western land, should first meditate on an image of the Buddha, which is sixteen cubits high, seated on a lotus-flower in the water of the lake. As was stated before, the real body and its measurements are unlimited, incomprehensible to the ordinary mind. But by the efficacy of the ancient prayer of that Tathāgata, those who think of and remember him shall certainly be able to accomplish their aim.

925   The Buddha's speech continues for many pages, then the text says:

When the Buddha had finished this speech, Vaidehi, together with her five hundred female attendants, guided by the Buddha's words, could see the scene of the far-stretching World of the Highest Happiness, and could also see the body of the Buddha and the bodies of the two Bodhisattvas. With her mind filled with joy she praised them, saying: 'Never have I seen such a wonder!' Instantly she became wholly and fully enlightened, and attained a spirit of resignation, prepared to endure whatever consequences might yet arise. Her five hundred female attendants too cherished the thought of obtaining the highest perfect knowledge, and sought to be born in the Buddha-country. The World-Honoured One predicted that they would all be born in that Buddha-country, and be able to obtain *samādhi* of the presence of many Buddhas.

926   In a digression on the fate of the unenlightened, the Buddha sums up the yoga exercise as follows:

But, being harassed by pains, he will have no time to think of the Buddha. Some good friend will then say to him: 'Even if you cannot exercise the remembrance of the Buddha, you may, at least, utter the name, "Buddha Amitāyus."' Let him do so serenely with his voice uninterrupted; let him be continually thinking of the Buddha until he has completed ten times the thought, repeating the formula, 'Adoration to Buddha Amitāyus.' On the strength of his merit in uttering the Buddha's name he will, during every repetition, expiate the sins which involve him in births and deaths during eighty millions of *kalpas*. He will, while dying, see a golden lotus-flower like the disc of the sun appearing before his eyes; in a moment he will be born in the World of Highest Happiness.

927   The above quotations form the essential content of the yoga exercise which interests us here. The text is divided into sixteen meditations, from

which I have chosen only certain parts, but they will suffice to portray the intensification of the meditation, culminating in *samādhi*, the highest ecstasy and enlightenment.

928   The exercise begins with the concentration on the setting sun. In southern latitudes the intensity of the rays of the setting sun is so strong that a few moments of gazing at it are enough to create an intense after-image. With closed eyes one continues to see the sun for some time. As is well known, one method of hypnosis consists in fixating a shining object, such as a diamond or a crystal. Presumably the fixation of the sun is meant to produce a similar hypnotic effect. On the other hand it should not have a soporific effect, because a 'meditation' of the sun must accompany the fixation. This meditation is a reflecting, a 'making-clear', in fact a *realization* of the sun, its form, its qualities and its meanings. Since the round form plays such an important role in the subsequent meditations, we may suppose that the sun's disc serves as a model for the later fantasies of circular structures, just as, by reason of its intense light, it prepares the way for the resplendent visions that come afterwards. In this manner, so the text says, 'the perception is to be formed'.

929   The next meditation, that of the water, is no longer based on any sense-impression but creates through active imagination the image of a reflecting expanse of water. This, as we know, throws back the full light of the sun. It should now be imagined that the water changes into ice, 'shining and transparent'. Through this procedure the immaterial light of the sun-image is transformed into the substance of water and this in turn into the solidity of ice. A concretization of the vision is evidently aimed at, and this results in a materialization of the fantasy-creation, which appears in the place of physical nature, of the world as we know it. A different reality is created, so to speak, out of soul-stuff. The ice, of a bluish colour by nature, changes into blue lapis lazuli, a solid, stony substance, which then becomes a 'ground', 'transparent and shining'. With this 'ground' an immutable, absolutely real foundation has been created. The blue translucent floor is like a lake of glass, and through its transparent layers one's gaze penetrates into the depths below.

930   The so-called 'golden banner' then shines forth out of these depths. It should be noted that the Sanskrit word *dhvaja* also means 'sign' or 'symbol' in general. So we could speak just as well of the appearance of the 'symbol'. It is evident that the symbol 'extending to the eight points of the compass' represents the ground plan of an eight-rayed system. As the text says, the 'eight corners of the ground are perfectly filled up' by the banner. The system shines 'like a thousand millions of suns', so that the shining after-image of the sun has enormously increased its radiant energy, and its illuminative power has now been intensified to an immeasurable degree. The strange idea of the 'golden ropes' spread over the system like a net presumably means that the system is tied together and secured in this way, so that it can no longer fall apart. Unfortunately the

text says nothing about a possible failure of the method, or about the phenomena of disintegration which might supervene as the result of a mistake. But disturbances of this kind in an imaginative process are nothing unexpected to an expert – on the contrary, they are a regular occurrence. So it is not surprising that a kind of inner reinforcement of the image is provided in the yoga vision by means of golden ropes.

931   Although not explicitly stated in the text, the eight-rayed system is already the Amitābha land. In it grow wonderful trees, as is meet and proper, for this is paradise. Especial importance attaches to the water of the Amitābha land. In accordance with the octagonal system, it is arranged in the form of eight lakes, and the source of these waters is a central jewel, *cintāmani*, the wishing pearl, a symbol of the 'treasure hard to attain',[4] the highest value. In Chinese art it appears as a moonlike image, frequently associated with a dragon.[5] The wondrous sounds of the water consist of two pairs of opposites which proclaim the dogmatic ground truths of Buddhism: 'suffering and non-existence, impermanence and non-self', signifying that all existence is full of suffering, and that everything that clings to the ego is impermanent. Not-being and not-being-ego deliver us from these errors. Thus the singing water is something like the teaching of the Buddha – a redeeming water of wisdom, an *aqua doctrinae*, to use an expression of Origen. The source of this water, the pearl without peer, is the Tathāgata, the Buddha himself. Hence the imaginative reconstruction of the Buddha-image follows immediately afterwards, and while this structure is being built up in the meditation it is realized that the Buddha is really nothing other than the activating psyche of the yogi – the meditator himself. It is not only that the image of the Buddha is produced out of 'one's own mind and thought', but the psyche which produces these thought-forms *is the Buddha himself*.

932   The image of the Buddha sits in the round lotus in the centre of the octagonal Amitābha land. He is distinguished by the great compassion with which he 'receives all beings', including the meditator. This means that the inmost being which is the Buddha is bodied forth in the vision and revealed as the true self of the meditator. He experiences himself as the only thing that exists, as the highest consciousness, even the Buddha. In order to attain this final goal it was necessary to pass through all the laborious exercises of mental reconstruction, to get free of the deluded ego-consciousness which is responsible for the sorrowful illusion of the world, and to reach that other pole of the psyche where the world as illusion is abolished.

933 Although it appears exceedingly obscure to the European, this yoga text is not a mere literary museum piece. It lives in the psyche of every Indian, in this form and in many others, so that his life and thinking are permeated by it down to the smallest details. It was not Buddhism that nurtured and educated this psyche, but yoga. Buddhism itself was born of the spirit of

yoga, which is older and more universal than the historical reformation wrought by the Buddha. Anyone who seeks to understand Indian art, philosophy and ethics from the inside must of necessity befriend this spirit. Our habitual understanding from the outside breaks down here, because it is hopelessly inadequate to the nature of Indian spirituality. And I wish particularly to warn against the oft-attempted imitation of Indian practices and sentiments. As a rule nothing comes of it except an artificial stultification of our Western intelligence. Of course, if anyone should succeed in giving up Europe from every point of view, and could actually *be* nothing but a yogi and sit in the lotus position with all the practical and ethical consequences that this entails, evaporating on a gazelle-skin under a dusty banyan tree and ending his days in nameless non-being, then I should have to admit that such a person understood yoga in the Indian manner. But anyone who cannot do this should not behave as if he did. He cannot and should not give up his Western understanding; on the contrary, he should apply it honestly, without imitation or sentimentality, to understanding as much of yoga as is possible for the Western mind. The secrets of yoga mean as much or even more to the Indian than our own Christian mysteries mean to us, and just as we would not allow any foreigner to make our *mysterium fidei* ludicrous, so we should not belittle these strange Indian ideas and practices or scorn them as absurd errors. By so doing we only block the way to a sensible understanding. Indeed, we in Europe have already gone so far in this direction that the spiritual content of our Christian dogma has disappeared in a rationalistic and 'enlightened' fog of alarming density, and this makes it all too easy for us to undervalue those things which we do not know and do not understand.

934   If we wish to understand at all, we can do so only in the European way. One can, it is true, understand many things with the heart, but then the head often finds it difficult to follow up with an intellectual formulation that gives suitable expression to what has been understood. There is also an understanding with the head, particularly of the Christian kind, where there is sometimes too little room for the heart. We must therefore leave it to the goodwill and co-operation of the reader to use first one and then the other. So let us first attempt, with the head, to find or build that hidden bridge which may lead to a European understanding of yoga.

935   For this purpose we must again take up the series of symbols we have already discussed, but this time we shall consider their sense-content. The *sun*, with which the series begins, is the source of warmth and light, the indubitable central point of our visible world. As the giver of life it is always and everywhere either the divinity itself or an image of the same. Even in the world of Christian ideas, the sun is a favourite allegory of Christ. A second source of life, especially in southern countries, is *water*, which also plays an important role in Christian allegory, for instance, as the four rivers of paradise and the waters which issued from the side of the Temple (Ezekiel 47). The latter were compared to the blood that flowed

from the wound in Christ's side. In this connection I would also mention Christ's talk with the woman of Samaria at the well, and the rivers of living water flowing from the body of Christ (John 7:38). A meditation on sun and water evokes these and similar associations without fail, so that the meditator will gradually be led from the foreground of visible appearances into the background, that is, to the spiritual meaning behind the object of meditation. He is transported to the psychic sphere, where sun and water, divested of their physical objectivity, become symbols of psychic contents, images of the source of life in the individual psyche. For indeed our consciousness does not create itself – it wells up from unknown depths. In childhood it awakens gradually, and all through life it wakes each morning out of the depths of sleep from an unconscious condition. It is like a child that is born daily out of the primordial womb of the unconscious. In fact, closer investigation reveals that it is not only influenced by the unconscious but continually emerges out of it in the form of numberless spontaneous ideas and sudden flashes of thought. Meditation on the meaning of sun and water is therefore something like a descent into the fountainhead of the psyche, into the unconscious itself.

936   Here, then, is a great difference between the Eastern and the Western mind. It is the same difference as the one we met before: the difference between the high and the low altar. The West is always seeking uplift, but the East seeks a sinking or deepening. Outer reality, with its bodiliness and weight, appears to make a much stronger and sharper impression on the European than it does on the Indian. Therefore the European seeks to raise himself above this world, while the Indian likes to turn back into the maternal depths of Nature.

937   Just as the Christian contemplative, for instance in the *Exercitia spiritualia* of Loyola, strives to comprehend the holy image as concretely as possible, with all the senses, so the yogi solidifies the water he contemplates first to ice and then to lapis lazuli, thereby creating a firm 'ground', as he calls it. He makes, so to speak, a solid body for his vision. In this way he endows the figures of his psychic world with a concrete reality which takes the place of the outer world. At first he sees nothing but a reflecting blue surface, like that of a lake or ocean (also a favourite symbol of the unconscious in our Western dreams); but under the shining surface unknown depths lie hidden, dark and mysterious.

938   As the text says, the blue is *transparent*, which informs us that the gaze of the meditator can penetrate into the depths of the psyche's secrets. There he sees what could not be seen before, i.e. what was unconscious. Just as sun and water are the physical sources of life, so, as symbols, they express the essential secret of the life of the unconscious. In the *banner*, the symbol the yogi sees through the floor of lapis lazuli, he beholds, as it were, an image of the source of consciousness, which before was invisible and apparently without form. Through *dhyāna*, through the sinking and deepening of contemplation, the unconscious has evidently

taken on form. It is as if the light of consciousness had ceased to illuminate the objects of the outer world of the senses and now illumines the darkness of the unconscious. If the world of the senses and all thought of it are completely extinguished, then the inner world springs into relief more distinctly.

939   Here the Eastern text skips over a psychic phenomenon that is a source of endless difficulties for the European. If a European tries to banish all thought of the outer world and to empty his mind of everything outside, he immediately becomes the prey of his own subjective fantasies, which have nothing whatever to do with the images mentioned in our text. Fantasies do not enjoy a good reputation; they are considered cheap and worthless and are therefore rejected as useless and meaningless. They are the *kleshas*, the disorderly and chaotic instinctual forces which yoga proposes to yoke. The *Exercitia spiritualia* pursue the same goal; in fact both methods seek to attain success by providing the meditator with an object to contemplate and showing him the image he has to concentrate on in order to shut out the allegedly worthless fantasies. Both methods, Eastern as well as Western, try to reach the goal by a direct path. I do not wish to question the possibilities of success when the meditation exercise is conducted in some kind of ecclesiastical setting. But, outside of some such setting, the thing does not as a rule work, or it may even lead to deplorable results. By throwing light on the unconscious one gets first of all into the chaotic sphere of the personal unconscious, which contains all that one would like to forget, and all that one does not wish to admit to oneself or to anybody else, and which one prefers to believe is not true anyhow. One therefore expects to come off best if one looks as little as possible into this dark corner. Naturally anyone who proceeds in that way will never get round this corner and will never obtain even a trace of what yoga promises. Only the man who goes through this darkness can hope to make any further progress. I am therefore in principle against the uncritical appropriation of yoga practices by Europeans, because I know only too well that they hope to avoid their own dark corners. Such a beginning is entirely meaningless and worthless.

940   This is also the deeper reason why we in the West have never developed anything comparable to yoga, aside from the very limited application of the Jesuit *Exercitia*. We have an abysmal fear of that lurking horror, our personal unconscious. Hence the European much prefers to tell others 'how to do it'. That the improvement of the whole begins with the individual, even with myself, never enters our heads. Besides, many people think it morbid to glance into their own interiors – it makes you melancholic, a theologian once assured me.

941   I have just said that we have developed nothing that could be compared with yoga. This is not entirely correct. True to our European bias, we have evolved a medical psychology dealing specifically with the *kleshas*. We call it the 'psychology of the unconscious'. The movement inaugurated by

Freud recognized the importance of the human shadow-side and its influence on consciousness, and then got entangled in this problem. Freudian psychology is concerned with the very thing that our text passes over in silence and assumes is already dealt with. The yogi is perfectly well aware of the world of the *kleshas*, but his religion is such a natural one that he knows nothing of the *moral conflict* which the *kleshas* represent for us. An ethical dilemma divides us from our shadow. The spirit of India grows out of nature; with us spirit is opposed to nature.

942   The floor of lapis lazuli is not transparent for us because the question of the *evil in nature* must first be answered. This question *can* be answered, but surely not with shallow rationalistic arguments and intellectual patter. The ethical responsibility of the individual can give a valid answer, but there are no cheap recipes and no licences – one must pay to the last penny before the floor of lapis lazuli can become transparent. Our *sutra* presupposes that the shadow world of our personal fantasies – the personal unconscious – has been traversed, and goes on to describe a symbolical figure which at first strikes us as very strange. This is a geometrical structure raying out from a centre and divided into eight parts – an ogdoad. In the centre there is a lotus with the Buddha sitting in it, and the decisive experience is the final knowledge that the meditator himself is the Buddha, whereby the fateful knots woven in the opening story are apparently resolved. The concentrically constructed symbol evidently expresses the highest concentration, which can be achieved only when the previously described withdrawal and canalization of interest away from the impressions of the sense-world and from object-bound ideas is pushed to the limit and applied to the background of consciousness. The conscious world with its attachment to objects, and even the centre of consciousness, the ego, are extinguished, and in their place the splendour of the Amitābha land appears with ever-increasing intensity.

943   Psychologically this means that behind or beneath the world of personal fantasies and instincts a still deeper layer of the unconscious becomes visible, which in contrast to the chaotic disorder of the *kleshas* is pervaded by the highest order and harmony, and, in contrast to their multiplicity, symbolizes the all-embracing unity of the *bodhimandala*, the magic circle of enlightenment.

944   What has our psychology to say about this Indian assertion of a suprapersonal, world-embracing unconscious that appears when the darkness of the personal unconscious grows transparent? Modern psychology knows that the personal unconscious is only the top layer, resting on a foundation of a wholly different nature which we call the collective unconscious. The reason for this designation is the circumstance that, unlike the personal unconscious and its purely personal contents, the images in the deeper unconscious have a distinctly mythological character. That is to say, in form and content they coincide with those widespread primordial ideas which underlie the myths. They are no longer of a

personal but of a purely suprapersonal nature and are therefore common to all men. For this reason they are to be found in the myths and legends of all peoples and all times, as well as in individuals who have not the slightest knowledge of mythology.

945   Our Western psychology has, in fact, got as far as yoga in that it is able to establish scientifically a deeper layer of unity in the unconscious. The mythological motifs, whose presence has been demonstrated by the exploration of the unconscious, form in themselves a multiplicity, but this culminates in a concentric or radial order which constitutes the true centre or essence of the collective unconscious. On account of the remarkable agreement between the insights of yoga and the results of psychological research, I have chosen the Sanskrit term *mandala* for this central symbol.

946   You will now surely ask: but how in the world does science come to such conclusions? There are two paths to this end. The first is the historical path. If we study, for instance, the introspective method of mediaeval natural philosophy, we find that it repeatedly used the circle, and in most cases the circle divided into four parts, to symbolize the central principle, obviously borrowing this idea from the ecclesiastical allegory of the quaternity as found in numerous representations of the *Rex gloriae* with the four evangelists, the four rivers of paradise, the four winds, and so on.

947   The second is the path of empirical psychology. At a certain stage in the psychological treatment patients sometimes paint or draw such mandalas spontaneously, either because they dream them or because they suddenly feel the need to compensate the confusion in their psyches through representations of an ordered unity. For instance, our Swiss national saint, the Blessed Brother Nicholas of Flüe, went through a process of this kind, and the result can still be seen in the picture of the Trinity in the parish church at Sachseln. With the help of circular drawings in a little book by a German mystic,[6] he succeeded in assimilating the great and terrifying vision that had shaken him to the depths.

948   But what has our empirical psychology to say about the Buddha sitting in the lotus? Logically one would expect Christ to be enthroned in the centre of our Western mandalas. This was once true, as we have already said, in the Middle Ages. But our modern mandalas, spontaneously produced by numerous individuals without any preconceived ideas or suggestions from outside, contain no Christ-figure, still less a Buddha in the lotus position. On the other hand, the equal-armed Greek cross, or even an unmistakable imitation of the swastika, is to be found fairly often. I cannot discuss this strange fact here, though in itself it is of the greatest interest.

949   Between the Christian and the Buddhist mandala there is a subtle but enormous difference. The Christian during contemplation would never say '*I* am Christ', but will confess with Paul: 'Not I, but Christ liveth in me' (Galatians 2:20). Our *sutra*, however, says: 'Thou wilt know that *thou* art the Buddha.' At bottom the two confessions are identical, in that the

Buddhist only attains this knowledge when he is *anātman*, 'without self'. But there is an immeasurable difference in the formulation. The Christian attains his end *in Christ*, the Buddhist knows *he* is the Buddha. The Christian gets *out* of the transitory and ego-bound world of consciousness, but the Buddhist *still* reposes on the eternal ground of his inner nature, whose oneness with Deity, or with universal Being, is confirmed in other Indian testimonies.

NOTES

1 [Delivered as a lecture to the Schweizerische Gesellschaft der Freunde ostasiatischer Kultur, in Zürich, Basel and Bern, during March–May 1943, and published as 'Zur Psychologie östlicher Meditation' in the Society's *Mitteilungen* (St. Gallen), V (1943), 33–53; repub. in *Symbolik des Geistes* (Zürich, 1948), pp. 447-72. Previously trans. by Carol Baumann in *Art and Thought*, a volume in honour of Ananda K. Coomaraswamy (London, 1948), pp. 169–79.

   The work of Heinrich Zimmer's which the author refers to in the opening sentence was his *Kunstform und Yoga im indischen Kultbild* (1926), the central argument of which has been restated in his posthumous English works, particularly *Myths and Symbols in Indian Art and Civilization* (1946) and *The Art of Indian Asia* (1955). – EDITORS.]

2 In *Buddhist Mahāyāna Sūtras* (*SBE*, XLIX), part II, pp. 159–201, trans. by J. Takakusu, slightly modified.

3 Jambunadi = Jambu-tree. A river formed of the juice of the fruit of the Jambu-tree flows in a circle round Mount Meru and returns to the tree.

4 Cf. *Symbols of Transformation,* part II, chs. 6 and 7, especially par. 510.

5 Cf. *Psychology and Alchemy,* fig. 61.

6 Cf. Stoeckli, *Die Visionen des Seligen Bruder Klaus.*

Part IV

Buddhism and the way of psychic healing

14 Death and psychic transformation

From: 'Psychological Commentary on
The Tibetan Book of the Dead'[1]

831   Before embarking upon the psychological commentary, I should like to
say a few words about the text itself. *The Tibetan Book of the Dead*, or the
Bardo Thödol, is a book of instructions for the dead and dying. Like *The
Egyptian Book of the Dead*, it is meant to be a guide for the dead man
during the period of his *Bardo* existence, symbolically described as an
intermediate state of forty-nine days' duration between death and rebirth.
The text falls into three parts. The first part, called *Chikhai Bardo*,
describes the psychic happenings at the moment of death. The second part,
or *Chönyid Bardo*, deals with the dream state which supervenes immediately after death, and with what are called 'karmic illusions'. The
third part, or *Sidpa Bardo*, concerns the onset of the birth instinct and of
prenatal events. It is characteristic that supreme insight and illumination,
and hence the greatest possibility of attaining liberation, are vouchsafed
during the actual process of dying. Soon afterwards, the 'illusions' begin
which lead eventually to reincarnation, the illuminative lights growing
ever fainter and more multifarious, and the visions more and more
terrifying. This descent illustrates the estrangement of consciousness from
the liberating truth as it approaches nearer and nearer to physical rebirth.
The purpose of the instruction is to fix the attention of the dead man, at
each successive stage of delusion and entanglement, on the ever-present
possibility of liberation, and to explain to him the nature of his visions.
The text of the *Bardo Thödol* is recited by the lama in the presence of the
corpse.

832   I do not think I could better discharge my debt of thanks to the two
previous translators of the *Bardo Thödol*, the late Lama Kazi Dawa-
Samdup and Dr Evans-Wentz, than by attempting, with the aid of a
psychological commentary, to make the magnificent world of ideas and
the problems contained in this treatise a little more intelligible to the
Western mind. I am sure that all who read this book with open eyes, and
who allow it to impress itself upon them without prejudice, will reap a
rich reward.

833   The *Bardo Thödol*, fitly named by its editor, Dr W. Y. Evans-Wentz, *The
Tibetan Book of the Dead*, caused a considerable stir in English-speaking

countries at the time of its first appearance in 1927. It belongs to that class of writings which are not only of interest to specialists in Mahāyāna Buddhism, but which also, because of their deep humanity and their still deeper insight into the secrets of the human psyche, make an especial appeal to the layman who is seeking to broaden his knowledge of life. For years, ever since it was first published, the *Bardo Thödol* has been my constant companion, and to it I owe not only many stimulating ideas and discoveries, but also many fundamental insights. Unlike *The Egyptian Book of the Dead*, which always prompts one to say too much or too little, the *Bardo Thödol* offers one an intelligible philosophy addressed to human beings rather than to gods or primitive savages. Its philosophy contains the quintessence of Buddhist psychological criticism; and, as such, one can truly say that it is of an unexampled sublimity. Not only the 'wrathful' but also the 'peaceful' deities are conceived as samsaric projections of the human psyche, an idea that seems all too obvious to the enlightened European, because it reminds him of his own banal simplifications. But though the European can easily explain away these deities as projections, he would be quite incapable of positing them at the same time as real. The *Bardo Thödol* can do that, because, in certain of its most essential metaphysical premises, it has enlightened as well as the unenlightened European at a disadvantage. The ever-present, unspoken assumption of the *Bardo Thödol* is the antinomian character of all metaphysical assertions, and also the idea of the qualitative difference of the various levels of consciousness and of the metaphysical realities conditioned by them. The background of this unusual book is not the niggardly European 'either–or', but a magnificently affirmative 'both-and'. This statement may appear objectionable to the Western philosopher, for the West loves clarity and unambiguity; consequently, one philosopher clings to the position 'God is', while another clings equally fervently to the negation, 'God is not.' What would these hostile brethren make of an assertion like the following [p. 96]?

> Recognizing the voidness of thine own intellect to be Buddhahood, and knowing it at the same time to be thine own consciousness, thou shalt abide in the state of the divine mind of the Buddha.

834   Such an assertion is, I fear, as unwelcome to our Western philosophy as it is to our theology. The *Bardo Thödol* is in the highest degree psychological in its outlook; but, with us, philosophy and theology are still in the mediaeval, pre-psychological stage where only the assertions are listened to, explained, defended, criticized and disputed, while the authority that makes them has, by general consent, been deposed as outside the scope of discussion.

835   Metaphysical assertions, however, are *statements of the psyche*, and are therefore psychological. To the Western mind, which compensates its well-known feelings of resentment by a slavish regard for 'rational'

explanations, this obvious truth seems all too obvious, or else it is seen as an inadmissible negation of metaphysical 'truth'. Whenever the Westerner hears the word 'psychological', it always sounds to him like '*only* psychological'. For him the 'soul' is something pitifully small, unworthy, personal, subjective, and a lot more besides. He therefore prefers to use the word 'mind' instead, though he likes to pretend at the same time that a statement which may in fact be very subjective indeed is made by the 'mind', naturally by the 'Universal Mind', or even – at a pinch – by the 'Absolute' itself. This rather ridiculous presumption is probably a compensation for the regrettable smallness of the soul. It almost seems as if Anatole France had uttered a truth which were valid for the whole Western world when, in his *Penguin Island*, Cathérine d'Alexandrie offers this advice to God: 'Donnez-leur une âme, mais une petite!'

836   It is the psyche which, by the divine creative power inherent in it, makes the metaphysical assertion; it posits the distinctions between metaphysical entities. Not only is it the condition of all metaphysical reality, it *is* that reality.

837   With this great psychological truth the *Bardo Thödol* opens. The book is not a ceremonial of burial, but a set of instructions for the dead, a guide through the changing phenomena of the *Bardo* realm, that state of existence which continues for forty-nine days after death until the next incarnation. If we disregard for the moment the supratemporality of the soul – which the East accepts as a self-evident fact – we, as readers of the *Bardo Thödol*, shall be able to put ourselves without difficulty in the position of the dead man, and shall consider attentively the teaching set forth in the opening section, which is outlined in the quotation above. At this point, the following words are spoken, not presumptuously, but in a courteous manner [pp. 95.f.]:

> O nobly born (so and so), listen. Now thou art experiencing the Radiance of the Clear Light of Pure Reality. Recognize it. O nobly born, thy present intellect, in real nature void, not formed into anything as regards characteristics or colour, naturally void, is the very Reality, the All-Good.
>
> Thine own intellect, which is now voidness, yet not to be regarded as of the voidness of nothingness, but as being the intellect itself, unobstructed, shining, thrilling, and blissful, is the very consciousness, the All-good Buddha.

838   This realization is the *dharma-kāya* state of perfect enlightenment; or, as we should express it in our own language, the creative ground of all metaphysical assertion is consciousness, as the invisible, intangible manifestation of the soul. The 'Voidness' is the state transcendent over all assertion and all predication. The fullness of its discriminative manifestations still lies latent in the soul.

839   The text continues:

Thine own consciousness, shining, void, and inseparable from the Great
Body of Radiance, hath no birth, nor death, and is the Immutable Light
– Buddha Amitābha.

840   The soul is assuredly not small, but the radiant Godhead itself. The West
finds this statement either very dangerous, if not downright blasphemous,
or else accepts it unthinkingly and then suffers from a theosophical
inflation. Somehow we always have a wrong attitude to these things. But
if we can master ourselves far enough to refrain from our chief error of
always wanting to *do* something with things and put them to practical use,
we may perhaps succeed in learning an important lesson from these
teachings, or at least in appreciating the greatness of the *Bardo Thödol*,
which vouchsafes to the dead man the ultimate and highest truth, that even
the gods are the radiance and reflection of our own souls. No sun is thereby
eclipsed for the Oriental as it would be for the Christian, who would feel
robbed of his God; on the contrary, his soul is the light of the Godhead,
and the Godhead is the soul. The East can sustain this paradox better than
the unfortunate Angelus Silesius, who even today would be psychologically far in advance of his time.

841   It is highly sensible of the *Bardo Thödol* to make clear to the dead man
the primacy of the psyche, for that is the one thing which life does not
make clear to us. We are so hemmed in by things which jostle and oppress
that we never get a chance, in the midst of all these 'given' things, to
wonder by whom they are 'given'. It is from this world of 'given' things
that the dead man liberates himself; and the purpose of the instruction is
to help him towards this liberation. We, if we put ourselves in his place,
shall derive no lesser reward from it, since we learn from the very first
paragraphs that the 'giver' of all 'given' things dwells within us. This is
a truth which in the face of all evidence, in the greatest things as in the
smallest, is never known, although it is often so very necessary, indeed
vital, for us to know it. Such knowledge, to be sure, is suitable only for
contemplatives who are minded to understand the purpose of existence,
for those who are Gnostics by temperament and therefore believe in a
saviour who, like the saviour of the Mandaeans, is called 'knowledge of
life' (Manda d'Hayye). Perhaps it is not granted to many of us to see the
world as something 'given'. A great reversal of standpoint, calling for
much sacrifice, is needed before we can see the world as 'given' by the
very nature of the psyche. It is so much more straightforward, more
dramatic, impressive, and therefore more convincing, to see all the things
that happen to me than to observe how I make them happen. Indeed, the
animal nature of man makes him resist seeing himself as the maker of his
circumstances. That is why attempts of this kind were always the object
of secret initiations, culminating as a rule in a figurative death which
symbolized the total character of this reversal. And, in point of fact, the
instruction given in the *Bardo Thödol* serves to recall to the dead man the

experiences of his initiation and the teachings of his guru, for the instruction is, at bottom, nothing less than an initiation of the dead into the *Bardo* life, just as the initiation of the living was a preparation for the Beyond. Such was the case, at least, with all the mystery cults in ancient civilizations from the time of the Egyptian and Eleusinian mysteries. In the initiation of the living, however, this 'Beyond' is not a world beyond death, but a reversal of the mind's intentions and outlook, a psychological 'Beyond' or, in Christian terms, a 'redemption' from the trammels of the world and of sin. Redemption is a separation and deliverance from an earlier condition of darkness and unconsciousness, and leads to a condition of illumination and releasedness, to victory and transcendence over everything 'given'.

842   Thus far the *Bardo Thödol* is, as Dr Evans-Wentz also feels, an initiation process whose purpose it is to restore to the soul the divinity it lost at birth. Now it is characteristic of Oriental religious literature that the teaching invariably begins with the most important item, with the ultimate and highest principles which, with us, would come last – as for instance in Apuleius, where Lucius is worshipped as Helios only right at the end. Accordingly, in the *Bardo Thödol*, the initiation is a series of diminishing climaxes ending with rebirth in the womb. The only 'initiation process' that is still alive and practised today in the West is the analysis of the unconscious as used by doctors for therapeutic purposes. This penetration into the ground-layers of consciousness is a kind of rational maieutics in the Socratic sense, a bringing-forth of psychic contents that are still germinal, subliminal and as yet unborn. Originally, this therapy took the form of Freudian psychoanalysis and was mainly concerned with sexual fantasies. This is the realm that corresponds to the last and lowest region of the *Bardo*, known as the *Sidpa Bardo*, where the dead man, unable to profit by the teachings of the *Chikhai* and *Chönyid Bardo*, begins to fall a prey to sexual fantasies and is attracted by the vision of mating couples. Eventually he is caught by a womb and born into the earthly world again. Meanwhile, as one might expect, the Oedipus complex starts functioning. If his karma destines him to be reborn as a man, he will fall in love with his mother-to-be and will find his father hateful and disgusting. Conversely, the future daughter will be highly attracted by her father-to-be and repelled by her mother. The European passes through this specifically Freudian domain when his unconscious contents are brought to light under analysis, but he goes in the reverse direction. He journeys back through the world of infantile sexual fantasy to the womb. It has even been suggested in psychoanalytical circles that the trauma *par excellence* is the birth experience itself – nay more, psychoanalysts even claim to have probed back to memories of intra-uterine origin. Here Western reason reaches its limit, unfortunately. I say 'unfortunately' because one rather wishes that Freudian psychoanalysis could have happily pursued these so called intra-uterine experiences still further back. Had it succeeded in this bold

undertaking, it would surely have come out beyond the *Sidpa Bardo* and penetrated from behind into the lower reaches of the *Chönyid Bardo*. It is true that, with the equipment of our existing biological ideas, such a venture would not have been crowned with success; it would have needed a wholly different kind of philosophical preparation from that based on current scientific assumptions. But, had the journey back been consistently pursued, it would undoubtedly have led to the postulate of a pre-uterine existence, a true *Bardo* life, if only it had been possible to find at least some trace of an experiencing subject. As it was, the psychoanalysts never got beyond purely conjectural traces of intra-uterine experiences, and even the famous 'birth trauma' has remained such an obvious truism that it can no longer explain anything, any more than can the hypothesis that life is a disease with a bad prognosis because its outcome is always fatal.

843   Freudian psychoanalysis, in all essential aspects, never went beyond the experiences of the *Sidpa Bardo*; that is, it was unable to extricate itself from sexual fantasies and similar 'incompatible' tendencies which cause anxiety and other affective states. Nevertheless, Freud's theory is the first attempt made by the West to investigate, as if from below, from the animal sphere of instinct, the psychic territory that corresponds in Tantric Lamaism to the *Sidpa Bardo*. A very justifiable fear of metaphysics prevented Freud from penetrating into the sphere of the 'occult'. In addition to this, the *Sidpa* state, if we are to accept the psychology of the *Sidpa Bardo*, is characterized by the fierce wind of karma, which whirls the dead man along until he comes to the 'womb-door'. In other words, the *Sidpa* state permits of no going back, because it is sealed off against the *Chönyid* state by an intense striving downwards, towards the animal sphere of instinct and physical rebirth. That is to say, anyone who penetrates into the unconscious with purely biological assumptions will become stuck in the instinctual sphere and be unable to advance beyond it, for he will be pulled back again and again into physical existence. It is therefore not possible for Freudian theory to reach anything except an essentially negative valuation of the unconscious. It is a 'nothing but'. At the same time, it must be admitted that this view of the psyche is typically Western, only it is expressed more blatantly, more plainly and more ruthlessly than others would have dared to express it, though at bottom they think no differently. As to what 'mind' means in this connection, we can only cherish the hope that it will carry conviction. But, as even Max Scheler[2] noted with regret, the power of this 'mind' is, to say the least of it, doubtful.

844   I think, then, we can state it as a fact that with the aid of psychoanalysis the rationalizing mind of the West has pushed forward into what one might call the neuroticism of the *Sidpa* state, and has there been brought to an inevitable standstill by the uncritical assumption that everything psychological is subjective and personal. Even so, this advance has been a great gain, inasmuch as it has enabled us to take one more step behind our

conscious lives. This knowledge also gives us a hint of how we ought to read the *Bardo Thödol* – that is, backwards. If, with the help of our Western science, we have to some extent succeeded in understanding the psychological character of the *Sidpa Bardo*, our next task is to see if we can make anything of the preceding *Chönyid Bardo*.

845   The *Chönyid* state is one of karmic illusion – that is to say, illusions which result from the psychic residua of previous existences. According to the Eastern view, karma implies a sort of psychic theory of heredity based on the hypothesis of reincarnation, which in the last resort is an hypothesis of the supratemporality of the soul. Neither our scientific knowledge nor our reason can keep in step with this idea. There are too many ifs and buts. Above all, we know desperately little about the possibilities of continued existence of the individual soul after death, so little that we cannot even conceive how anyone could prove anything at all in this respect. Moreover, we know only too well, on epistemological grounds, that such a proof would be just as impossible as the proof of God. Hence we may cautiously accept the idea of karma only if we understand it as *psychic heredity* in the very widest sense of the word. Psychic heredity does exist – that is to say, there is inheritance of psychic characteristics such as predisposition to disease, traits of character, special gifts, and so forth. It does no violence to the psychic nature of these complex facts if natural science reduces them to what appear to be physical aspects (nuclear structures in cells, and so on). They are essential phenomena of life which express themselves, in the main, psychically, just as there are other inherited characteristics which express themselves, in the main, physiologically, on the physical level. Among these inherited psychic factors there is a special class which is not confined either to family or to race. These are the universal dispositions of the mind, and they are to be understood as analogous to Plato's forms (*eidola*), in accordance with which the mind organizes its contents. One could also describe these forms as *categories* analogous to the logical categories which are always and everywhere present as the basic postulates of reason. Only, in the case of our 'forms', we are not dealing with categories of reason but with categories of the *imagination*. As the products of imagination are always in essence visual, their forms must, from the outset, have the character of images and moreover of *typical* images, which is why, following St Augustine, I call them 'archetypes'. Comparative religion and mythology are rich mines of archetypes, and so is the psychology of dreams and psychoses. The astonishing parallelism between these images and the ideas they serve to express has frequently given rise to the wildest migration theories, although it would have been far more natural to think of the remarkable similarity of the human psyche at all times and in all places. Archetypal fantasy forms are, in fact, reproduced spontaneously anytime and anywhere, without there being any conceivable trace of direct transmission. The original structural components of the psyche are of no

less surprising a uniformity than are those of the visible body. The archetypes are, so to speak, organs of the pre-rational psyche. They are eternally inherited forms and ideas which have at first no specific content. Their specific content only appears in the course of the individual's life, when personal experience is taken up in precisely these forms. If the archetypes were not pre-existent in identical forms everywhere, how could one explain the fact, postulated at almost every turn by the *Bardo Thödol*, that the dead do not know that they are dead, and that this assertion is to be met with just as often in the dreary, half baked literature of European and American Spiritualism? Although we find the same assertion in Swedenborg, knowledge of his writings can hardly be sufficiently widespread for this little bit of information to have been picked up by every small-town medium. And a connection between Swedenborg and the *Bardo Thödol* is completely unthinkable. It is a primordial, universal idea that the dead simply continue their earthly existence and do not know that they are disembodied spirits – an archetypal idea which enters into immediate, visible manifestation whenever anyone sees a ghost. It is significant, too, that ghosts all over the world have certain features in common. I am naturally aware of the unverifiable spiritualistic hypothesis, though I have no wish to make it my own. I must content myself with the hypothesis of an omnipresent, but differentiated, psychic structure which is inherited and which necessarily gives a certain form and direction to all experience. For, just as the organs of the body are not mere lumps of indifferent, passive matter, but are dynamic, functional complexes which assert themselves with imperious urgency, so also the archetypes, as organs of the psyche, are dynamic, instinctual complexes which determine psychic life to an extraordinary degree. That is why I also call them *dominants* of the unconscious. The layer of unconscious psyche which is made up of these universal dynamic forms I have termed the *collective unconscious.*

846   So far as I know, there is no inheritance of individual prenatal, or pre-uterine, memories, but there are undoubtedly inherited archetypes which are, however, devoid of content, because, to begin with, they contain no personal experiences. They only emerge into consciousness when personal experiences have rendered them visible. As we have seen, *Sidpa* psychology consists in wanting to live and to be born. (The *Sidpa Bardo* is the '*Bardo* of Seeking Rebirth'.) Such a state, therefore, precludes any experience of transubjective psychic realities, unless the dead man refuses categorically to be born back again into the world of consciousness. According to the teachings of the *Bardo Thödol*, it is still possible for him, in each of the *Bardo* states, to reach the *dharma-kāya* by transcending the four-faced Mount Meru, provided that he does not yield to his desire to follow the 'dim lights'. This is as much as to say that the individual must desperately resist the dictates of reason, as we understand it, and give up the supremacy of egohood, regarded by reason as sacrosanct. What this

means in practice is complete capitulation to the objective powers of the psyche, with all that this entails; a kind of figurative death, corresponding to the Judgement of the Dead in the *Sidpa Bardo*. It means the end of all conscious, rational, morally responsible conduct of life, and a voluntary surrender to what the *Bardo Thödol* calls 'karmic illusion'. Karmic illusion springs from belief in a visionary world of an extremely irrational nature, which neither accords with nor derives from our rational judgements but is the exclusive product of uninhibited imagination. It is sheer dream or 'fantasy', and every well-meaning person will instantly caution us against it; nor indeed can one see at first sight what is the difference between fantasies of this kind and the phantasmagoria of a lunatic. Very often only a slight *abaissement du niveau mental* is needed to unleash this world of illusion. The terror and darkness of this moment are reflected in the experiences described in the opening sections of the *Sidpa Bardo*. But the contents of the *Chönyid Bardo* reveal the archetypes, the karmic images which appear first in their terrifying form. The *Chönyid* state is equivalent to a deliberately induced psychosis.

847   One often hears and reads about the dangers of yoga, particularly of the ill-reputed *kundalini* yoga. The deliberately induced psychotic state, which in certain unstable individuals might easily lead to a real psychosis, is a danger that needs to be taken very seriously indeed. These things really are dangerous and ought not to be meddled with in our typically Western way. It is a meddling with fate, which strikes at the very roots of human existence and can let loose a flood of sufferings of which no sane person ever dreamed. These sufferings correspond to the hellish torments of the *Chönyid* state, described in the text as follows:

> Then the Lord of Death will place round thy neck a rope and drag thee along; he will cut off thy head, tear out thy heart, pull out thy intestines, lick up thy brain, drink thy blood, eat thy flesh, and gnaw thy bones; but thou wilt be incapable of dying. Even when thy body is hacked to pieces, it will revive again. The repeated hacking will cause intense pain and torture.[3]

848   These tortures aptly describe the real nature of the danger: it is a disintegration of the wholeness of the *Bardo* body, which is a kind of 'subtle body' constituting the visible envelope of the psychic self in the after-death state. The psychological equivalent of this dismemberment is psychic dissociation. In its deleterious form it would be schizophrenia (split mind). This most common of all mental illnesses consists essentially in a marked *abaissement du niveau mental* which abolishes the normal checks imposed by the conscious mind and thus gives unlimited scope to the play of the unconscious 'dominants'.

849   The transition, then, from the *Sidpa* state to the *Chönyid* state is a dangerous reversal of the aims and intentions of the conscious mind. It is a sacrifice of the ego's stability and a surrender to the extreme uncertainty

of what must seem like a chaotic riot of phantasmal forms. When Freud coined the phrase that the ego was 'the true seat of anxiety', he was giving voice to a very true and profound intuition. Fear of self-sacrifice lurks deep in every ego, and this fear is often only the precariously controlled demand of the unconscious forces to burst out in full strength. No one who strives for selfhood (individuation) is spared this dangerous passage, for that which is feared also belongs to the wholeness of the self – the subhuman, or suprahuman, world of psychic 'dominants' from which the ego originally emancipated itself with enormous effort, and then only partially, for the sake of a more or less illusory freedom. This liberation is certainly a very necessary and very heroic undertaking, but it represents nothing final: it is merely the creation of a *subject*, who, in order to find fulfilment, has still to be confronted by an *object*. This, at first sight, would appear to be the world, which is swelled out with projections for that very purpose. Here we seek and find our difficulties, here we seek and find our enemy, here we seek and find what is dear and precious to us; and it is comforting to know that all evil and all good is to be found out there, in the visible object, where it can be conquered, punished, destroyed or enjoyed. But nature herself does not allow this paradisal state of innocence to continue for ever. There are, and always have been, those who cannot help but see that the world and its experiences are in the nature of a symbol, and that it really reflects something that lies hidden in the subject himself, in his own transubjective reality. It is from this profound intuition, according to lamaist doctrine, that the *Chönyid* state derives its true meaning, which is why the *Chönyid Bardo* is entitled The '*Bardo* of Experiencing of Reality'.

850   The reality experienced in the *Chönyid* state is, as the last section [pp. 143ff.] of this *Bardo* teaches, the reality of thought. The 'thought forms' appear as realities, fantasy takes on real form, and the terrifying dream evoked by karma and played out by the unconscious 'dominants' begins. The first to appear (if we read the text backwards) is the all-destroying God of Death, the epitome of all terrors; he is followed by the twenty-eight 'power-holding' and sinister goddesses and the fifty-eight 'blood-drinking' goddesses. In spite of their demonic aspect, which appears as a confusing chaos of terrifying attributes and monstrosities, a certain order is already discernible. We find that there are companies of gods and goddesses who are arranged according to the four directions and are distinguished by typical mystic colours. It gradually becomes clearer that all these deities are organized into mandalas, or circles, containing a cross of the four colours. The colours are co-ordinated with the four aspects of wisdom:

1 White = the light-path of the mirror-like wisdom;
2 Yellow = the light-path of the wisdom of equality;
3 Red = the light-path of the discriminative wisdom;
4 Green = the light-path of the all-performing wisdom.

851   On a higher level of insight, the dead man knows that the real thought-forms all emanate from himself, and that the four light-paths of wisdom which appear before him are the radiations of his own psychic faculties. This takes us straight to the psychology of the lamaistic mandala, which I have already discussed in the book I brought out with the late Richard Wilhelm, *The Secret of the Golden Flower*.

852   Continuing our ascent backwards through the region of the *Chönyid Bardo*, we come finally to the vision of the Four Great Ones: the green Amogha-Siddhi, the red Amitābha, the yellow Ratna-Sambhava, and the white Vajra-Sattva. The ascent ends with the effulgent blue light of the *Dharmadhātu*, the Buddha-body, which glows in the midst of the mandala from the heart of Vairochana.

853   With this final vision the karmic illusions cease; consciousness, weaned away from all form and from all attachment to objects, returns to the timeless, inchoate state of the *dharma-kāya*. Thus (reading backwards) the *Chikhai* state, which appeared at the moment of death, is reached.

854   I think these few hints will suffice to give the attentive reader some idea of the psychology of the *Bardo Thödol*. The book describes a way of initiation in reverse, which, unlike the eschatological expectations of Christianity, prepares the soul for a descent into physical being. The thoroughly intellectualistic and rationalistic worldly-mindedness of the European makes it advisable for us to reverse the sequence of the *Bardo Thödol* and to regard it as an account of Eastern initiation experiences, though one is perfectly free, if one chooses, to substitute Christian symbols for the gods of the *Chönyid Bardo*. At any rate, the sequence of events as I have described it offers a close parallel to the phenomenology of the European unconscious when it is undergoing an 'initiation process', that is to say, when it is being analysed. The transformation of the unconscious that occurs under analysis makes it the natural analogue of the religious initiation ceremonies, which do, however, differ in principle from the natural process in that they anticipate the natural course of development and substitute for the spontaneous production of symbols a deliberately selected set of symbols prescribed by tradition. We can see this in the *Exercitia* of Ignatius Loyola, or in the yoga meditations of the Buddhists and Tantrists.

855   The reversal of the order of the chapters, which I have suggested here as an aid to understanding, in no way accords with the original intention of the *Bardo Thödol*. Nor is the psychological use we make of it anything but a secondary intention, though one that is possibly sanctioned by lamaist custom. The real purpose of this singular book is the attempt, which must seem very strange to the educated European of the twentieth century, to enlighten the dead on their journey through the regions of the *Bardo*. The Catholic Church is the only place in the world of the white man where any provision is made for the souls of the departed. Inside the Protestant camp, with its world-affirming optimism, we only find a few

mediumistic 'rescue circles', whose main concern is to make the dead aware of the fact that they *are* dead.[4] But, generally speaking, we have nothing in the West that is in any way comparable to the *Bardo Thödol*, except for certain secret writings which are inaccessible to the wider public and to the ordinary scientist. According to tradition, the *Bardo Thödol*, too, seems to have been included among the 'hidden' books, as Dr Evans-Wentz makes clear in his Introduction. As such, it forms a special chapter in the magical 'cure of the soul' which extends even beyond death. This cult of the dead is rationally based on the belief in the supratemporality of the soul, but its irrational basis is to be found in the psychological need of the living to do something for the departed. This is an elementary need which forces itself upon even the most 'enlightened' individuals when faced by the death of relatives and friends. That is why, enlightenment or no enlightenment, we still have all manner of ceremonies for the dead. If Lenin had to submit to being embalmed and put on show in a sumptuous mausoleum like an Egyptian pharaoh, we may be quite sure it was not because his followers believed in the resurrection of the body. Apart, however, from the Masses said for the soul in the Catholic Church, the provisions we make for the dead are rudimentary and on the lowest level, not because we cannot convince ourselves of the soul's immortality, but because we have rationalized the above-mentioned psychological need out of existence. We behave as if we did not have this need, and because we cannot believe in a life after death we prefer to do nothing about it. Simpler-minded people follow their own feelings, and, as in Italy, build themselves funeral monuments of gruesome beauty. The Catholic Masses for the soul are on a level considerably above this, because they are expressly intended for the psychic welfare of the deceased and are not a mere gratification of lachrymose sentiments. But the highest application of spiritual effort on behalf of the departed is surely to be found in the instructions of the *Bardo Thödol*. They are so detailed and thoroughly adapted to the apparent changes in the dead man's condition that every serious-minded reader must ask himself whether these wise old lamas might not, after all, have caught a glimpse of the fourth dimension and twitched the veil from the greatest of life's secrets.

856   Even if the truth should prove to be a disappointment, one almost feels tempted to concede at least some measure of reality to the vision of life in the *Bardo*. At any rate, it is unexpectedly original, if nothing else, to find the after-death state, of which our religious imagination has formed the most grandiose conceptions, painted in lurid colours as a terrifying dream state of a progressively degenerative character.[5] The supreme vision comes not at the end of the *Bardo*, but right at the beginning, at the moment of death; what happens afterward is an ever-deepening descent into illusion and obscuration, down to the ultimate degradation of new physical birth. The spiritual climax is reached at the moment when life ends. Human life, therefore, is the vehicle of the highest perfection it is

possible to attain; it alone generates the karma that makes it possible for the dead man to abide in the perpetual light of the Voidness without clinging to any object, and thus to rest on the hub of the wheel of rebirth, freed from all illusion of genesis and decay. Life in the *Bardo* brings no eternal rewards or punishments, but merely a descent into a new life which shall bear the individual nearer to his final goal. But this eschatological goal is what he himself brings to birth as the last and highest fruit of the labours and aspirations of earthly existence. This view is not only lofty, it is manly and heroic.

857   The degenerative character of *Bardo* life is corroborated by the spiritual-istic literature of the West, which again and again gives one a sickening impression of the utter inanity and banality of communications from the 'spirit world'. The scientific mind does not hesitate to explain these reports as emanations from the unconscious of the mediums and of those taking part in the séance, and even to extend this explanation to the description of the Hereafter given in *The Tibetan Book of the Dead*. And it is an undeniable fact that the whole book is created out of the archetypal contents of the unconscious. Behind these there lie – and in this our Western reason is quite right – no physical or metaphysical realities, but 'merely' the reality of psychic facts, the data of psychic experience. Now whether a thing is 'given' subjectively or objectively, the fact remains that it *is*. The *Bardo Thödol* says no more than this, for its five Dhyāni-Buddhas are themselves no more than psychic data. That is just what the dead man has to recognize, if it has not already become clear to him during life that his own psychic self and the giver of all data are one and the same. The world of gods and spirits is truly 'nothing but' the collective unconscious inside me. To turn this sentence round so that it reads 'The collective unconscious is the world of gods and spirits outside me' no intellectual acrobatics are needed, but a whole human lifetime, perhaps even many lifetimes of increasing completeness. Notice that I do not say 'of in-creasing perfection', because those who are 'perfect' make another kind of discovery altogether.

858   The *Bardo Thödol* began by being a 'closed' book, and so it has remained, no matter what kind of commentaries may be written upon it. For it is a book that will only open itself to spiritual understanding, and this is a capacity which no man is born with, but which he can only acquire through special training and social experience. It is good that such to all intents and purposes 'useless' books exist. They are meant for those 'queer folk' who no longer set much store by the uses, aims and meaning of present-day 'civilization'.

NOTES

1 [Originally published as 'Psychologischer Kommentar zum Bardo Thödol' (preceded by an 'Einführung', partially translated in the first two paragraphs here),

in *Das Tibetanische Totenbuch*, translated into German by Louise Göpfert-March (Zürich, 1935). As ultimately revised for the 5th (revised and expanded) Swiss edition (1953), the commentary was translated by R. F. C. Hull for publication in the 3rd (revised and expanded) English edition (the original) of *The Tibetan Book of the Dead, or The After-Death Experience on the 'Bardo' Plane*, according to Lama Kazi Dawa-Samdup's English rendering, edited by W. Y. Evans-Wentz, with foreword by Sir John Woodroffe (London and New York, 1957). With only minor alterations, it is the translation presented here. – EDITORS.]

2 [German philosopher and sociologist (1874–1928) working mainly in the field of values. – EDITORS.]

3 [Actually from the *Sidpa Bardo* section (p. 166), but similar torments figure in the 'Wrathful Deities' section (pp. 131ff.) of the *Chönyid Bardo*. – EDITORS.]

4 Information on this spiritualistic activity will be found in Lord Dowding's writings: *Many Mansions* (1943), *Lychgate* (1945), *God's Magic* (1946).

5 A similar view in Aldous Huxley, *Time Must Have a Stop* (1945).

15 The reality of the psyche in Buddhist thought

From: 'Psychological Commentary on *The Tibetan Book of the Great Liberation*' [1]

THE DIFFERENCE BETWEEN EASTERN AND WESTERN THINKING

759   Dr Evans-Wentz has entrusted me with the task of commenting on a text which contains an important exposition of Eastern 'psychology'. The very fact that I have to use quotation marks shows the dubious applicability of this term. It is perhaps not superfluous to mention that the East has produced nothing equivalent to what we call psychology, but rather philosophy or metaphysics. Critical philosophy, the mother of modern psychology, is as foreign to the East as to mediaeval Europe. Thus the word 'mind', as used in the East, has the connotation of something metaphysical. Our Western conception of mind has lost this connotation since the Middle Ages, and the word has now come to signify a 'psychic function'. Despite the fact that we can neither know nor pretend to know what 'psyche' is, we can deal with the phenomenon of 'mind'. We do not assume that the mind is a metaphysical entity or that there is any connection between an individual mind and a hypothetical Universal Mind. Our psychology is, therefore, a science of mere phenomena without any metaphysical implications. The development of Western philosophy during the last two centuries has succeeded in isolating the mind in its own sphere and in severing it from its primordial oneness with the universe. Man himself has ceased to be the microcosm and *eidolon* of the cosmos, and his 'anima' is no longer the consubstantial *scintilla* or spark of the *Anima Mundi*, the World Soul.

760   Psychology accordingly treats all metaphysical claims and assertions as mental phenomena, and regards them as statements about the mind and its structure that derive ultimately from certain unconscious dispositions. It does not consider them to be absolutely valid or even capable of establishing a metaphysical truth. We have no intellectual means of ascertaining whether this attitude is right or wrong. We only know that there is no evidence for, and no possibility of proving, the validity of a metaphysical postulate such as 'Universal Mind'. If the mind asserts the existence of a Universal Mind, we hold that it is merely making an assertion. We do not

assume that by such an assertion the existence of a Universal Mind has been established. There is no argument against this reasoning, but no evidence, either, that our conclusion is ultimately right. In other words, it is just as possible that our mind is nothing but a perceptible manifestation of a Universal Mind. Yet we do not know, and we cannot even see, how it would be possible to recognize whether this is so or not. Psychology therefore holds that the mind cannot establish or assert anything beyond itself.

761   If, then, we accept the restrictions imposed upon the capacity of our mind, we demonstrate our commonsense. I admit it is something of a sacrifice, inasmuch as we bid farewell to that miraculous world in which mind-created things and beings move and live. This is the world of the primitive, where even inanimate objects are endowed with a living, healing, magic power, through which they participate in us and we in them. Sooner or later we had to understand that their potency was really ours, and that their signficance was our projection. The theory of knowledge is only the last step out of humanity's childhood, out of a world where mind-created figures populated a metaphysical heaven and hell.

762   Despite this inevitable epistemological criticism, however, we have held fast to the religious belief that the organ of faith enables man to know God. The West thus developed a new disease: the conflict between science and religion. The critical philosophy of science became as it were negatively metaphysical – in other words, materialistic – on the basis of an error in judgement; matter was assumed to be a tangible and recognizable reality. Yet this is a thoroughly metaphysical concept hypostatized by uncritical minds. Matter is a hypothesis. When you say 'matter', you are really creating a symbol for something unknown, which may just as well be 'spirit' or anything else; it may even be God. Religious faith, on the other hand, refuses to give up its pre-critical *Weltanschauung*. In contradiction to the saying of Christ, the faithful try to *remain* children instead of becoming *as* children. They cling to the world of childhood. A famous modern theologian confesses in his autobiography that Jesus has been his good friend 'from childhood on'. Jesus is the perfect example of a man who preached something different from the religion of his forefathers. But the *imitatio Christi* does not appear to include the mental and spiritual sacrifice which he had to undergo at the beginning of his career and without which he would never have become a saviour.

763   The conflict betwen science and religion is in reality a misunderstanding of both. Scientific materialism has merely introduced a new hypostasis, and that is an intellectual sin. It has given another name to the supreme principle of reality and has assumed that this created a new thing and destroyed an old thing. Whether you call the principle of existence 'God', 'matter', 'energy', or anything else you like, you have created nothing; you have simply changed a symbol. The materialist is a metaphysician *malgré lui*. Faith, on the other hand, tries to retain a primitive mental

condition on merely sentimental grounds. It is unwilling to give up the primitive, childlike relationship to mind-created and hypostatized figures; it wants to go on enjoying the security and confidence of a world still presided over by powerful, responsible and kindly parents. Faith may include a *sacrificium intellectus* (provided there is an intellect to sacrifice), but certainly not a sacrifice of feeling. In this way the faithful *remain* children instead of becoming *as* children, and they do not gain their life because they have not lost it. Furthermore, faith collides with science and thus gets its deserts, for it refuses to share in the spiritual adventure of our age.

764   Any honest thinker has to admit the insecurity of all metaphysical positions, and in particular of all creeds. He has also to admit the unwarrantable nature of all metaphysical assertions and face the fact that there is no evidence whatever for the ability of the human mind to pull itself up by its own bootstrings, that is, to establish anything transcendental.

765   Materialism is a metaphysical reaction against the sudden realization that cognition is a mental faculty and, if carried beyond the human plane, a projection. The reaction was 'metaphysical' in so far as the man of average philosophical education failed to see through the implied hypostasis, not realizing that 'matter' was just another name for the supreme principle. As against this, the attitude of faith shows how reluctant people were to accept philosophical criticism. It also demonstrates how great is the fear of letting go one's hold on the securities of childhood and of dropping into a strange, unknown world ruled by forces unconcerned with man. Nothing really changes in either case; man and his surroundings remain the same. He has only to realize that he is shut up inside his mind and cannot step beyond it, even in insanity; and that the appearance of his world or of his gods very much depends upon his own mental condition.

766   In the first place, the structure of the mind is responsible for anything we may assert about metaphysical matters, as I have already pointed out. We have also begun to understand that the intellect is not an *ens per se*, or an independent mental faculty, but a psychic function dependent upon the conditions of the psyche as a whole. A philosophical statement is the product of a certain personality living at a certain time in a certain place, and not the outcome of a purely logical and impersonal procedure. To that extent it is chiefly subjective; whether it has an objective validity or not depends on whether there are few or many persons who argue in the same way. The isolation of man within his mind as a result of epistemological criticism has naturally led to psychological criticism. This kind of criticism is not popular with the philosophers, since they like to consider the philosophic intellect as the perfect and unconditioned instrument of philosophy. Yet this intellect of theirs is a function dependent upon an individual psyche and determined on all sides by subjective conditions, quite apart from environmental influence. Indeed, we have already become

so accustomed to this point of view that 'mind' has lost its universal character altogether. It has become a more or less individualized affair, with no trace of its former cosmic aspect as the *anima rationalis*. Mind is understood nowadays as a subjective, even an arbitrary, thing. Now that the formerly hypostatized 'universal ideas' have turned out to be mental principles, it is dawning upon us to what an extent our whole experience of so-called 'reality' is psychic; as a matter of fact, everything thought, felt, or perceived is a psychic image, and the world itself exists only so far as we are able to produce an image of it. We are so deeply impressed with the truth of our imprisonment in, and limitation by, the psyche that we are ready to admit the existence in it even of things we do *not* know: we call them 'the unconscious'.

767   The seemingly universal and metaphysical scope of the mind has thus been narrowed down to the small circle of individual consciousness, profoundly aware of its almost limitless subjectivity and of its infantile-archaic tendency to heedless projection and illusion. Many scientifically minded persons have even sacrificed their religious and philosophical leanings for fear of uncontrolled subjectivism. By way of compensation for the loss of a world that pulsed with our blood and breathed with our breath, we have developed an enthusiasm for *facts* – mountains of facts, far beyond any single individual's power to survey. We have the pious hope that this incidental accumulation of facts will form a meaningful whole, but nobody is quite sure, because no human brain can possibly comprehend the gigantic sum-total of this mass-produced knowledge. The facts bury us, but whoever dares to speculate must pay for it with a bad conscience – and rightly so, for he will instantly be tripped up by the facts.

768   Western psychology knows the mind as the mental functioning of a psyche. It is the 'mentality' of an individual. An impersonal Universal Mind is still to be met with in the sphere of philosophy, where it seems to be a relic of the orignal human 'soul'. This picture of our Western outlook may seem a little drastic, but I do not think it is far from the truth. At all events, something of the kind presents itself as soon as we are confronted with the Eastern mentality. In the East, mind is a cosmic factor, the very essence of existence; while in the West we have just begun to understand that it is the essential condition of cognition, and hence of the cognitive existence of the world. There is no conflict between religion and science in the East, because no science is there based upon the passion for facts, and no religion upon mere faith; there is religous cognition and cognitive religion.[2] With us, man is incommensurably small and the grace of God is everything; but in the East, man is God and he redeems himself. The gods of Tibetan Buddhism belong to the sphere of illusory separateness and mind-created projections, and yet they exist; but so far as we are concerned an illusion remains an illusion, and thus is nothing at all. It is a paradox, yet nevertheless true, that with us a thought has no proper reality; we treat it as if it were a nothingness. Even though the thought be true in itself, we

hold that it exists only by virtue of certain facts which it is said to formulate. We can produce a most devastating fact like the atom bomb with the help of this ever-changing phantasmagoria of virtually non-existent thoughts, but it seems wholly absurd to us that one could ever establish the reality of thought itself.

769   'Psychic reality' is a controversial concept, like 'psyche' or 'mind'. By the latter terms some understand consciousness and its contents, others allow the existence of 'dark' or 'subconscious' representations. Some include instincts in the psychic realm, others exclude them. The vast majority consider the psyche to be a result of biochemical processes in the brain cells. A few conjecture that it is the psyche that makes the cortical cells function. Some identify 'life' with psyche. But only an insignificant minority regards the psychic phenomenon as a category of existence *per se* and draws the necessary conclusions. It is indeed paradoxical that *the* category of existence, the indispensable *sine qua non* of all existence, namely the psyche, should be treated as if it were only semi-existent. Psychic existence is the only category of existence of which we have *immediate* knowledge, since nothing can be known unless it first appears as a psychic image. Only psychic existence is immediately verifiable. To the extent that the world does not assume the form of a psychic image, it is virtually non-existent. This is a fact which, with few exceptions – as, for instance, in Schopenhauer's philosophy – the West has not yet fully realized. But Schopenhauer was influenced by Buddhism and by the Upanishads.

770   Even a superficial acquaintance with Eastern thought is sufficient to show that a fundamental difference divides East and West. The East bases itself upon psychic reality, that is, upon the psyche as the main and unique condition of existence. It seems as if this Eastern recognition were a psychological or temperamental fact rather than a result of philosophical reasoning. It is a typically introverted point of view, contrasted with the equally typical extraverted point of view of the West.[3] Introversion and extraversion are known to be temperamental or even constitutional attitudes which are never intentionally adopted in normal circumstances. In exceptional cases they may be produced at will, but only under very special conditions. Introversion is, if one may so express it, the 'style' of the East, a habitual and collective attitude, just as extraversion is the 'style' of the West. Introversion is felt here as something abnormal, morbid or otherwise objectionable. Freud identifies it with an autoerotic, 'narcissistic' attitude of mind. He shares his negative position with the National Socialist philosophy of modern Germany,[4] which accuses introversion of being an offence against community feeling. In the East, however, our cherished extraversion is depreciated as illusory desirousness, as existence in the *samsāra*, the very essence of the *nidāna*-chain which culminates in the sum of the world's sufferings.[5] Anyone with practical knowledge of the mutual depreciation of values between introvert and extravert will understand the

emotional conflict between the Eastern and the Western standpoint. For those who know something of the history of European philosophy the bitter wrangling about 'universals' which began with Plato will provide an instructive example. I do not wish to go into all the ramifications of this conflict between introversion and extraversion, but I must mention the religious aspects of the problem. The Christian West considers man to be wholly dependent upon the grace of God, or at least upon the Church as the exclusive and divinely sanctioned earthly instrument of man's redemption. The East, however, insists that man is the sole cause of his higher development, for it believes in 'self-liberation'.

771   The religious point of view always expresses and formulates the essential psychological attitude and its specific prejudices, even in the case of people who have forgotten, or who have never heard of, their own religion. In spite of everything, the West is thoroughly Christian as far as its psychology is concerned. Tertullian's *anima naturaliter christiana* holds true throughout the West – not, as he thought, in the religious sense, but in a psychological one. Grace comes from elsewhere; at all events from outside. Every other point of view is sheer heresy. Hence it is quite understandable why the human psyche is suffering from undervaluation. Anyone who dares to establish a connection between the psyche and the idea of God is immediately accused of 'psychologism' or suspected of morbid 'mysticism'. The East, on the other hand, compassionately tolerates those 'lower' spiritual stages where man, in his blind ignorance of karma, still bothers about sin, and tortures his imagination with a belief in absolute gods, who, if he only looked deeper, are nothing but the veil of illusion woven by his own unenlightened mind. The psyche is therefore all-important; it is the all-pervading Breath, the Buddha-essence; it is the Buddha-Mind, the One, the *dharma-kāya*. All existence emanates from it, and all separate forms dissolve back into it. This is the basic psychological prejudice that permeates Eastern man in every fibre of his being, seeping into all his thoughts, feelings and deeds, no matter what creed he professes.

772   In the same way Western man is Christian, no matter to what denomination his Christianity belongs. For him man is small inside, he is next to nothing; moreover, as Kierkegaard says, 'before God man is always wrong'. By fear, repentance, promises, submission, self-abasement, good deeds and praise he propitiates the great power, which is not himself but *totaliter aliter*, the Wholly Other, altogether perfect and 'outside', the only reality.[6] If you shift the formula a bit and substitute for God some other power, for instance the world or money, you get a complete picture of Western man – assiduous, fearful, devout, self-abasing, enterprising, greedy and violent in his pursuit of the goods of this world: possessions, health, knowledge, technical mastery, public welfare, political power, conquest, and so on. What are the great popular movements of our time? Attempts to grab the money or property of others and to protect our own. The mind is chiefly employed in devising suitable 'isms' to hide the real

motives or to get more loot. I refrain from describing what would happen to Eastern man should he forget his ideal of Buddhahood, for I do not want to give such an unfair advantage to my Western prejudices. But I cannot help raising the question of whether it is possible, or indeed advisable, for either to imitate the other's standpoint. The difference between them is so vast that one can see no reasonable possibility of this, much less its advisability. You cannot mix fire and water. The Eastern attitude stultifies the Western, and vice versa. You cannot be a good Christian and redeem yourself, nor can you be a Buddha and worship God. It is much better to accept the conflict, for it admits only of an irrational solution, if any.

773   By an inevitable decree of fate the West is becoming acquainted with the peculiar facts of Eastern spirituality. It is useless either to belittle these facts, or to build false and treacherous bridges over yawning gaps. Instead of learning the spiritual techniques of the East by heart and imitating them in a thoroughly Christian way – *imitatio Christi*! – with a correspondingly forced attitude, it would be far more to the point to find out whether there exists in the unconscious an introverted tendency similar to that which has become the guiding spiritual principle of the East. We should then be in a position to build on our own ground with our own methods. If we snatch these things direct from the East, we have merely indulged our Western acquisitiveness, confirming yet again that 'everything good is outside', whence it has to be fetched and pumped into our barren souls.[7] It seems to me that we have really learned something from the East when we understand that the psyche contains riches enough without having to be primed from outside, and when we feel capable of evolving out of ourselves with or without divine grace. But we cannot embark upon this ambitious enterprise until we have learned how to deal with our spiritual pride and blasphemous self-assertiveness. The Eastern attitude violates the specifically Christian values, and it is no good blinking this fact. If our new attitude is to be genuine, i.e. grounded in our own history, it must be acquired with full consciousness of the Christian values and of the conflict between them and the introverted attitude of the East. We must get at the Eastern values from within and not from without, seeking them in ourselves, in the unconscious. We shall then discover how great is our fear of the unconscious and how formidable are our resistances. Because of these resistances we doubt the very thing that seems so obvious to the East, namely, the *self-liberating power of the introverted mind*.

774   This aspect of the mind is practically unknown to the West, though it forms the most important component of the unconscious. Many people flatly deny the existence of the unconscious, or else they say that it consists merely of instincts, or of repressed or forgotten contents that were once part of the conscious mind. It is safe to assume that what the East calls 'mind' has more to do with our 'unconscious' than with mind as we understand it, which is more or less identical with consciousness. To us, consciousness is inconceivable without an ego; it is equated with the

relation of contents to an ego. If there is no ego there is nobody to be conscious of anything. The ego is therefore indispensable to the conscious process. The Eastern mind, however, has no difficulty in conceiving of a consciousness without an ego. Consciousness is deemed capable of transcending its ego condition; indeed, in its 'higher' forms, the ego disappears altogether. Such an ego-less mental condition can only be unconscious to us, for the simple reason that there would be nobody to witness it. I do not doubt the existence of mental states transcending consciousness. But they lose their consciousness to exactly the same degree that they transcend consciousness. I cannot imagine a conscious mental state that does not relate to a subject, that is, to an ego. The ego may be depotentiated – divested, for instance, of its awareness of the body – but so long as there is awareness of something, there must be somebody who is aware. The unconscious, however, is a mental condition of which no ego is aware. It is only by indirect means that we eventually become conscious of the existence of an unconscious. We can observe the manifestation of unconscious fragments of the personality, detached from the patient's consciousness, in insanity. But there is no evidence that the unconscious contents are related to an unconscious centre analogous to the ego; in fact there are good reasons why such a centre is not even probable.

775   The fact that the East can dispose so easily of the ego seems to point to a mind that is not to be identified with our 'mind'. Certainly the ego does not play the same role in Eastern thought as it does with us. It seems as if the Eastern mind were less egocentric, as if its contents were more loosely connected with the subject, and as if greater stress were laid on mental states which include a depotentiated ego. It also seems as if *hatha* yoga were chiefly useful as a means for extinguishing the ego by fettering its unruly impulses. There is no doubt that the higher forms of yoga, in so far as they strive to reach *samādhi*, seek a mental condition in which the ego is practically dissolved. Consciousness in our sense of the word is rated a definitely inferior condition, the state of *avidyā* (ignorance), whereas what we call the 'dark background of consciousness' is understood to be a 'higher' consciousness.[8] Thus our concept of the 'collective unconscious' would be the European equivalent of *buddhi*, the enlightened mind.

776   In view of all this, the Eastern form of 'sublimation' amounts to a withdrawal of the centre of psychic gravity from ego-consciousness, which holds a middle position between the body and the ideational processes of the psyche. The lower, semi-physiological strata of the psyche are subdued by *askesis*, i.e. exercises, and kept under control. They are not exactly denied or suppressed by a supreme effort of the will, as is customary in Western sublimation. Rather, the lower psychic strata are adapted and shaped through the patient practice of *hatha* yoga until they no longer interfere with the development of 'higher' consciousness. This peculiar process seems to be aided by the fact that the ego and its desires are checked by the greater importance which the East habitually attaches to

the 'subjective factor'.[9] By this I mean the 'dark background' of consciousness, the unconscious. The introverted attitude is characterized in general by an emphasis on the *a priori* data of apperception. As is well known, the act of apperception consists of two phases: first the perception of the object, second the assimilation of the perception to a pre-existing pattern or concept by means of which the object is 'comprehended'. The psyche is not a nonentity devoid of all quality; it is a definite system made up of definite conditions and it reacts in a specific way. Every new representation, be it a perception or a spontaneous thought, arouses associations which derive from the storehouse of memory. These leap immediately into consciousness, producing the complex picture of an 'impression', though this is already a sort of interpretation. The unconscious disposition upon which the quality of the impression depends is what I call the 'subjective factor'. It deserves the qualification 'subjective' because objectivity is hardly ever conferred by a first impression. Usually a rather laborious process of verification, comparison and analysis is needed to modify and adapt the immediate reactions of the subjective factor.

777   The prominence of the subjective factor does not imply a *personal subjectivism*, despite the readiness of the extraverted attitude to dismiss the subjective factor as 'nothing but' subjective. The psyche and its structure are real enough. They even transform material objects into psychic images, as we have said. They do not perceive waves, but sound; not wave-lengths, but colours. Existence is as we see and understand it. There are innumerable things that can be seen, felt and understood in a great variety of ways. Quite apart from merely personal prejudices, the psyche assimilates external facts in its own way, which is based ultimately upon the laws or patterns of apperception. These laws do not change, although different ages or different parts of the world call them by different names. On a primitive level people are afraid of witches; on the modern level we are apprehensively aware of microbes. There everybody believes in ghosts, here everybody believes in vitamins. Once upon a time men were possessed by devils, now they are not less obsessed by ideas, and so on.

778   The subjective factor is made up, in the last resort, of the eternal patterns of psychic functioning. Anyone who relies upon the subjective factor is therefore basing himself on the reality of psychic law. So he can hardly be said to be wrong. If by this means he succeeds in extending his consciousness downwards, to touch the basic laws of psychic life, he is in possession of that truth which the psyche will naturally evolve if not fatally interfered with by the non-psychic, i.e. the external, world. At any rate, his truth could be weighed against the sum of all knowledge acquired through the investigation of externals. We in the West believe that a truth is satisfactory only if it can be verified by external facts. We believe in the most exact observation and exploration of nature; our truth must coincide with the behaviour of the external world, otherwise it is merely

'subjective'. In the same way that the East turns its gaze from the dance of *prakriti* (physis) and from the multitudinous illusory forms of *māyā*, the West shuns the unconscious and its futile fantasies. Despite its introverted attitude, however, the East knows very well how to deal with the external world. And despite its extraversions the West, too, has a way of dealing with the psyche and its demands; it has an institution called the Church, which gives expression to the unknown psyche of man through its rites and dogmas. Nor are natural science and modern techniques by any means the invention of the West. Their Eastern equivalents are somewhat old fashioned, or even primitive. But what we have to show in the way of spiritual insight and psychological technique must seem, when compared with yoga, just as backward as Eastern astrology and medicine when compared with Western science. I do not deny the efficacy of the Christian Church; but, if you compare the *Exercitia* of Ignatius Loyola with yoga, you will take my meaning. There is a difference, and a big one. To jump straight from that level into Eastern yoga is no more advisable than the sudden transformation of Asian peoples into half-baked Europeans. I have serious doubts as to the blessings of Western civilization, and I have similar misgivings as to the adoption of Eastern spirituality by the West. Yet the two contradictory worlds have met. The East is in full trans-formation; it is thoroughly and fatally disturbed. Even the most efficient methods of European warfare have been successfully imitated. The trouble with us seems to be far more psychological. Our blight is ideologies – they are the long-expected Antichrist! National Socialism comes as near to being a religious movement as any movement since AD 622.[10] Communism claims to be paradise come to earth again. We are far better protected against failing crops, inundations, epidemics and invasions from the Turk than we are against our own deplorable spiritual inferiority, which seems to have little resistance to psychic epidemics.

779   In its religious attitude, too, the West is extraverted. Nowadays it is gratuitously offensive to say that Christianity implies hostility, or even indifference, to the world and the flesh. On the contrary, the good Christian is a jovial citizen, an enterprising businessman, an excellent soldier, the very best in every profession there is. Worldly goods are often interpreted as special rewards for Christian behaviour, and in the Lord's Prayer the adjective ἐπιούσιος, *supersubstantialis*,[11] referring to the bread, has long since been omitted, for the real bread obviously makes so very much more sense! It is only logical that extraversion, when carried to such lengths, cannot credit man with a psyche which contains anything not imported into it from outside, either by human teaching or by divine grace. From this point of view it is downright blasphemy to assert that man has it in him to accomplish his own redemption. Nothing in our religion encourages the idea of the self-liberating power of the mind. Yet a very modern form of psychology – 'analytical' or 'complex' psychology – envisages the possibility of there being certain processes in the unconscious which, by

virtue of their symbolism, compensate the defects and anfractuosities of the conscious attitude. When these unconscious compensations are made conscious through the analytical technique, they produce such a change in the conscious attitude that we are entitled to speak of a new level of consciousness. The method cannot, however, produce the actual process of unconscious compensation; for that we depend upon the unconscious psyche or the 'grace of God' – names make no difference. But the unconscious process itself hardly ever reaches consciousness without technical aid. When brought to the surface, it reveals contents that offer a striking contrast to the general run of conscious thinking and feeling. If that were not so, they would not have a compensatory effect. The first effect, however, is usually a conflict, because the conscious attitude resists the intrusion of apparently incompatible and extraneous tendencies, thoughts, feelings, etc. Schizophrenia yields the most startling examples of such intrusions of utterly foreign and unacceptable contents. In schizophrenia it is, of course, a question of pathological distortions and exaggerations, but anybody with the slightest knowledge of the normal material will easily recognize the sameness of the underlying patterns. It is, as a matter of fact, the same imagery that one finds in mythology and other archaic thought-forms.

780   Under normal conditions, every conflict stimulates the mind to activity for the purpose of creating a satisfactory solution. Usually – i.e. in the West – the conscious standpoint arbitrarily decides against the unconscious, since anything coming from inside suffers from the prejudice of being regarded as inferior or somehow wrong. But in the cases with which we are here concerned it is tacitly agreed that the apparently incompatible contents shall not be suppressed again, and that the conflict shall be accepted and suffered. At first no solution appears possible, and this fact, too, has to be borne with patience. The suspension thus created 'constellates' the unconscious – in other words, the conscious suspense produces a new compensatory reaction in the unconscious. This reaction (usually manifested in dreams) is brought to conscious realization in its turn. The conscious mind is thus confronted with a new aspect of the psyche, which arouses a different problem or modifies an old one in an unexpected way. The procedure is continued until the original conflict is satisfactorily resolved. The whole process is called the 'transcendent function'. It is a process and a method at the same time. The production of unconscious compensations is a spontaneous *process*; the conscious realization is a *method*. The function is called 'transcendent' because it facilitates the transition from one psychic condition to another by means of the mutual confrontation of opposites.

781   This is a very sketchy description of the transcendent function, and for details I must refer the reader to the relevant literature.[12] But I felt it necessary to call attention to these psychological observations and methods because they indicate the way by which we may find access to the sort of

'mind' referred to in our text. This is the image-creating mind, the matrix of all those patterns that give apperception its peculiar character. These patterns are inherent in the unconscious 'mind'; they are its structural elements, and they alone can explain why certain mythological motifs are more or less ubiquitous, even where migration as a means of transmission is exceedingly improbable. Dreams, fantasies and psychoses produce images to all appearances identical with mythological motifs of which the individuals concerned had absolutely no knowledge, not even indirect knowledge acquired through popular figures of speech or through the symbolic language of the Bible.[13] The psychopathology of schizophrenia, as well as the psychology of the unconscious, demonstrate the production of archaic material beyond a doubt. Whatever the structure of the unconscious may be, one thing is certain: it contains an indefinite number of motifs or patterns of an archaic character, in principle identical with the root ideas of mythology and similar thought-forms.

782   Because the unconscious is the matrix mind, the quality of creativeness attaches to it. It is the birthplace of thought forms such as our text considers the Universal Mind to be. Since we cannot attribute any particular form to the unconscious, the Eastern assertion that the Universal Mind is without form, the *arupaloka*, yet is the source of all forms, seems to be psychologically justified. In so far as the forms or patterns of the unconscious belong to no time in particular, being seemingly eternal, they convey a peculiar feeling of timelessness when consciously realized. We find similar statements in primitive psychology: for instance, the Australian word *aljira*[14] means 'dream' as well as 'ghostland' and the 'time' in which the ancestors lived and still live. It is, as they say, the 'time when there was no time'. This looks like an obvious concretization and projection of the unconscious with all its characteristic qualities – its dream manifestations, its ancestral world of thought-forms, and its timelessness.

783   An introverted attitude, therefore, which withdraws its emphasis from the external world (the world of consciousness) and localizes it in the subjective factor (the background of consciousness) necessarily calls forth the characteristic manifestations of the unconscious, namely, archaic thought-forms imbued with 'ancestral' or 'historic' feeling, and, beyond them, the sense of indefiniteness, timelessness, oneness. The extraordinary feeling of oneness is a common experience in all forms of 'mysticism' and probably derives from the general contamination of contents, which increases as consciousness dims. The almost limitless contamination of images in dreams, and particularly in the products of insanity, testifies to their unconscious origin. In contrast to the clear distinction and differentiation of forms in consciousness, unconscious contents are incredibly vague and for this reason capable of any amount of contamination. If we tried to conceive of a state in which nothing is distinct, we should certainly feel the whole as one. Hence it is not unlikely that the peculiar experience of oneness derives from the subliminal awareness of all-contamination in the unconscious.

784   By means of the transcendent function we not only gain access to the 'One Mind' but also come to understand why the East believes in the possibility of self-liberation. If, through introspection and the conscious realization of unconscious compensations, it is possible to transform one's mental condition and thus arrive at a solution of painful conflicts, one would seem entitled to speak of 'self-liberation'. But, as I have already hinted, there is a hitch in this proud claim to self-liberation, for a man cannot produce these unconscious compensations at will. He has to rely upon the possibility that they *may* be produced. Nor can he alter the peculiar character of the compensation: *est ut est aut non est* – 'it is as it is or it isn't at all'. It is a curious thing that Eastern philosophy seems to be almost unaware of this highly important fact. And it is precisely this fact that provides the psychological justification for the Western point of view. It seems as if the Western mind had a most penetrating intuition of man's fateful dependence upon some dark power which must co-operate if all is to be well. Indeed, whenever and wherever the unconscious fails to co-operate, man is instantly at a loss, even in his most ordinary activities. There may be a failure of memory, of co-ordinated action, or of interest and concentration; and such failure may well be the cause of serious annoyance, or of a fatal accident, a professional disaster, or a moral collapse. Formerly, men called the gods unfavourable; now we prefer to call it a neurosis, and we seek the cause in lack of vitamins, in endocrine disturbances, overwork or sex. The co-operation of the unconscious, which is something we never think of and always take for granted, is, when it suddenly fails, a very serious matter indeed.

785   In comparison with other races – the Chinese for instance – the white man's mental equilibrium, or, to put it bluntly, his brain, seems to be his tender spot. We naturally try to get as far away from our weaknesses as possible, a fact which may explain the sort of extraversion that is always seeking security by dominating its surroundings. Extraversion goes hand in hand with mistrust of the inner man, if indeed there is any consciousness of him at all. Moreover, we all tend to undervalue the things we are afraid of. There must be some such reason for our absolute conviction that *nihil est in intellectu quod non antea fuerit in sensu*, which is the motto of Western extraversion. But, as we have emphasized, this extraversion is psychologically justified by the vital fact that unconscious compensation lies beyond man's control. I know that yoga prides itself on being able to control even the unconscious processes, so that nothing can happen in the psyche as a whole that is not ruled by a supreme consciousness. I have not the slightest doubt that such a condition is more or less possible. But it is possible only at the price of becoming identical with the unconscious. Such an identity is the Eastern equivalent of our Western fetish of 'complete objectivity', the machine-like subservience to one goal, to one idea or cause, at the cost of losing every trace of inner life. From the Eastern point of view this complete objectivity is appalling, for it amounts

to complete identity with the *samsāra*; to the West, on the other hand, *samādhi* is nothing but a meaningless dream-state. In the East, the inner man has always had such a firm hold on the outer man that the world had no chance of tearing him away from his inner roots; in the West, the outer man gained the ascendency to such an extent that he was alienated from his innermost being. The One Mind, Oneness, indefiniteness, and eternity remained the prerogative of the One God. Man became small, futile and essentially in the wrong.

786   I think it is becoming clear from my argument that the two standpoints, however contradictory, each have their psychological justification. Both are one-sided in that they fail to see and take account of those factors which do not fit in with their typical attitude. The one underrates the world of consciousness, the other the world of the One Mind. The result is that, in their extremism, both lose one half of the universe; their life is shut off from total reality, and is apt to become artificial and inhuman. In the West, there is the mania for 'objectivity', the asceticism of the scientist or of the stockbroker, who throws away the beauty and universality of life for the sake of the ideal, or not so ideal, goal. In the East, there is the wisdom, peace, detachment and inertia of a psyche that has returned to its dim origins, having left behind all the sorrow and joy of existence as it is and, presumably, ought to be. No wonder that one-sidedness produces very similar forms of monasticism in both cases, guaranteeing to the hermit, the holy man, the monk or the scientist unswerving singleness of purpose. I have nothing against one-sidedness as such. Man, the great experiment of nature, or his own great experiment, is evidently entitled to all such undertakings – if he can endure them. Without one-sidedness the spirit of man could not unfold in all its diversity. But I do not think there is any harm in trying to understand both sides.

787   The extraverted tendency of the West and the introverted tendency of the East have one important purpose in common: both make desperate efforts to conquer the mere naturalness of life. It is the assertion of mind over matter, the *opus contra naturam*, a symptom of the youthfulness of man, still delighting in the use of the most powerful weapon ever devised by nature: the conscious mind. The afternoon of humanity, in a distant future, may yet evolve a different ideal. In time, even conquest will cease to be the dream.

NOTES

1 [Written in English in 1939 and first published in *The Tibetan Book of the Great Liberation*, the texts of which were translated from Tibetan by various hands and edited by W. Y. Evans-Wentz (London and New York, 1954), pp. xxix–lxiv. The commentary is republished here with only minor alterations. – EDITORS.]
2 I am purposely leaving out of account the modernized East.
3 *Psychological Types*, defs. 19 and 34.
4 Written in the year 1939.

5 *Samyutta-nikāya* 12, *Nidāna-samyutta*.

6 [Cf. Otto, *The Idea of the Holy*, pp. 26ff. – EDITORS.]

7 'Whereas who holdeth not God as such an inner possession, but with every means must fetch Him from without . . . verily such a man hath Him not, and easily something cometh to trouble him', Meister Eckhart (Büttner, II, p. 185). Cf. *Meister Eckhart*, trans. by Evans, II, p. 8.

8 In so far as 'higher' and 'lower' are categorical judgements of consciousness, Western psychology does not differentiate unconscious contents in this way. It appears that the East recognizes subhuman psychic conditions, a real 'sub-consciousness' comprising the instincts and semi-physiological psychisms, but classed as a 'higher consciousness'.

9 *Psychological Types*, paras 621ff.

10 [Date of Mohammed's flight (*hegira*) to Medina: beginning of Moslem era.]

11 This is not the unacceptable translation of ἐπιούσιος by Jerome but the ancient spiritual interpretation by Tertullian, Origen and others.

12 *Psychological Types*, def. 51. [Cf. also 'The Transcendent Function'.]

13 Some people find such statements incredible. But either they have no knowledge of primitive psychology, or they are ignorant of the results of psychopathological research. Specific observations occur in my *Symbols of Transformation* and *Psychology and Alchemy*, part II; Nelken, 'Analytische Beobachtungen über Phantasien eines Schizophrenen', pp. 504ff.; Spielrein, 'Über den psychologischen Inhalt eines Falls von Schizophrenie', pp. 329ff.; and C. A. Meier, 'Spontanmanifestationen des kollektiven Unbewussten'.

14 Lévy-Bruhl, *La Mythologie primitive*, pp. xxiii ff.

16 Zen, enlightenment, and psychotherapy

From: 'Foreword to Suzuki's *Introduction to Zen Buddhism*'[1]

877   Daisetz Teitaro Suzuki's works on Zen Buddhism are among the best contributions to the knowledge of living Buddhism that recent decades have produced, and Zen itself is the most important fruit to have sprung from the tree whose roots are the collections of the Pali Canon.[2] We cannot be sufficiently grateful to the author, first for having brought Zen closer to Western understanding, and second for the manner in which he has performed this task. Oriental religious conceptions are usually so very different from our Western ones that even the bare translation of the words often presents the greatest difficulties, quite apart from the meaning of the terms used, which in certain circumstances are better left untranslated. I need only mention the Chinese 'Tao', which no European translation has yet got near. The original Buddhist writings contain views and ideas which are more or less unassimilable for ordinary Europeans. I do not know, for instance, just what kind of mental (or perhaps climatic?) background or preparation is necessary before one can form any completely clear idea of what is meant by the Buddhist *kamma*. Judging by all we know of the nature of Zen, here too we are up against a central conception of unsurpassed singularity. This strange conception is called *satori*, which may be translated as 'enlightenment'. '*Satori* is the *raison d'être* of Zen without which Zen is not Zen', says Suzuki.[3] It should not be too difficult for the Western mind to grasp what a mystic understands by 'enlightenment', or what is known as such in religious parlance. *Satori*, however, designates a special kind and way of enlightenment which is practically impossible for the European to appreciate. By way of illustration, I would refer the reader to the enlightenment of Hyakujo (Pai-chang Huai-hai, AD 724–814) and of the Confucian poet and statesman Kozankoku (Huang Shan-ku),[4] as described by Suzuki.

878   The following may serve as a further example: A monk once went to Gensha, and wanted to learn where the entrance to the path of truth was. Gensha asked him, 'Do you hear the murmuring of the brook?' 'Yes, I hear it', answered the monk. 'There is the entrance', the Master instructed him.

879   I will content myself with these few examples, which aptly illustrate the opacity of *satori* experiences. Even if we take example after example, it

still remains exceedingly obscure how any enlightenment comes and of what it consists – in other words, by what or about what one is enlightened. Kaiten Nukariya, who was himself a professor at the So-to-shu Buddhist College in Tokyo, says, speaking of enlightenment:

> Having set ourselves free from the mistaken conception of self, next we must awaken our innermost wisdom, pure and divine, called the Mind of Buddha, or Bodhi, or Prajna by Zen masters. It is the divine light, the inner heaven, the key to all moral treasures, the centre of thought and consciousness, the source of all influence and power, the seat of kindness, justice, sympathy, impartial love, humanity and mercy, the measure of all things. When this innermost wisdom is fully awakened, we are able to realize that each and every one of us is identical in spirit, in essence, in nature with the universal life or Buddha, that each ever lives face to face with Buddha, that each is beset by the abundant grace of the Blessed One, that He arouses his moral nature, that He opens his spiritual eyes, that He unfolds his new capacity, that He appoints his mission, and that life is not an ocean of birth, disease, old age, and death, nor the vale of tears, but the holy temple of Buddha, the Pure Lane, where he can enjoy the bliss of Nirvana.[5]

880   That is how an Oriental, himself an adept in Zen, describes the essence of enlightenment. One must admit that this passage would need only a few trifling alterations in order to find its way into a Christian mystical book of devotion. Yet somehow it sends us away empty as regards understanding the *satori* experience described again and again in the literature. Presumably Nukariya is addressing himself to Western rationalism, of which he himself acquired a good dose, and that is why it all sounds so flatly edifying. The abstruse obscurity of the Zen anecdotes is distinctly preferable to this adaptation *ad usum Delphini*: it conveys a great deal more by saying less.

881   Zen is anything but a philosophy in the Western sense of the word.[6] This is also the opinion of Rudolf Otto, who says in his foreword to Ohazama's book on Zen that Nukariya has 'imported the magical world of Oriental ideas into our Western philosophical categories' and confused it with these. 'If psycho-physical parallelism, that most wooden of all doctrines, is invoked in order to explain this mystical intuition of Non-duality and Oneness and the *coincidentia oppositorum*, then one is completely outside the sphere of the *koan*, the *kwatsu*, and *satori*.'[7] It is far better to allow oneself to become deeply imbued at the outset with the exotic obscurity of the Zen anecdotes, and to bear in mind the whole time that *satori* is a *mysterium ineffabile*, as indeed the Zen masters wish it to be. Between the anecdote and the mystical enlightenment there is, to our way of thinking, a gulf, and the possibility of bridging it can at best be hinted but never in practice achieved.[8] One has the feeling of touching upon a true secret, and not one that is merely imagined or pretended. It is

not a question of mystification and mumbo-jumbo, but rather of an experience which strikes the experient dumb. *Satori* comes upon one unawares, as something utterly unexpected.

882   When, in the sphere of Christianity, visions of the Holy Trinity, the Madonna, the Crucified, or of the patron saint are vouchsafed after long spiritual preparation, one has the impression that this is all more or less as it should be. That Jakob Böhme should obtain a glimpse into the *centrum naturae* by means of a sunbeam reflected in a tin platter is also understandable. It is harder to digest Meister Eckhart's vision of the 'little naked boy', not to speak of Swedenborg's 'man in the purple coat', who wanted to dissuade him from overeating, and whom, in spite – or perhaps because – of this, he recognized as the Lord God.[9] Such things are difficult to swallow, bordering as they do on the grotesque. Many of the Zen anecdotes, however, not only border on the grotesque but are right there in the middle of it, and sound like the most crashing nonsense.

883   For anyone who has devoted himself, with love and sympathetic understanding, to studying the flowerlike mind of the Far East, many of these puzzling things, which drive the naive European from one perplexity to another, simply disappear. Zen is indeed one of the most wonderful blossoms of the Chinese spirit[10] – a spirit fertilized by the immense world of Buddhist thought. Anyone who has really tried to understand Buddhist doctrine – even if only to the extent of giving up certain Western prejudices – will begin to suspect treacherous depths beneath the bizarre surface of individual *satori* experiences, or will sense disquieting difficulties which the religion and philosophy of the West have up to now thought fit to disregard. If he is a philosopher, he is exclusively concerned with the kind of understanding that has nothing to do with life. And if he is a Christian, he has of course no truck with heathens ('God, I thank thee that I am not as other men are'). There is no *satori* within these Western limits – that is a purely Oriental affair. But is this really so? Have we in fact no *satori*?

884   When one reads the Zen texts attentively, one cannot escape the impression that, however bizarre, *satori* is a *natural occurrence*, something so very simple,[11] even, that one fails to see the wood for the trees, and in attempting to explain it invariably says the very thing that throws others into the greatest confusion. Nukariya is therefore right when he says that any attempt to explain or analyse the content of Zen, or of the enlightenment, is futile. Nevertheless he does venture to assert that enlightenment 'implies an insight into the nature of self',[12] and that it is an 'emancipation of mind from illusion concerning self'.[13] The illusion concerning the nature of self is the common confusion of the self with the ego. Nukariya understands by 'self' the All-Buddha, i.e. total consciousness of life. He quotes Pan Shan, who says: 'The moon of mind comprehends all the universe in its light', adding: 'It is Cosmic life and Cosmic spirit, and at the same time individual life and individual spirit.'[14]

885   However one may define the self, it is always something other than the ego, and inasmuch as a higher insight of the ego leads over to the self, the self is a more comprehensive thing which includes the experience of the ego and therefore transcends it. Just as the ego is a certain experience I have of myself, so is the self an experience of my ego. It is, however, no longer experienced in the form of a broader or higher ego, but in the form of a non-ego.

886   Such thoughts were familiar to the anonymous author of the *Theologia Germanica*:

> In whatsoever creature the Perfect shall be known, therein creature-nature, created state, I-hood, selfhood, and the like must all be given up and done away.[15]
>
> Now that I arrogate anything good to myself, as if I were, or had done, or knew, or could perform any good thing, or that it were mine; that is all out of blindness and folly. For if the real truth were in me, I should understand that I am not that good thing, and that it is not mine nor of me.
>
> Then the man says: 'Behold! I, poor fool that I was, thought it was I, but behold! it is, and was, of a truth, God!'[16]

887   This tells us a good deal about the 'content of enlightenment'. The occurrence of *satori* is interpreted and formulated as a *breakthrough*, by a consciousness limited to the ego-form, into the non-ego-like self. This view is in accord not only with the essence of Zen, but also with the mysticism of Meister Eckhart:

> When I flowed out from God, all things declared, 'God is!' Now this cannot make me blessed, for thereby I acknowledge myself a creature. But in the breakthrough[17] I stand empty in the will of God, and empty also of God's will, and of all his works, even of God himself – then I am more than all creatures, then I am neither God nor creature: I am what I was, and that I shall remain, now and ever more! Then I receive a thrust which carries me above all angels. By this thrust I become so rich that God cannot suffice me, despite all that he is as God and all his godly works; for in this breakthrough I receive what God and I have in common. I am what I was,[18] I neither increase nor diminish, for I am the unmoved mover that moves all things. Here God can find no more place in man, for man by his emptiness has won back that which he was eternally and ever shall remain.[19]

888   Here the Master may actually be describing a *satori* experience, a supersession of the ego by the self, which is endued with the 'Buddha nature' or divine universality. Since, out of scientific modesty, I do not presume to make a metaphysical statement, but am referring only to a change of consciousness that can be experienced, I treat *satori* first of all

as a psychological problem. For anyone who does not share or understand this point of view, the 'explanation' will consist of nothing but words which have no tangible meaning. He is then incapable of throwing a bridge from these abstractions to the facts reported; that is to say, he cannot understand how the scent of the blossoming laurel or the tweaked nose[20] could bring about so formidable a change of consciousness. Naturally the simplest thing would be to relegate all these anecdotes to the realm of amusing fairy-tales, or, if one accepts the facts as they are, to write them off as instances of self-deception. (Another favourite explanation is 'auto-suggestion', that pathetic white elephant from the arsenal of intellectual inadequacies!) But no serious and responsible investigation can pass over these facts unheedingly. Of course, we can never decide definitely whether a person is *really* 'enlightened' or 'released', or whether he merely imagines it. We have no criteria to go on. Moreover, we know well enough that an imaginary pain is often far more agonizing than a so-called 'real' one, since it is accompanied by a subtle moral suffering caused by a dull feeling of secret self-accusation. In this sense, therefore, it is not a question of 'actual fact' but of *psychic reality*, i.e. the psychic process known as *satori*.

889   Every psychic process is an image and an 'imagining', otherwise no consciousness could exist and the occurrence would lack phenomenality. Imagination itself is a psychic process, for which reason it is completely irrelevant whether the enlightenment be called 'real' or 'imaginary'. The person who has the enlightenment, or alleges that he has it, thinks at all events that he is enlightened. What others think about it decides nothing whatever for him in regard to his experience. Even if he were lying, his lie would still be a psychic fact. Indeed, even if all the reports of religious experiences were nothing but deliberate inventions and falsifications, a very interesting psychological treatise could still be written about the incidence of such lies, and with the same scientific objectivity with which one describes the psychopathology of delusional ideas. The fact that there is a religious movement upon which many brilliant minds have worked over a period of many centuries is sufficient reason for at least venturing a serious attempt to bring such processes within the realm of scientific understanding.

890   Earlier, I raised the question of whether we have anything like *satori* in the West. If we discount the sayings of our Western mystics, a superficial glance discloses nothing that could be likened to it in even the faintest degree. The possibility that there are stages in the development of consciousness plays no role in our thinking. The mere thought that there is a tremendous psychological difference between consciousness of the existence of an object and 'consciousness of the consciousness' of an object borders on a quibble that hardly needs answering. For the same reason, one could hardly bring oneself to take such a problem seriously enough to consider the psychological conditions in which it arose. It is significant that questions of this kind do not, as a rule, arise from any

intellectual need, but, where they exist, are nearly always rooted in an originally religious practice. In India it was yoga and in China Buddhism which supplied the driving force for these attempts to wrench oneself free from bondage to a state of consciousness that was felt to be incomplete. So far as Western mysticism is concerned, its texts are full of instructions as to how man can and must release himself from the 'I-ness' of his consciousness, so that through knowledge of his own nature he may rise above it and attain the inner (godlike) man. John of Ruysbroeck makes use of an image which was also known to Indian philosophy, that of the tree whose roots are above and its branches below:[21] 'And he must climb up into the tree of faith, which grows from above downwards, for its roots are in the Godhead.'[22] He also says, like the yogi: 'Man must be free and without ideas, released from all attachments and empty of all creatures.'[23] 'He must be untouched by joy and sorrow, profit and loss, rising and falling, concern for others, pleasure and fear, and not be attached to any creature.'[24] It is in this that the 'unity' of his being consists, and this means 'being turned inwards'. Being turned inwards means that 'a man is turned within, into his own heart, that he may understand and feel the inner working and the inner words of God'.[25] This new state of consciousness born of religious practice is distinguished by the fact that outward things no longer affect an ego-bound consciousness, thus giving rise to mutual attachment, but that an empty consciousness stands open to another influence. This 'other' influence is no longer felt as one's own activity, but as that of a non-ego which has the conscious mind as its object.[26] It is as if the subject-character of the ego had been overrun, or taken over, by another subject which appears in place of the ego.[27] This is a well-known religious experience, already formulated by St Paul.[28] Undoubtedly a new state of consciousness is described here, separated from the earlier state by an incisive process of religious transformation.

891   It could be objected that consciousness in itself has not changed, only the consciousness of something, just as though one had turned over the page of a book and now saw a different picture with the same eyes. I am afraid this is no more than an arbitrary interpretation, for it does not fit the facts. The fact is that in the texts it is not merely a different picture or object that is described, but rather an experience of transformation, often occurring amid the most violent psychic convulsions. The blotting out of one picture and its replacement by another is an everyday occurrence which has none of the attributes of a transformation experience. *It is not that something different is seen, but that one sees differently.* It is as though the spatial act of seeing were changed by a new dimension. When the Master asks: 'Do you hear the murmuring of the brook?' he obviously means something quite different from ordinary 'hearing'.[29] Consciousness is something like perception, and like the latter is subject to conditions and limitations. You can, for instance, be conscious at various levels, within a narrower or wider field, more on the surface or deeper down.

These differences in degree are often differences in kind as well, since they depend on the development of the personality as a whole, that is to say, on the nature of the perceiving subject.

892   The intellect has no interest in the nature of the perceiving subject so far as the latter only thinks logically. The intellect is essentially concerned with elaborating the contents of consciousness and with methods of elaboration. A rare philosophic passion is needed to compel the attempt to get beyond intellect and break through to a 'knowledge of the knower'. Such a passion is practically indistinguishable from the driving force of religion; consequently this whole problem belongs to the religious transformation process, which is incommensurable with intellect. Classical philosophy subserves this process on a wide scale, but this can be said less and less of the newer philosophy. Schopenhauer is still – with qualifications – classical, but Nietzsche's *Zarathustra* is no longer philosophy at all: it is a dramatic process of transformation which has completely swallowed up the intellect. It is no longer concerned with thought, but, in the highest sense, with the thinker of thought – and this on every page of the book. A new man, a completely transformed man, is to appear on the scene, one who has broken the shell of the old and who not only looks upon a new heaven and a new earth, but has created them. Angelus Silesius puts it rather more modestly than Zarathustra:

> My body is a shell in which a chick lies closed about;
> Brooded by the spirit of eternity, it waits its hatching out.[30]

893   *Satori* corresponds in the Christian sphere to an experience of religious transformation. As there are different degrees and kinds of such an experience, it may not be superfluous to define more accurately the category which corresponds most closely to the Zen experience. This is without doubt the mystic experience, which differs from other types in that its preliminary stages consist in 'letting onself go', in 'emptying oneself of images and ideas', as opposed to those religious experiences which, like the exercises of Ignatius Loyola, are based on the practice of envisaging sacred images. In this latter class I would include transformation through faith and prayer and through collective experience in Protestantism, since a very definite expectation plays the decisive role here, and not by any means 'emptiness' or 'freeness'. The characteristically Eckhartian assertion that 'God is Nothingness' may well be incompatible in principle with the contemplation of the Passion, with faith and collective expectations.

894   Thus the correspondence between *satori* and Western experience is limited to those few Christian mystics whose paradoxical statements skirt the edge of heterodoxy or actually overstep it. As we know, it was this that drew down on Meister Eckhart's writings the condemnation of the Church. If Buddhism were a 'Church' in our sense of the word, she would undoubtedly find Zen an insufferable nuisance. The reason for this is the extreme individualism of its methods, and also the iconoclastic attitude of

many of the Masters.[31] To the extent that Zen is a movement, collective forms have arisen in the course of the centuries, as can be seen from Suzuki's *Training of the Zen Buddhist Monk* (Kyoto, 1934). But these concern externals only. Apart from the typical mode of life, the spiritual training or development seems to lie in the method of the *koan*. The *koan* is understood to be a paradoxical question, statement or action of the Master. Judging by Suzuki's description, it seems to consist chiefly of master-questions handed down in the form of anecdotes. These are submitted by the teacher to the student for meditation. A classic example is the Wu anecdote. A monk once asked the Master: 'Has a dog a Buddha nature too?' Whereupon the Master replied: 'Wu!' As Suzuki remarks, this 'Wu' means quite simply 'bow-wow', obviously just what the dog himself would have said in answer to such a question.[32]

895   At first sight it seems as if the posing of such a question as an object of meditation would anticipate or prejudice the end-result, and that it would therefore determine the content of the experience, just as in the Jesuit exercises or in certain yoga meditations the content is determined by the task set by the teacher. The *koans*, however, are so various, so ambiguous and above all so boundlessly paradoxical that even an expert must be completely in the dark as to what might be considered a suitable solution. In addition, the descriptions of the final result are so obscure that in no single case can one discover any rational connection between the *koan* and the experience of enlightenment. Since no logical sequence can be demonstrated, it remains to be supposed that the *koan* method puts not the smallest restraint upon the freedom of the psychic process and that the end-result therefore springs from nothing but the individual disposition of the pupil. The complete destruction of the rational intellect aimed at in the training creates an almost perfect lack of conscious presuppositions. These are excluded as far as possible, but not unconscious presuppositions – that is, the existing but unrecognized psychological disposition, which is anything but empty or a *tabula rasa*. It is a nature-given factor, and when it answers – this being obviously the *satori* experience – it is an answer of Nature, who has succeeded in conveying her reaction direct to the conscious mind.[33] What the unconscious nature of the pupil presents to the teacher or to the *koan* by way of an answer is, manifestly, *satori*. This seems, at least to me, to be the view which, to judge by the descriptions, formulates the nature of *satori* more or less correctly. It is also supported by the fact that the 'glimpse into one's own nature', the 'original man', and the depths of one's being are often a matter of supreme concern to the Zen master.[34]

896   Zen differs from all other exercises in meditation, whether philosophical or religious, in its total lack of presuppositions. Often Buddha himself is sternly rejected, indeed, almost blasphemously ignored, although – or perhaps just because – he could be the strongest spiritual presupposition of the whole exercise. But he too is an image and must

therefore be set aside. Nothing must be present except what is actually there, that is, man with all his unconscious presuppositions, of which, precisely because they are unconscious, he can never, never rid himself. The answer which appears to come from the void, the light which flares up from the blackest darkness, these have always been experienced as a wonderful and blessed illumination.

897   The world of consciousness is inevitably a world full of restrictions, of walls blocking the way. It is of necessity one-sided, because of the nature of consciousness itself. No consciousness can harbour more than a very small number of simultaneous perceptions. All else must lie in shadow, withdrawn from sight. Any increase in the simultaneous contents immediately produces a dimming of consciousness, if not confusion to the point of disorientation. Consciousness not only requires, but is of its very nature strictly limited to, the few and hence the distinct. We owe our general orientation simply and solely to the fact that through attention we are able to register a fairly rapid succession of images. But attention is an effort of which we are not capable all the time. We have to make do, so to speak, with a minimum of simultaneous perceptions and successions of images. Hence in wide areas possible perceptions are continuously excluded, and consciousness is always bound to the narrowest circle. What would happen if an individual consciousness were able to take in at a single glance a simultaneous picture of every possible perception is beyond imagining. If man has already succeeded in building up the structure of the world from the few distinct things that he can perceive at one and the same time, what godlike spectacle would present itself to his eyes if he were able to perceive a great deal more all at once and distinctly? This question applies only to perceptions that are *possible* to us. If we now add to these the unconscious contents – i.e. contents which are not yet, or no longer, capable of consciousness – and then try to imagine a total vision, why, this is beyond the most audacious fantasy. It is, of course, completely unimaginable in any conscious form, but in the unconscious it is a fact, since everything subliminal holds within it the ever-present possibility of being perceived and represented in consciousness. The unconscious is an irrepresentable totality of all subliminal psychic factors, a 'total vision' *in potentia*. It constitutes the total disposition from which consciousness singles out tiny fragments from time to time.

898   Now if consciousness is emptied as far as possible of its contents, they will fall into a state of unconsciousness, at least for the time being. In Zen, this displacement usually results from the energy being withdrawn from conscious contents and transferred either to the conception of 'emptiness' or to the *koan*. As both of these must be static, the succession of images is abolished and with it the energy which maintains the kinetics of consciousness. The energy thus saved goes over to the unconscious and reinforces its natural charge to bursting-point. This increases the readiness of the unconscious contents to break through into conscious-

ness. But since the emptying and shutting down of consciousness is no easy matter, a special training of indefinite duration[35] is needed in order to set up that maximum tension which leads to the final breakthrough of unconscious contents.

899 The contents that break through are far from being random ones. As psychiatric experience with insane patients shows, specific relations exist between the conscious contents and the delusional ideas that break through in delirium. They are the same relations as exist between the dreams and the waking consciousness of normal people. The connection is an essentially compensatory relationship:[36] the unconscious contents bring to the surface everything that is necessary[37] in the broadest sense for the completion and wholeness of conscious orientation. If the fragments offered by, or forced up from, the unconscious are meaningfully built into conscious life, a form of psychic existence results which corresponds better to the whole of the individual's personality, and so abolishes the fruitless conflicts between his conscious and unconscious self. Modern psychotherapy is based on this principle, in so far as it has been able to free itself from the historical prejudice that the unconscious consists only of infantile and morally inferior contents. There is certainly an inferior corner in it, a lumber room full of dirty secrets, though these are not so much unconscious as hidden and only half-forgotten. But all this has about as much to do with the whole of the unconscious as a decayed tooth has with the total personality. The unconscious is the matrix of all metaphysical statements, of all mythology, of all philosophy (so far as this is not merely critical), and of all expressions of life that are based on psychological premisses.

900 Every invasion of the unconscious is an answer to a definite conscious situation, and this answer follows from the totality of possible ideas present, i.e. from the total disposition which, as explained above, is a simultaneous picture *in potentia* of psychic existence. The splitting-up into single units, its one-sided and fragmentary character, is of the essence of consciousness. The reaction coming from the disposition always has a total character, as it reflects a nature which has not been divided up by any discriminating consciousness.[38] Hence its overpowering effect. It is the unexpected, all-embracing, completely illuminating answer, which works all the more as illumination and revelation since the conscious mind has got itself wedged into a hopeless blind alley.[39]

901 When, therefore, after many years of the hardest practice and the most strenuous demolition of rational understanding, the Zen devotee receives an answer – the only true answer – from Nature herself, everything that is said of *satori* can be understood. As one can see for oneself, it is the *naturalness* of the answer that strikes one most about the Zen anecdotes. Yes, one can accept with a sort of old-roguish satisfaction the story of the enlightened pupil who gave his Master a slap in the face as a reward.[40] And how much wisdom there is in the Master's 'Wu', the answer to the

question about the Buddha-nature of the dog! One must always bear in mind, however, that there are a great many people who cannot distinguish between a metaphysical joke and nonsense, and just as many who are so convinced of their own cleverness that they have never in their lives met any but fools.

902   Great as is the value of Zen Buddhism for understanding the religious transformation process, its use among Western people is very problematical. The mental education necessary for Zen is lacking in the West. Who among us would place such implicit trust in a superior Master and his incomprehensible ways? This respect for the greater human personality is found only in the East. Could any of us boast that he believes in the possibility of a boundlessly paradoxical transformation experience, to the extent, moreover, of sacrificing many years of his life to the wearisome pursuit of such a goal? And finally, who would dare to take upon himself the responsibility for such an unorthodox transformation experience – except a man who was little to be trusted, one who, maybe for pathological reasons, has too much to say for himself? Just such a person would have no cause to complain of any lack of following among us. But let a 'Master' set us a hard task, which requires more than mere parrot talk, and the European begins to have doubts, for the steep path of self-development is to him as mournful and gloomy as the path to hell.

903   I have no doubt that the *satori* experience does occur also in the West, for we too have men who glimpse ultimate goals and spare themselves no pains to draw near to them. But they will keep silent, not only out of shyness, but because they know that any attempt to convey their experience to others is hopeless. There is nothing in our civilization to foster these strivings, not even the Church, the custodian of religious values. Indeed, it is the function of the Church to oppose all original experience, because this can only be unorthodox. The only movement inside our civilization which has, or should have, some understanding of these endeavours is psychotherapy. It is therefore no accident that it is a psychotherapist who is writing this foreword.

904   Psychotherapy is at bottom a dialectical relationship between doctor and patient. It is an encounter, a discussion between two psychic wholes, in which knowledge is used only as a tool. The goal is transformation – not one that is predetermined, but rather an indeterminable change, the only criterion of which is the disappearance of ego-hood. No efforts on the part of the doctor can compel this experience. The most he can do is to smooth the path for the patient and help him to attain an attitude which offers the least resistance to the decisive experience. If knowledge plays no small part in our Western procedure, this is equivalent to the importance of the traditional spiritual atmosphere of Buddhism in Zen. Zen and its technique could only have arisen on the basis of Buddhist culture, which it presupposes at every turn. You cannot annihilate a rationalistic intellect that was never there – no Zen adept was ever the product of ignorance and lack

of culture. Hence it frequently happens with us also that a conscious ego and a cultivated understanding must first be produced through analysis before one can even think about abolishing ego-hood or rationalism. What is more, psychotherapy does not deal with men who, like Zen monks, are ready to make any sacrifice for the sake of truth, but very often with the most stubborn of all Europeans. Thus the tasks of psychotherapy are much more varied, and the individual phases of the long process much more contradictory, than is the case in Zen.

905   For these and many other reasons a direct transplantation of Zen to our Western conditions is neither commendable nor even possible. All the same, the psychotherapist who is seriously concerned with the question of the aim of his therapy cannot remain unmoved when he sees the end towards which this Eastern method of psychic 'healing' – i.e. 'making whole' – is striving. As we know, this question has occupied the most adventurous minds of the East for more than two thousand years, and in this respect methods and philosophical doctrines have been developed which simply put all Western attempts along these lines into the shade. Our attempts have, with few exceptions, all stopped short at either magic (mystery cults, amongst which we must include Christianity) or intellectualism (philosophy from Pythagoras to Schopenhauer). It is only the tragedies of Goethe's *Faust* and Nietzsche's *Zarathustra* which mark the first glimmerings of a breakthrough of total experience in our Western hemisphere.[41] And we do not know even today what these most promising of all products of the Western mind may at length signify, so overlaid are they with the materiality and concreteness of our thinking, as moulded by the Greeks.[42] Despite the fact that our intellect has developed almost to perfection the capacity of the bird of prey to espy the tiniest mouse from the greatest height, yet the pull of the earth drags it down, and the *samskaras* entangle it in a world of confusing images the moment it no longer seeks for booty but turns one eye inwards *to find him who seeks.* Then the individual falls into the throes of a daemonic rebirth, beset with unknown terrors and dangers and menaced by deluding mirages in a labyrinth of error. The worst of all fates threatens the venturer: mute, abysmal loneliness in the age he calls his own. What do we know of the hidden motives for Goethe's 'main business', as he called his *Faust*, or of the shudders of the 'Dionysus experience'? One has to read the *Bardo Thödol*, *The Tibetan Book of the Dead*, backwards, as I have suggested, in order to find an Eastern parallel to the torments and catastrophes of the Western 'way of release' to wholeness. This is the issue here – not good intentions, clever imitations or intellectual acrobatics. And this, in shadowy hints or in greater or lesser fragments, is what the psychotherapist is faced with when he has freed himself from over-hasty and shortsighted doctrinal opinions. If he is a slave to his quasi-biological credo he will always try to reduce what he has glimpsed to the banal and the known, to a rationalistic denominator which satisfies only those who are content with

illusions. But the foremost of all illusions is that anything can ever satisfy anybody. That illusion stands behind all that is unendurable in life and in front of all progress, and it is one of the most difficult things to overcome. If the psychotherapist can take time off from his helpful activities for a little reflection, or if by any chance he is forced into seeing through his own illusions, it may dawn on him how hollow and flat, how inimical to life, are all rationalistic reductions when they come upon something that is alive, that wants to grow. Should he follow this up, he will soon get an idea of what it means to 'open wide that gate / Past which man's steps have ever flinching trod'.[43]

906   I would not under any circumstances like it to be understood that I am making any recommendations or offering any advice. But when one begins to talk about Zen in the West I consider it my duty to show the European where our entrance lies to that 'longest road' which leads to *satori*, and what kind of difficulties bestrew the path which only a few of our great ones have trod – beacons, perhaps, on high mountains, shining out into the dim future. It would be a disastrous mistake to assume that *satori* or *samādhi* is to be met with anywhere below these heights. As an experience of totality it cannot be anything cheaper or smaller than the whole. What this means psychologically can be seen from the simple reflection that consciousness is always only a part of the psyche and therefore never capable of psychic wholeness: for that the indefinite extension of the unconscious is needed. But the unconscious can neither be caught with clever formulas nor exorcized by means of scientific dogmas, for something of destiny clings to it – indeed, it is sometimes destiny itself, as *Faust* and *Zarathustra* show all too clearly. The attainment of wholeness requires one to stake one's whole being. Nothing less will do; there can be no easier conditions, no substitutes, no compromises. Considering that both *Faust* and *Zarathustra*, despite the highest recognition, stand on the borderline of what is comprehensible to the European, one could hardly expect the educated public, which has only just begun to hear about the obscure world of the psyche, to form any adequate conception of the spiritual state of a man caught in the toils of the individuation process – which is my term for 'becoming whole'. People then drag out the vocabulary of pathology and console themselves with the terminology of neurosis and psychosis, or else they whisper about the 'creative secret'. But what can a man 'create' if he doesn't happen to be a poet? This misunderstanding has caused not a few persons in recent times to call themselves – by their own grace – 'artists', just as if art had nothing to do with ability. But if you have nothing at all to create, then perhaps you create yourself.

907   Zen shows how much 'becoming whole' means to the East. Preoccupation with the riddles of Zen may perhaps stiffen the spine of the faint-hearted European or provide a pair of spectacles for his psychic myopia, so that from his 'damned hole in the wall'[44] he may enjoy at least a glimpse of the world of psychic experience, which till now lay shrouded

in fog. No harm can be done, for those who are too frightened will be effectively protected from further corruption, as also from everything of significance, by the helpful idea of 'auto-suggestion'.[45] I should like to warn the attentive and sympathetic reader, however, not to underestimate the spiritual depth of the East, or to assume that there is anything cheap and facile about Zen.[46] The assiduously cultivated credulity of the West in regard to Eastern thought is in this case a lesser danger, as in Zen there are fortunately none of those marvellously incomprehensible words that we find in Indian cults. Neither does Zen play about with complicated *hatha* yoga techniques,[47] which delude the physiologically minded European into the false hope that the spirit can be obtained by just sitting and breathing. On the contrary, Zen demands intelligence and will-power, as do all greater things that want to become realities.

NOTES

1 [Originally published as a foreword to Suzuki, *Die grosse Befreiung: Einführung in den Zen-Buddhismus* (Leipzig, 1939). The Suzuki text had been translated into German by Heinrich Zimmer from the original edition of *An Introduction to Zen Buddhism*. The foreword by Jung was published in an earlier translation by Constance Rolfe in a new edition of the Suzuki work (London and New York 1949). – EDITORS.]

2 The origin of Zen, as Oriental authors themselves admit, is to be found in Buddha's Flower Sermon. On this occasion he held up a flower to a gathering of disciples without uttering a word. Only Kasyapa understood him. Cf. Shuei Ohazama, *Zen: Der lebendige Buddhismus in Japan*, p. 3.

3 *Introduction to Zen Buddhism* (1949), p. 95.

4 ibid., pp. 89 and 92f.

5 *The Religion of the Samurai*, p. 133.

6 'Zen is neither psychology nor philosophy.'

7 In Ohazama, p. viii.

8 If in spite of this I attempt 'explanations' in what follows, I am nevertheless fully aware that in the sense of *satori* I have said nothing valid. All the same, I had to make an attempt to manoeuvre our Western understanding into at least the proximity of an understanding – a task so difficult that in doing it one must take upon oneself certain crimes against the spirit of Zen.

9 Cf. Spamer, ed., *Texte aus der deutschen Mystik des 14. und 15. Jahrhunderts*, p. 143; Evans, *Meister Eckhart*, I, p. 438; William White, *Emanuel Swedenborg*, I, p. 243.

10 'There is no doubt that Zen is one of the most precious and in many respects the most remarkable [of the] spiritual possessions bequeathed to Eastern people' (Suzuki, *Essays on Zen Buddhism*, I, p. 264).

11 'Before a man studies Zen, to him mountains are mountains and waters are waters; after he gets an insight into the truth of Zen, through the instruction of a good master, mountains to him are not mountains and waters are not waters; after this when he really attains to the abode of rest, mountains are once more mountains and waters are waters' (ibid., pp. 22f.).

12 *Religion of the Samurai*, p. 123.

13 ibid., p. 124.

14 ibid., p. 132.

15 *Theologia Germanica*, ed. by Trask, p. 115.

16 ibid., pp. 120–1.
17 There is a similar image in Zen: when a Master was asked what Buddhahood consisted in, he answered, 'The bottom of a pail is broken through' (Suzuki, *Essays*, I, p. 229). Another analogy is the 'bursting of the bag' (*Essays*, II, p. 117).
18 Cf. Suzuki, *Essays*, I, pp. 231, 255. Zen means catching a glimpse of the original nature of man, or the recognition of the original man (p. 157).
19 Cf. Evans, *Meister Eckhart*, p. 221; also *Meister Eckhart: A Modern Translation*, by Blakney, pp. 231f.
20 Suzuki, *Introduction*, pp. 93, 84.
21 'Its root is above, its branches below – this eternal fig tree! . . . That is *brahma*, that is called the Immortal' (*Katha Upanishad*, 6, 1, trans. by Hume, *The Thirteen Principal Upanishads*, p. 358).
22 John of Ruysbroeck, *The Adornment of the Spiritual Marriage*, p. 47. One can hardly suppose that this Flemish mystic, who was born in 1273, borrowed this image from any Indian text.
23 ibid., p. 51.
24 P. 57, modified.
25 ibid., p. 62, modified.
26 'O Lord . . . instruct me in the doctrine of the non-ego, which is grounded in the self-nature of mind.' Cited from the *Lankavatāra Sutra*, in Suzuki, *Essays*, I, p. 89.
27 A Zen Master says: 'Buddha is none other than the mind, or rather, him who strives to see this mind.'
28 Galatians 2:20: 'It is no longer I who live, but Christ who lives in me.'
29 Suzuki says of this change, 'The old way of viewing things is abandoned and the world acquires a new signification . . . a new beauty which exists in the "refreshing breeze" and in the "shining jewel"' (*Essays*, I, p. 249). See also p. 138.
30 From *Der Cherubinischer Wandersmann*. [Trans. by W. R. Trask (unpub.).]
31 '*Satori* is the most intimate individual experience' (*Essays*, I, p. 261).
    A Master says to his pupil: 'I have really nothing to impart to you, and if I tried to do so you might have occasion to make me an object of ridicule. Besides, whatever I can tell you is my own and can never be yours' (*Introduction*, p. 91).
    A monk says to the Master: 'I have been seeking for the Buddha, but do not yet know how to go on with my research.' Said the Master: 'It is very much like looking for an ox when riding on one' (*Essays*, II, p. 74).
    A Master says: 'The mind that does not understand is the Buddha: there is no other' (ibid., p. 72).
32 *Essays*, II, pp. 84, 90.
33 'Zen consciousness is to be nursed to maturity. When it is fully matured, it is sure to break out as satori, which is an insight into the unconscious' (*Essays*, II, p. 60).
34 The fourth maxim of Zen is: 'Seeing into one's nature and the attainment of Buddhahood' (ibid., I, p. 18). When a monk asked Hui-neng for instruction, the Master told him: 'Show me your original face before you were born' (ibid., I, p. 224). A Japaneze Zen book says: 'If you wish to seek the Buddha, you ought to see into your own nature; for this nature is the Buddha himself' (ibid., I, p. 231). A *satori* experience shows a Master the 'original man' (ibid., I, p. 255). Hui-neng said: 'Think not of good, think not of evil, but see what at the moment your own original features are, which you had even before coming into existence' (ibid., II, p. 42).
35 Bodhidarma, the founder of Zen in China, says: 'The incomparable doctrine of Buddhism can be comprehended only after a long hard discipline and by enduring what is most difficult to endure, and by practising what is most difficult to practise. Men of inferior virtue and wisdom are not allowed to understand anything about it. All the labours of such ones will come to naught' (ibid., I, p. 188).

36 This is more probable than one that is merely 'complementary'.

37 This 'necessity' is a working hypothesis. People can, and do, hold very different views on this point. For instance, are religious ideas 'necessary'? Only the course of the individual's life can decide this, i.e. his individual experience. There are no abstract criteria.

38 'When the mind discriminates, there is manifoldness of things; when it does not it looks into the true state of things' (*Essays*, I, p. 99).

39 See the passage beginning 'Have your mind like unto space . . . .' (Suzuki, *Essays*, I, p. 223).

40 *Introduction to Zen Buddhism*, p. 94.

41 In this connection I must also mention the English mystic William Blake. Cf. an excellent account in Percival, *William Blake's Circle of Destiny*.

42 The genius of the Greeks lay in the breakthrough of consciousness into the materiality of the world, thus robbing the world of its original dreamlike quality.

43 *Faust, Part I*, trans. by Wayne, p. 54.

44 ibid., p. 44.

45 *Introduction*, p. 95.

46 'It is no pastime but the most serious task in life; no idlers will ever dare attempt it' (Suzuki, *Essays*, I, p. 27; cf. also p. 92).

47 Says a Master: 'If thou seekest Buddhahood by thus sitting cross-legged, thou murderest him. So long as thou freest thyself not from sitting so, thou never comest to the truth' (*Essays*, I, p. 235; cf. also II, p. 83f).

17 Mandalas and the path to psychic wholeness

From: *Memories, Dreams, Reflections*

In 1918–19 I was in Château d'Oex as Commandant de la Région Anglaise des Internés de Guerre. While I was there I sketched every morning in a notebook a small circular drawing, a mandala, which seemed to correspond to my inner situation at the time. With the help of these drawings I could observe my psychic transformations from day to day. One day, for example, I received a letter from an aesthetic lady in which she again stubbornly maintained that the fantasies arising from my unconscious had artistic value and should be considered art. The letter got on my nerves. It was far from stupid and therefore dangerously persuasive. The modern artist, after all, seeks to create art out of the unconscious. The utilitarianism and self-importance concealed behind this thesis touched a doubt in myself, namely, my uncertainty as to whether the fantasies I was producing were really spontaneous and natural, and not ultimately my own arbitrary inventions. I was by no means free from the bigotry and hubris of consciousness which wants to believe that any halfway decent inspiration is due to one's own merit, whereas inferior reactions come merely by chance, or even derive from alien sources. Out of this irritation and disharmony within myself there proceeded, the following day, a changed mandala: part of the periphery had burst open and the symmetry was destroyed.

Only gradually did I discover what the mandala really is: 'Formation, Transformation, Eternal Mind's eternal recreation'.[1] And that is the self, the wholeness of the personality, which if all goes well is harmonious, but which cannot tolerate self-deceptions.

My mandalas were cryptograms concerning the state of the self which were presented to me anew each day. In them I saw the self – that is, my whole being – actively at work. To be sure, at first I could only dimly understand them; but they seemed to me highly significant, and I guarded them like precious pearls. I had the distinct feeling that they were something central, and in time I acquired through them a living conception of the self. The self, I thought, was like the monad which I am, and which is my world. The mandala represents this monad, and corresponds to the microcosmic nature of the psyche.

I no longer know how many mandalas I drew at this time. There were a great many. While I was working on them, the question arose repeatedly: What is this process leading to? Where is its goal? From my own experience, I knew by now that I could not presume to choose a goal which would seem trustworthy to me. It had been proved to me that I had to abandon the idea of the superordinate position of the ego. After all, I had been brought up short when I had attempted to maintain it. I had wanted to go on with the scientific analysis of myths which I had begun in *Symbols of Transformation*. That was still my goal – but I must not think of that! I was being compelled to go through this process of the unconscious. I had to let myself be carried along by the current, without a notion of where it would lead me. When I began drawing the mandalas, however, I saw that everything, all the paths I had been following, all the steps I had taken, were leading back to a single point – namely, to the mid-point. It became increasingly plain to me that the mandala is the centre. It is the exponent of all paths. It is the path to the centre, to individuation.

During those years, between 1918 and 1920, I began to understand that the goal of psychic development is the self. There is no linear evolution; there is only a circumambulation of the self. Uniform development exists, at most, only at the beginning; later, everything points towards the centre. This insight gave me stability, and gradually my inner peace returned. I knew that in finding the mandala as an expression of the self I had attained what was for me the ultimate. Perhaps someone else knows more, but not I.

Some years later (in 1927) I obtained confirmation of my ideas about the centre and the self by way of a dream. I represented its essence in a mandala which I called 'Window on Eternity'. The picture is reproduced in *The Secret of the Golden Flower*.[2] A year later I painted a second picture, likewise a mandala,[3] with a golden castle in the centre. When it was finished, I asked myself, 'Why is this so Chinese?' I was impressed by the form and choice of colours, which seemed to me Chinese, although there was nothing outwardly Chinese about it. Yet that was how it affected me. It was a strange coincidence that shortly afterwards I received a letter from Richard Wilhelm enclosing the manuscript of a Taoist-alchemical treatise entitled *The Secret of the Golden Flower*, with a request that I write a commentary on it. I devoured the manuscript at once, for the text gave me an undreamed-of confirmation of my ideas about the mandala and the circumambulation of the centre. That was the first event which broke through my isolation. I became aware of an affinity; I could establish ties with something and someone.

In remembrance of this coincidence, this 'synchronicity', I wrote underneath the picture which had made so Chinese an impression upon me: 'In 1928, when I was painting this picture, showing the golden, well-fortified castle, Richard Wilhelm in Frankfurt sent me the thousand-year-old Chinese text on the yellow castle, the germ of the immortal body.'

From: 'Concerning Mandala Symbolism'[4]

629   The Sanskrit word *mandala* means 'circle'. It is the Indian term for the circles drawn in religious rituals. In the great temple of Madura, in southern India, I saw how a picture of this kind was made. It was drawn by a woman on the floor of the *mandapam* (porch), in coloured chalks, and measured about ten feet across. A pandit who accompanied me said in reply to my questions that he could give me no information about it. Only the women who drew such pictures knew what they meant. The woman herself was non-committal; she evidently did not want to be disturbed in her work. Elaborate mandalas, executed in red chalk, can also be found on the whitewashed walls of many huts. The best and most significant mandalas are found in the sphere of Tibetan Buddhism.[5] I shall use as an example a Tibetan mandala, to which my attention was drawn by Richard Wilhelm.

630   A mandala of this sort is known in ritual usage as a *yantra*, an instrument of contemplation. It is meant to aid concentration by narrowing down the psychic field of vision and restricting it to the centre. Usually the mandala contains three circles, painted in black or dark blue. They are meant to shut out the outside and hold the inside together. Almost regularly the outer rim consists of fire, the fire of *concupiscentia*, 'desire,' from which proceed the torments of hell. The horrors of the burial ground are generally depicted on the outer rim. Inside this is a garland of lotus leaves, characterizing the whole mandala as a *padma* 'lotus-flower'. Then comes a kind of monastery courtyard with four gates. It signifies sacred seclusion and concentration. Inside this courtyard there are as a rule the four basic colours, red, green, white and yellow, which represent the four directions and also the psychic functions, as *The Tibetan Book of the Dead*[6] shows. Then, usually marked off by another magic circle, comes the centre as the essential object or goal of contemplation.

631   This centre is treated in very different ways, depending on the requirements of the ritual, the grade of initiation of the contemplator, and the sect he belongs to. As a rule it shows Shiva in his world-creating emanations. Shiva, according to Tantric doctrine, is the One Existent, the Timeless in its perfect state. Creation begins when this unextended point – known as *Shiva-bindu* – appears in the eternal embrace of its feminine side, the *shakti*. It then emerges from the state of being-in-itself and attains the state of being-for-itself, if I may use the Hegelian terminology.

632   In *kundalini* yoga symbolism, Shakti is represented as a snake wound three and a half times round the *lingam*, which is Shiva in the form of a phallus. This image shows the *possibility* of manifestation in space. From *shakti* comes *māyā*, the building material of all individual things; she is, in consequence, the creatrix of the real world. This is thought of as illusion, as being and not-being. It *is*, and yet remains dissolved in Shiva. Creation therefore begins with an act of division of the opposites that are

Figure 17.1 A Tibetan mandala. Reproduced from Jung's *Collected Works*, Vol. 9i.

united in the deity. From their splitting arises, in a gigantic explosion of energy, the multiplicity of the world.

633   The goal of contemplating the processes depicted in the mandala is that the yogi shall become inwardly aware of the deity. Through contemplation, he recognizes himself as God again, and thus returns from the illusion of individual existence into the universal totality of the divine state.

634   As I have said, *mandala* means 'circle'. There are innumerable variants of the motif shown here, but they are all based on the squaring of a circle. Their basic motif is the premonition of a centre of personality, a kind of central point within the psyche, to which everything is related, by which everything is arranged, and which is itself a source of energy. The energy of the central point is manifested in the almost irresistible compulsion and urge to *become what one is*, just as every organism is driven to assume the form that is characteristic of its nature, no matter what the circumstances. This centre is not felt or thought of as the ego but, if one may so express it, as the *self*. Although the centre is represented by an innermost point, it is surrounded by a periphery containing everything that belongs to the self – the paired opposites that make up the total personality. This totality comprises consciousness first of all, then the personal unconscious, and finally an indefinitely large segment of the collective unconscious whose archetypes are common to all mankind. A certain number of these, however, are permanently or temporarily included within the scope of the personality and, through this contact, acquire an individual stamp as the shadow, anima and animus, to mention only the best-known figures. The self, though on the one hand simple, is on the other hand an extremely composite thing, a 'conglomerate soul', to use the Indian expression.

635   Lamaic literature gives very detailed instructions as to how such a circle must be painted and how it should be used. Form and colour are laid down by tradition, so the variants move within fairly narrow limits. The ritual use of the mandala is actually non-Buddhist; at any rate it is alien to the original Hīnayāna Buddhism and appears first in Mahāyāna Buddhism.

636   The mandala shown here depicts the state of one who has emerged from contemplation into the absolute state. That is why representation of hell and the horrors of the burial ground are missing. The diamond thunderbolt, the *dorje* in the centre, symbolizes the perfect state where masculine and feminine are united. The world of illusions has finally vanished. All energy has gathered together in the initial state.

637   The four *dorjes* in the gates of the inner courtyard are meant to indicate that life's energy is streaming inwards; it has detached itself from the objects and now returns to the centre. When the perfect union of all energies in the four aspects of wholeness is attained, there arises a static state subject to no more change. In Chinese alchemy this state is called the 'Diamond Body', corresponding to the *corpus incorruptibile* of mediaeval alchemy, which is identical with the *corpus glorificationis* of Christian tradition, the incorruptible body of resurrection. This mandala shows, then,

the union of all opposites, and is embedded between *yang* and *yin*, heaven and earth; the state of everlasting balance and immutable duration.

638   For our more modest psychological purposes we must abandon the colourful metaphysical language of the East. What yoga aims at in this exercise is undoubtedly a psychic change in the adept. The ego is the expression of individual existence. The yogin exchanges his ego for Shiva or the Buddha; in this way he induces a shifting of the psychological centre of personality from the personal ego to the impersonal non-ego, which is now experienced as the real 'Ground' of the personality.

NOTES

1 *Faust, Part II*, trans. by Philip Wayne (Penguin Classics, 1959), p. 79.
2 Cf. 'Concerning Mandala Symbolism', in *The Archetypes and the Collective Unconscious* (CW9i), figs 5ff. and pp. 363ff.
3 *The Secret of the Golden Flower*, fig. 10. See also 'Concerning Mandala Symbolism', fig. 36 and p. 377.
4 [First published, as 'Über Mandalasymbolik', in *Gestaltungen des Unbewussten*, Psychologische Abhandlungen, VII (Zürich, 1950).– EDITORS.]
5 Cf. *Psychology and Alchemy*, pars. 122ff.
6 [Cf. Jung, Psychological Commentary on *The Tibetan Book of the Dead*, par. 850. – EDITORS.]

18 Deliverance from suffering

From: 'On the Discourses of the Buddha'[1]

1575   It was neither the history of religion nor the study of philosophy that first drew me to the world of Buddhist thought, but my professional interests as a doctor. My task was the treatment of psychic suffering, and it was this that impelled me to become acquainted with the views and methods of that great teacher of humanity whose principal theme was the 'chain of suffering, old age, sickness, and death'. For although the healing of the sick naturally lies closest to the doctor's heart, he is bound to recognize that there are many diseases and states of suffering which, not being susceptible of a direct cure, demand from both patient and doctor some kind of attitude to their irremediable nature. Even though it may not amount to actual incurability, in all such cases there are inevitably phases of stagnation and hopelessness which seem unendurable and require treatment just as much as a direct symptom of illness. They call for a kind of moral attitude such as is provided by religious faith or a philosophical belief. In this respect the study of Buddhist literature was of great help to me, since it trains one to observe suffering objectively and to take a universal view of its causes. According to tradition, it was by objectively observing the chain of causes that the Buddha was able to extricate his consciousness from the snares of the ten thousand things, and to rescue his feelings from the entanglements of emotion and illusion. So also in our sphere of culture the suffering and the sick can derive considerable benefit from this prototype of the Buddhist mentality, however strange it may appear.

1576   The discourses of the Buddha, here presented in K. E. Neumann's new translation, have an importance that should not be underestimated. Quite apart from their profound meaning, their solemn, almost ritual form emits a penetrating radiance which has an exhilarating and exalting effect and cannot fail to work directly upon one's feelings. Against this use of the spiritual treasures of the East it might be – and, indeed, often has been – objected from the Christian point of view that the faith of the West offers consolations that are at least as significant, and that there is no need to invoke the spirit of Buddhism with its markedly rational attitude. Aside from the fact that in most cases the Christian faith of which people speak simply isn't there, and no one can tell how it might be obtained (except by the special providence of God), it is a truism that anything known becomes so familiar and hackneyed by frequent use that it gradually loses its meaning and hence its effect; whereas anything strange and unknown, and so completely different in its nature, can open doors hitherto locked and new possibilities of understanding. If a Christian insists so much on his faith when it does not even help him to ward off a neurosis, then his faith is vain, and it is better to accept humbly what he needs, no matter where he finds it, if only it helps. There is no need for him to deny his religious convictions if he acknowledges his debt to Buddhism, for he is only following the Pauline injunction: 'Prove all things; hold fast that which is good' (I Thessalonians 5:21).

1577   To this good which should be held fast one must reckon the discourses of the Buddha, which have much to offer even to those who cannot boast of any Christian convictions. They offer Western man ways and means of disciplining his inner psychic life, thus remedying an often regrettable defect in the various brands of Christianity. The teachings of the Buddha can give him a helpful training when either the Christian ritual has lost its meaning or the authority of religious ideas has collapsed, as all too frequently happens in psychogenic disorders.

1578   People have often accused me of regarding religion as 'mental hygiene'. Perhaps one may pardon a doctor his professional humility in not undertaking to prove the truth of metaphysical assertions and in shunning confessions of faith. I am content to emphasize the importance of having a *Weltanschauung* and the therapeutic necessity of adopting some kind of attitude to the problem of psychic suffering. Suffering that is not understood is hard to bear, while on the other hand it is often astounding to see how much a person can endure when he understands the why and the wherefore. A philosophical or religious view of the world enables him to do this, and such views prove to be, at the very least, psychic methods of healing if not of salvation. Even Christ and his disciples did not scorn to heal the sick, thereby demonstrating the therapeutic power of their mission. The doctor has to cope with actual suffering for better or worse, and ultimately has nothing to rely on except the mystery of divine Providence. It is no wonder, then, that he values religious ideas and attitudes, so far as they prove helpful, as therapeutic systems, and singles out the Buddha in particular, the essence of whose teaching is deliverance from suffering through the maximum development of consciousness, as one of the supreme helpers on the road to salvation. From ancient times physicians have sought a panacea, a *medicina catholica*, and their persistent efforts have unconsciously brought them nearer to the central ideas of the religion and philosophy of the East.

1579   Anyone who is familiar with methods of suggestion under hypnosis knows that plausible suggestions work better than those which run counter to the patient's own nature. Consequently, whether he liked it or not, the doctor was obliged to develop conceptions which corresponded as closely as possible with the actual psychological conditions. Thus, there grew up a realm of theory which not only drew upon traditional thought but took account of the unconscious products that compensated its inevitable one-sidedness – that is to say, all those psychic factors which Christian philosophy left unsatisfied. Among these were not a few aspects which, unknown to the West, had been developed in Eastern philosophy from very early times.

1580   So if, as a doctor, I acknowledge the immense help and stimulation I have received from the Buddhist teachings, I am following a line which can be traced back some two thousand years in the history of human thought.

NOTE

1 [Statement in the publisher's prospectus for *Die Reden Gotamo Buddhos*, translated from the Pali Canon by Karl Eugen Neumann, 3 vols (Zürich, Stuttgart, Vienna, 1956). Statements were also contributed to the prospectus by Thomas Mann and Albert Schweitzer. Neumann (1865–1915) had published an earlier version of his translation in 1911, which Jung cited in *Wandlungen und Symbole der Libido* (1911–12); cf. *Psychology of the Unconscious* (New York, 1916), p. 538, n. 25. The present statement was published as '*Zu Die Reden Gotamo Buddhos*' in *Gesam. Werke*, XI, Anhang.]

Sources and acknowledgements

Jung's passage to India: from *Memories, Dreams, Reflections*, recorded and edited by Aniela Jaffé, translated by Richard and Clara Winston, (London: Fontana, 1977), pp. 304–14.

Jung's way to China: from 'Richard Wilhelm: In Memoriam', *Collected Works*, edited by H. Read, M. Fordham and G. Adler, translated by R. F. C. Hull (London: Routledge, and Princeton, New Jersey: Princeton University Press, 1953–85), Vol. 15, paras 74–96.

In search of Indian spiritual values: from 'The Holy Men of India', *Collected Works*, Vol. 11, paras 950–63.

East–West psychological comparisons: from 'What India Can Teach Us', *Collected Works*, Vol. 10, paras 1002–13; and from Foreword to 'Lily Abegg, *The Mind of East Asia*', *Collected Works*, Vol. 18, paras 1483–5.

The allures of the East: from 'The Archetypes of the Collective Unconscious', *Collected Works*, Vol. 9i, paras 11 and 21–9; and 'The Spiritual Problems of Modern Man', *Collected Works*, Vol. 10, paras 188–90.

The Chinese world-view: from 'Synchronicity: An Acausal Connecting Principle', *Collected Works*, Vol. 8, paras 916–24; and 'On the Theory and Practice of Analytical Psychology', *Collected Works*, Vol. 18, paras 141–4.

Yin and *yang*: the unity of opposites: from *Psychological Types*, *Collected Works*, Vol. 6, paras 358–70.

Chinese alchemy and psychological individuation: from 'Commentary on *The Secret of the Golden Flower*', *Collected Works*, Vol. 13, paras 1–84.

A dialogue with the *I Ching*: from *Memories, Dreams, Reflections*, Appendix IV: 'Richard Wilhelm', pp. 405–6; and 'Foreword to the *I Ching*', *Collected Works*, Vol. 11, paras 964–1018.

Brahman and the uniting of opposites: from *Psychological Types*, *Collected Works*, Vol. 6, paras 189–92 and 327–44.

The psychological symbolism of *kundalini* yoga: from 'The Realities of Practical Psychotherapy', *Collected Works*, Vol. 16, paras 561 and 560; and 'Psychological Commentary on *kundalini* Yoga', lectures given by C. G. Jung in 1932, the second of two lectures reprinted in *Spring* 1976 from the text compiled by Mary Foote, pp. 21–9.

Yoga and the spiritual crisis of the West: from 'Yoga and the West', *Collected Works*, Vol. 11, paras 859–76.

Meditation and Western psychology: from 'The Psychology of Eastern Meditation', *Collected Works*, Vol. 11, paras 908–49.

Death and psychic transformation: from 'Psychological Commentary on *The Tibetan Book of the Dead*', *Collected Works*, Vol. 11, paras 831–58.

The reality of the psyche in Buddhist thought: from 'Psychological Commentary on *The Tibetan Book of the Great Liberation*', *Collected Works*, Vol. 11, paras 759–87.

Zen, enlightenment, and psychotherapy: from 'Foreword to Suzuki's *Introduction to Zen Buddhism*', *Collected Works*, Vol. 11, paras 877–907.

Mandalas and the path to psychic wholeness: from *Memories, Dreams, Reflections*, pp. 220–3; and 'Concerning Mandala Symbolism', *Collected Works*, Vol. 9i, paras 629–39.

Deliverance from suffering: from 'On the Discourses of the Buddha', *Collected Works*, Vol. 18, paras 1575–80.

Bibliography

WORKS INCORPORATING JUNG'S WRITINGS

Evans-Wentz, W. Y., trans. & ed. (1954) *The Tibetan Book of the Great Liberation* (London: Oxford University Press). Contains Jung's 'Psychological Commentary'.
—— (1960) *The Tibetan Book of the Dead* (London: Oxford University Press). Contains Jung's 'Psychological Commentary'.
Jung, C. G. (1953–83) *The Collected Works of C. G. Jung*, edited by H. Read, M. Fordham and G. Adler, translated by R. F. C. Hull (London: Routledge, and Princeton, New Jersey: Princeton University Press), especially Vols 6, 10, 11 and 13.
—— (1983) *Memories, Dreams, Reflections*, recorded and edited by Aniela Jaffé (London: Flamingo). Contains Jung's account of his trip to India, and Appendix on Richard Wilhelm.
Suzuki, D. T. (1949) *An Introduction to Zen Buddhism* (New York: Philosophical Library). Contains Jung's 'Foreword'.
Wilhelm, Richard, trans. (1989) *I Ching, or Book of Changes*, The Richard Wilhelm translation rendered into English by Cary F. Baynes (London: Arkana). Contains Jung's 'Foreword'.

GENERAL WORKS ON JUNG AND EASTERN THOUGHT

Coward, Harold, with contributions by J. Borelli, J. F. T. Jordans, and J. Henderson (1985) *Jung and Eastern Thought* (Albany: State University of New York Press). Especially strong on the yoga and Indian traditions, and includes a comprehensive bibliography.
Clarke, J. J. (1994) *Jung and Eastern Thought: A Dialogue with the Orient* (London and New York: Routledge). Offers a critical examination of all aspects of Jung's writings on Eastern thought, and discusses them in the wider context of the West's dialogue with the East.

WORKS DEALING WITH SPECIFIC ASPECTS OF JUNG'S WRITINGS

Avens, Roberts (1980) *Imagination is Reality: Western Nirvana in Jung, Hillman, Barfield & Cassirer* (Dallas, Texas: Spring Publications). Discusses the role of the mythical and the imaginal in modern thought, linking them and the idea of individuation with themes from Eastern thought.
Faber, Phillip A., and Saayman, Graham S. 'On the Relation of the Doctrines of Yoga

to Jung's Psychology', in Renos K. Papadopoulos and Graham S. Saayman, eds (1984) *Jung in Modern Perspective* (London: Wildwood House). A comparative study from the point of view of analytical psychology.

Fincher, Susanne F. (1991) *Creating Mandalas* (Boston and London: Shambhala). Includes discussions of Jung's views on the symbolism of the mandala.

Moacanin, Radmilla (1986) *Jung's Psychology and Tibetan Buddhism: Western and Eastern Paths to the Heart* (London: Wisdom Publications). Seeks to link Buddhism with analytical psychology, but without glossing over the differences.

Scott, Mary (1983) *Kundalini in the Physical World* (London: Routledge). Includes some discussion of Jung's psychological interpretation of *kundalini* yoga.

Spiegelman, J. M. and Miyuki, Mokusen (1985) *Buddhism and Jungian Psychology* (Phoenix, Arizona: Falcon Press). A collection of writings which seeks to link Buddhist concepts with Jungian psychology

Spiegelman, J. M., and Vasavada, Arwind. V (1987) *Hinduism and Jungian Psychology* (Phoenix, Arizona: Falcon Press). A collection of writings which seeks to build a bridge between Eastern and Western traditions.

DISCUSSIONS IN GENERAL WORKS ON JUNG

Hannah, Barbara (1976) *Jung, His Life and Work: A Biographical Memoir* (New York: Perigee Books). Includes a chapter on Jung's journey to India.

Progoff, Ira (1973) *Jung, Synchronicity and Human Destiny* (New York: Julian Press). Includes a chapter on Jung's use of the *I Ching*, as well as a discussion of the relationship between synchronicity and Eastern philosophy.

Stern, P. J. (1976) *C. G. Jung: The Haunted Prophet* (New York: Braziller). A highly critical examination of Jung including a discussion of his journey to India and his relationship with Eastern ideas.

Wehr, Gerhard (1987) *Jung: A Biography*, translated by David M. Weeks (Boston, Massachusetts: Shambhala). Includes a chapter on Jung's journey to India, and an Appendix on 'Western Consciousness and Eastern Spirituality'.

Whitmont, Edward C. (1969) *The Symbolic Quest: Basic Concepts of Analytical Psychology* (Princeton, New Jersey: Princeton University Press). Includes a discussion on the relationship between the *yang–yin* polarity and the male–female distinction in relation to Jung's writings.

DISCUSSIONS AND CRITICISMS OF JUNG'S WRITINGS ON THE EAST

Ajaya, S. (1984) *Psychotherapy East and West* (Homesdale, Pennsylvania: Himalayan International Institute). Includes a critical discussion of Jung's interpretation of yoga philosophy and meditation practices.

Bishop, Peter (1984) 'Jung, Eastern Religions, and the Language of the Imagination', *The Eastern Buddhist*, 17:1. A brief but wide-ranging discussion of Jung's writings on Eastern religious ideas.

Borelli, John (1977) 'Jung's Psychology and Yoga Spirituality', *Riverdale Studies*, 4. Examines Jung's criticism of the use of Eastern spiritual practices by Westerners.

Claxton, Guy, ed. (1986) *Beyond Therapy: The Impact of Eastern Religions on Psychological Theory and Practice* (London: Wisdom Publications). A collection of essays examining the impact of Eastern teachings on psychological theory and practice.

Grisson, Pierre (1968) 'The Golden Flower and its Fruit', *Studies in Comparative Religion*, 2:3. Highly critical comment on Jung's attempt to understand Eastern spirituality in Western psychological terms.

Grof, Stanislav (1985) *Beyond the Brain: Birth, Death and Transcendence in Psychotherapy* (New York: State University of New York Press). Discusses the contributions of Jung and Eastern philosophies to the development of transpersonal psychology.

Harding, Esther (1968) 'The Reality of the Psyche', in Joseph B. Wheelwright, ed. *The Reality of the Psyche* (New York: Putnam). Makes use of Jung's psychological interpretation of *kundalini* yoga.

Henderson, Joseph L. (1975) 'The Self and Individuation', *International Encyclopedia of Neurology, Psychiatry, Psychoanalysis and Psychology*, 1. Emphasizes the Hindu contribution to Jung's idea of the self.

Jones, R. H. (1979) 'Jung and Eastern Religious Traditions', *Religion*, 9:2. Criticizes Jung for distorting Eastern ideas through the conceptual lens of analytical psychology.

Mokusen, Miyuki (1977) 'The Psychodynamics of Buddhist Meditation', *The Eastern Buddhist*, 10:2. Relates Jungian analysis to practice of *zazen*.

Odajuyk, V.W. (1993) *Gathering the Light: A Psychology of Meditation* (Boston and London: Shambhala). Includes discussion of Jung's views on Eastern meditation.

Watts, Alan (1973) *Psychotherapy East and West* (Harmondsworth: Penguin Books). Includes a criticism of Jung for having a defective understanding of the Eastern idea of liberation.

Welwood, John, ed. (1985) *The Awakening Heart: East/West Approaches to Psychotherapy and the Healing Relationship* (Boston and London: Shambhala). Includes a discussion on the relationship between psychological change and spiritual growth, with particular reference to Jung and Eastern traditions.

ISSUES CONCERNING TRANSLATIONS OF EASTERN TEXTS

Cleary, Thomas, trans. & ed. (1991) *The Secret of the Golden Flower* (San Francisco, California: Harper). Points to inadequacies of the Richard Wilhelm text that Jung had access to.

Reynolds, John M., trans. & ed. (1989) *Self-Liberation through Seeing with Naked Awareness* (Barrytown, NY: Station Hill Press). Includes an Appendix which discusses the inadequacies of Evans-Wentz's translation of *The Tibetan Book of the Great Liberation* – of which this is a retitled and retranslated edition – and the implications of this for Jung's interpretation.

INFLUENCE OF JUNG'S WRITINGS ON THE EAST

Abegg, Lilly (1952) *The Mind of East Asia* (London and New York: Thames & Hudson). Makes use of Jung's introvert–extravert typology in study of psychological differences between East and West.

Sharpe, Eric J. (1992) *Comparative Religion: A History* (London: Duckworth). Examines Jung's influence on the development of psychological and comparative studies of religion.

Ulanov, Barry (1992) *Jung and the Ouside World* (Wilmette, Illinois: Chiron Publications). Includes a chapter on the influence of Jung's writings on Eastern thought, and discusses his influence on the study of comparative religion.

Index